GRAPHIC DESIGN ON THE DESKTOP

GRAPHIC DESIGN ON THE DESKTOP
A GUIDE FOR THE NON-DESIGNER

Marcelle Lapow Toor

Cornell University

VAN NOSTRAND REINHOLD
An International Thomson Publishing Company

New York • London • Bonn • Boston • Detroit • Madrid • Melbourne • Mexico City
Paris • Singapore • Tokyo • Toronto • Albany NY • Belmont CA • Cincinnati OH

Copyright © 1994 by Van Nostrand Reinhold

Library of Congress Catalog Number 94-16140

ISBN 0-442-01786-3

I(T)P Van Nostrand Reinhold, an International Thomson Publishing Company.
ITP logo is a trademark under license.

Printed in the United States of America.

Van Nostrand Reinhold

115 Fifth Avenue
New York, New York 10003

International Thomson Publishing
Berkshire House
168-173 High Holborn
London WCIV 7AA
England

Thomas Nelson Australia
102 Dodds Street
South Melbourne 3205
Australia

Nelson Canada
1120 Birchmount Road
Scarborough, Ontario
MIK 5G4, Canada

International Thomson Publishing GmbH
Königswinterer Strasse 418
53227 Bonn
Germany

International Thomson Publishing Asia
221 Henderson Road
#05 10 Henderson Building
Singapore 0315

International Thomson Publishing Japan
Hirakawacho Kyowa Building, 3F
2-2-1 Hirakawa-cho, Chiyoda-ku
Tokyo 102
Japan

EDWAA 16 15 14 13 12 11 10 9 8 7 6 5 4

Library of Congress Cataloging-in-Publication Data

Toor, Marcelle Lapow.
    Graphic design on the desktop: a guide for the non-designer
/ Marcelle Lapow Toor.
    Includes index.
    ISBN 0-442-01786-3
    1. Desktop publishing   I. Title
Z253.53.T66   1994
686.2'254536—dc20

94-16140
CIP

ᐧᐧ For my father, Harry Lapow

CONTENTS

Acknowledgments

Several people provided me with information, inspiration, support and encouragement in the preparation of this book. My daughter, Rachel Toor read and critiqued the original outline and helped me solidify my ideas. My son, Mark Toor gave me the support to pursue this task. My partner and mate, George Rhoads, fed me encouragement and numerous dinners. Jane Hardy, my colleague and friend, edited the early manuscript. Joan Ormondroyd, Cly Boehs and Sherrill Wainer read the early chapters and gave me good critical feedback.

My thanks to the graphic designers who provided me with illustrations of their work. They are identified in the captions and in the index. Mark Dimunation, Curator of Rare Books at Cornell University helped me locate illustrations from old and rare manuscripts. Art Science Studio/Lab provided the copy work for this book. My thanks to the reviewers who read the manuscript and made helpful suggestions. I wish to thank all the software publishers who contributed copy for the software bibliography.

Finally, I am grateful to all the people at VNR who made this book happen—especially Risa Cohen, my editor, for believing in this project, and Chris Grisonich who held my hand throughout the entire production process.

ANOTHER BOOK ON GRAPHIC DESIGN

efore the personal computer made its grand appearance, graphic design was limited to a group of people trained formally in the fine arts, commercial art, or design. The average person who claimed an inability to draw a straight line was a consumer of the printed page, not its creator.

The Macintosh computer that set off the desktop publishing revolution was presented to the world in 1985. Since then the ways in which we live and do business have changed. People in offices across the country are producing a variety of printed materials on their desktops: invitations, stationery, flyers, brochures, newsletters, and magazines. You name it–it's being done on a computer. In most cases it's being done by someone whose original job description did not include design, and who doesn't know a serif from a dingbat.

Years ago college-level courses in graphic design or commercial art were only to be found in art departments. Since the late 1980s, graphic design and desktop publishing courses have been springing up in other departments: Communication, Journalism, Business, English, and especially in continuing education and adult education programs. College students, and the public in general, want to learn the skills they need for the '90s. The terms "visual literacy," "visual perception," and "visual awareness" are easing their way into the vocabulary of our educational system.

DESKTOP PUBLISHING: THE BEGINNING

The term "desktop publishing," coined by Paul Brainard, president of Aldus Corporation, describes the

ability to produce publishable pages on a desktop using a micro-computer, a laser printer, and a page layout program.

Desktop publishing began a very short time ago. It can be traced to January 1985, when four corporations joined forces. Apple produced the Macintosh computer and LaserWriter printer. Adobe Systems, Inc., invented a computer language, PostScript, that enabled the computer to speak to the LaserWriter or other output device. Allied Linotype Company, a manufacturer and distributor of typesetting equipment, licensed its typefaces to Adobe. Aldus Corporation developed a software program, PageMaker, that made it possible for the computer to be used as an electronic drawing board, giving the computer operator the power and control over type, plus the ability to manipulate graphics and type freely on a page. This union of the four "A's" has left a permanent mark on the publishing, business, and education worlds.

Desktop publishing can be compared to photography. Anyone who has a camera can take a picture and get a likeness. However, if the person taking the picture has understanding and knowledge of composition, design, the interplay of light and dark, and negative space, and can work a camera, he or she might end up with a good photograph, instead of a simple snapshot. The same is true of the computer. Anyone with an understanding of the hardware and software can produce a newsletter or a brochure. In order for a person to produce a professional-looking publication, he or she must also have an understanding of visual communication, the principles of design, composition, and typography.

■ ■ ■

ABOUT THIS BOOK

The task of designing a publication for print can be confusing and overwhelming to a beginning designer, or the person in an office who has suddenly been designated "the designer." The function of *Graphic Design on the Desktop* is to lead the inexperienced designer, desktop operator or electronic publisher through the process of designing for the printed page. This book has been set up to guide the reader from concept to production, to demystify graphic design, and to provide practical information for designing more effective and more visually exciting publications using the computer as a design tool.

Graphic Design on the Desktop is organized to provide information in a sequential, step-by-step manner, presenting the information in an order to enhance the learning process. Each chapter builds on the information presented in the previous chapter. Graphic design tasks are examined in terms of concepts, ideas, and the thinking process involved. The thinking process you will go through to find a solution to your design problem is the same whether you are designing a simple flyer produced on the laser printer or a professionally-printed slick and elaborate five color annual report.

Each chapter in *Graphic Design on the Desktop* contains relevant quotes, hints, tips, and exercises pertaining to the chapter to guide the reader through the design process.

We have a rich heritage in visual communication, a history as old as the human race. Since the past is a wonderful resource for the present, most of the chapters in this book contain some brief historical information in order to put the topic covered in that chapter into perspective.

A glossary of desktop publishing terms and an annotated bibliography of desktop publishing software is located at the back of the book.

CHAPTER 1
What is Graphic Design?

We begin to look at graphic design in terms of visual communication and problem solving, in order to discover how it works and what it's all about. The creative process is discussed with suggestions for stimulating creativity. This chapter has questions for the beginning designer to consider before making an attempt to design anything for print.

CHAPTER 2
Type as Visual Communication

This chapter follows the previous one because type is the basic ingredient in graphic design. Chapter 2 begins with a brief history of the printed word, Johann Gutenberg's invention of movable type,

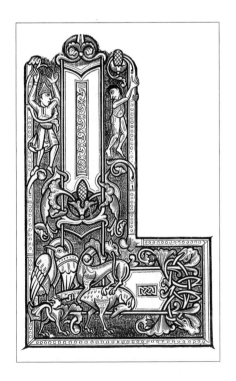

Decorative letter from 13th century Byzantine manuscript. From L'Ornament Polychrome, 1869.

and the printing press. Chapter 1 is about visual communication. In this chapter we look at type as a powerful communication tool and discuss how to choose a typeface to communicate a message to a particular audience. We examine how type can be used to convey an emotion and illustrate words. Letters are looked at in terms of shapes and forms with negative space which provides an introduction for the next chapter Logos, Symbols, and Trademarks.

CHAPTER 3
Logos, Symbols, and Trademarks

In this chapter, we begin to look at the relationship of letters to each other and how these letterforms are used in the design of a logo. Symbols have been around since the cave age. This chapter examines how we use symbols in general, and more specifically, as identifiers for businesses and other organizatons. The entire chapter has been devoted to the logo because the logo embodies what graphic design is all about in terms of conceptual thinking, problem solving, creating an image, and communicating a message. A case study of an actual logo design and the process involved are included in this chapter.

Proposed symbol for "Seahorse" Beach Concession in Ischia, an island off the coast of Naples. Designer: Tony DiSpigna. 1990.

CHAPTER 4
Influences on Contemporary Graphic Design:
Graphic Design Roots

Although visual communication has its roots in the stone age, contemporary graphic design has evolved from a series of art movements beginning in the late nineteenth and early twentieth century, and has been influenced by the findings of the Gestalt psychologists. This chapter unfolds the evolution of present day design based on the influences of the past.

We look at the basic principles of design: harmony, balance, contrast, tension, and the role each plays in the graphic design environment. We look at the Gestalt view of visual perception, how we make sense of images, how we recognize, interpret, and identify objects, how we can become more visually aware and more sensitive to our surroundings, and how we develop an aesthetic sense. We examine the importance of shapes, negative space, figure/ground, and their effect on the printed page.

CHAPTER 5
The Design Process

A good design is memorable and will elicit a response. This chapter examines the design process and answers the following questions: Where does a designer get ideas? Which design format is most appropriate for solving a particular design problem? What are the steps in the design process? What are the basic elements of a page? How does a designer create visual interest on a page? This chapter looks at all the issues surrounding the creation of an effective design.

CHAPTER 6
Type Terminology and Typesetting Basics

Before a page is designed the designer must have a basic understanding of type and its appearance and function on a page. Type in a printed piece, brochure, advertisement, or flyer needs to be readable, legible, and organized in a logical hierarchy. This chapter contains type terminology and typesetting hints that address the most common typographical errors made by desktop publishers when designing on the computer, as well as basic typesetting tips involving wordspacing; combining type styles; using dingbats; boxes and bullets; and using type as a graphic for visual interest.

The information in this chapter provides the groundwork for the next three chapters on designing specific pieces for print.

CHAPTER 7
Designing Informational Materials: Flyers, Posters, and Brochures

In this chapter we examine the elements involved in the design of flyers, posters, and brochures. We are led through an actual brochure design problem and its solution.

CHAPTER 8
Designing Editorial Materials: Newsletters and Magazines

Newsletters and magazines fall under the category of editorial design. This chapter looks at the factors to consider before designing periodicals. An actual magazine design problem is presented at the end of the chapter, and a solution is described.

CHAPTER 9
Advertising Design: Designing Ads and Business Materials
In this chapter we examine the advertisement and things to be considered before the actual design process begins.

This chapter includes pertinent information for the designing of business materials: letterheads, business cards, and envelopes along with some actual design problems and their solutions.

CHAPTER 10
Using Illustrations:
Photographs, Drawings and Information Graphics
This chapter discusses using the appropriate art to enhance a printed piece: clip art, photographs, charts, and graphs.

A photograph from a magazine or illustration from a book cannot be legally used without permission from the holder of the copyright. The designer needs to have some knowledge of the copyright laws. The end of this chapter discusses some copyright basics and answers the questions: What is a copyright? Who can claim copyright? What works are protected under the copyright laws? What do "public domain" and "fair use" mean in relation to copyright?

CHAPTER 11
Working With Color
After the design for the printed page is conceived and in rough form, colors must be selected. By understanding the psychology of colors, as we've been conditioned to them, the designer is able to select colors that will enhance the overall message to be communicated. Colors, like smells, elicit certain responses in us; some have positive associations, while others have negative associations. We discuss the way we use color in speech, in expressions like "seeing red" to express anger. We look at the vocabulary of color, hue, value and saturation, as well as the perception of color and how color can be used to help promote a message and enhance an overall design. We

Art deco border from *New Art Deco Borders and Motifs*. William Rowe. Dover Press. 1984.

discuss the use of PANTONE® Color Publications as guides in the selection of color for a design.

CHAPTER 12
The Printing Process

The design has been approved by the client. The process of preparing the finished piece for the printer begins. How do you prepare your design for the printer? What decisions need be made at this point? Will you use laser printer output for the mechanical? Will your budget allow for Linotronic output? Is it necessary for your printed piece? What do you need to know when you take your finished mechanical to the printer? How do you communicate with a printer and get quotes for the piece you have designed? What kind of paper will you use? This chapter suggests answers to these questions. The printing process and terminology are explained here. You will find out how to get quotes from printers and how to communicate with them to get the results you want.

Graphic design is discovery and excitement. Each piece to be designed presents a new and exciting challenge, a problem to be solved.

AN AD CAMPAIGN

An advertising campaign is a series of ads that basically have one message.

The three advertisements on this page are for a pet shop, The Pet Gallery. Humor is used in the clever headlines to stress the uniqueness of the pets found in the shop.

Ad campaign for The Pet Gallery.
Art Director: Sean Riley.
Copywriter: Raymond McKinney.
The Martin Agency, 1992.

Come see our chameleons.

Stop by and check out our assortment of exotic pets. But you'd better hurry. They're disappearing fast.

The Pet Gallery
2403 S. Wrightsville Ave, Nags Head, 441-1852

The rarest fish this side of a sushi bar.

We serve up the widest selection of freshwater and saltwater fish in town. (No reservations required.)

The Pet Gallery
2403 S. Wrightsville Ave, Nags Head, 441-1852

It won't wet the floor. Your mom might.

Our snakes make wonderful pets. And don't worry. Over time your mother will grow to love it.

The Pet Gallery
2403 S. Wrightsville Ave, Nags Head, 441-1852

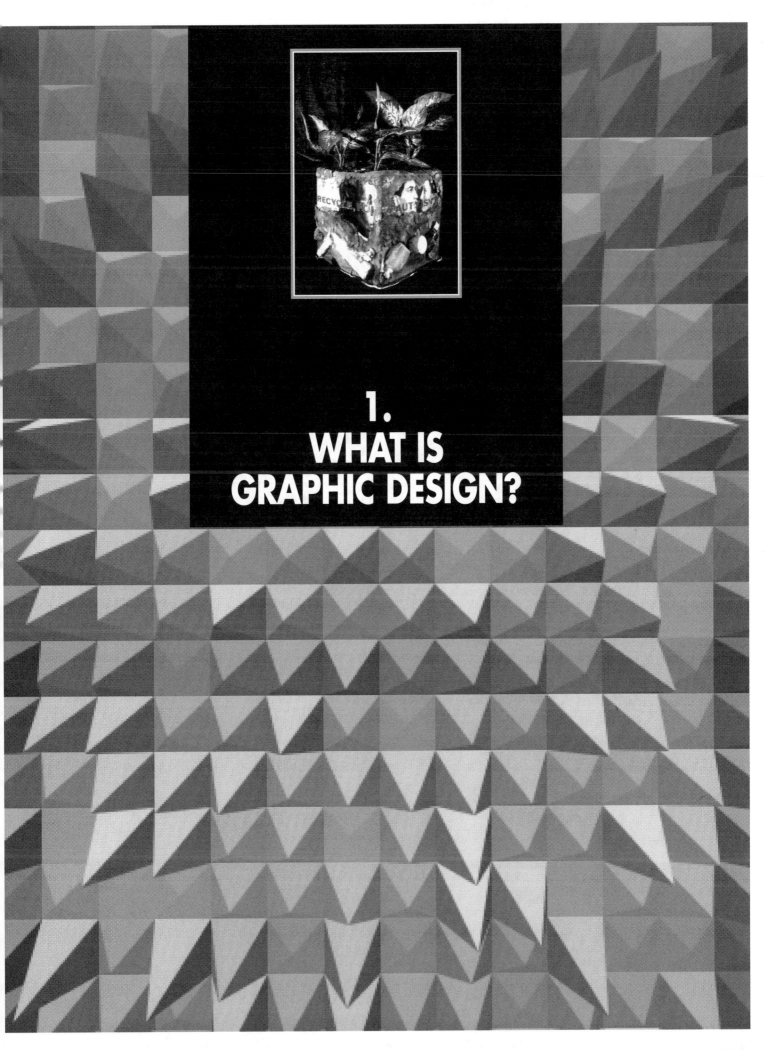

1.
WHAT IS
GRAPHIC DESIGN?

INSIDE THIS CHAPTER

WHAT IS GRAPHIC DESIGN?

hen the words "visual communication" are substituted for graphic design, we begin to get a clearer picture of what graphic design is about. Graphic design involves communication, design principles, aesthetics, marketing, and psychology. It is about creativity: concepts, ideas, solving problems, taking risks, and devising unique and surprising solutions. Graphic design is not the making of pretty pictures, or designing for the sake of design. The process involved in designing a printed piece is similar to the process of creating a painting. Both are concerned with communication. Unless the painter is working on commission within specific parameters, a problem is set up, and the artist proceeds to solve it. The solution may take the form of a painting, a landscape, or a portrait, but the problem is a *personal* one, and the finished product will communicate the artist's intentions to some audience. That is not the fine artist's main concern. The graphic designer, on the other hand, must solve a specific problem for someone else, the client, creating a design that is original and communicates a message to a designated audience. The design must suit both the message and the audience, and the result should be a solution that is attention-getting.

Graphic design is design with a purpose, a language of type and visual symbols, with a message to be communicated in a creative way. We are living in an age of information; an age in which visual images scream for our attention. The graffiti on walls of

Posters, flyers, and parts of newspapers pasted on a wall in New York City's Greenwich Village. Photographer: Harry Lapow, 1979.

buildings, and on buses, subways, and other public spaces compete for our attention with walls wearing posters and flyers announcing any number of events. The graphic designer must be able to create designs that will be noticed in this type of environment.

Graphic design, both good and bad, surrounds us in our everyday lives in signs on shops and public places, in newspapers, magazines, posters, flyers, ads, TV commercials, and in all the printed materials that come to us through the mail. Design is part of our everyday lives in what we see and what we do. Most people are unaware that they are involved in the making of design decisions daily: the placement of furniture in a room, the exact location selected for a stamp on an envelope, or the selection of the exact spot on a wall to hang paintings or posters. Graphic design incorporates this kind of organization and placement of objects. In graphic design, the objects are type and graphics, words and pictures, and they are moved around on a printed page at a drawing board or a computer monitor. It is the designer's job to organize this information.

■ ■ ■

The computer has changed the way designers work. Many designers have cast off the old tools, the drawing board, T-square, triangle, rubber cement, waxers, technical pens, etc., and replaced them with new electronic ones. A new tool for designers, the computer enables them to design and manipulate images and type, and gives them almost complete control over the finished product. Although the tools have changed, and will continue to change, the process involved in the actual designing remains the same.

Philip B. Meggs, graphic designer and author, discusses the new technology and its relation to graphic design in his book, *A History of Graphic Design.* "As has happened so often in the past, the tools are changing with the relentless advance of technology, but the essence of graphic design remains unchanged. The essence is to give order to information, form to ideas, and expression and feeling to artifacts that document human experience."

GRAPHIC DESIGN SHOULD BE THOUGHT OF AS:

■ Visual communication

- The marriage of images and words
- A visual language, with simplicity and legibility
- A vehicle to communicate specific information to a specific audience
- A cooperative effort between designer, client, photographer or illustrator, copywriter, printer.

 Hint: *Graphic design should never be thought of as design for design's sake. It is always a solution to a particular communication problem with a message to an audience.*

THE THINKING PROCESS
Defining the problem

Before any attempt is made at design, the purpose of the task must be clearly defined. The direction that appears to be the most obvious is not necessarily the best. Several factors must be considered and questions must be asked in order to determine the format of the actual piece. The following is a checklist of the six questions to ask before attempting any design task:

1. Who is the audience?

The audience is the key to solving any design problem. Create a personality profile of the audience you intend to address by answering the following questions:

- Who is the message aimed at?
- Where is this audience located?
- What is the age group?
- Does this group share anything in common?
- What size is the audience?
- What is the gender of the audience?

2. What is your objective?

Before beginning the design process for a printed piece consider whether it is possible to achieve your objective through door-to-door interviews, or a few phone calls, rather than a printed piece. Answer these questions about the piece:

- Are you trying to promote a particular product?

- ▶ Are you trying to promote a political or social view?
- ▶ Do you want to explain a simple idea?
- ▶ Do you wish to inform your audience about a particular event or product?
- ▶ Are you attempting only to entertain?

3. What is the message?

After answering questions 1 & 2 you should have a more defined image of your audience and your objectives.

- ▶ What do you want to say to this audience?
- ▶ What is the tone of that message (formal or informal)?

The tone will depend upon your audience and what you want to tell them.

4. What format will you use to convey the message? (See Chapter 5)

By now you should begin to get an idea of the format you need for your message: a personal letter, invitation, brochure, flyer, newsletter, poster, ad, etc. The question to be asked at this point is:

- ▶ What is your budget?

If you do not have the answer to this question before you begin to design, you might be wasting a great deal of your time and money. If you forget to ask your client this question and create an elaborate design in several colors when your client is on a tight budget, you are not solving the problem appropriately. Your client's pocketbook is your concern. It is the designer's responsibility to create a design that will sell the client or the client's product or service, but the designer should also try to save the client money, if possible.

Example:

If you are trying to promote a creative writing workshop for kids, sponsored by a not-for-profit organization, which is short on funds, the best and the least expensive approach would be a flyer (8 ½" x 11") reproduced on a laser printer or duplicating machine, posted in the local library and sent to all the schools in the area. The poster would reach the appropriate audience—kids and their parents—and would not drain the budget of the organization sponsoring it.

5. What is the image you wish to project for your client, and what has the organization done before? How will the people involved react to the change?

The graphic designer's job is to create an image for a client or organization. Advertising agencies create images that help presidential candidates get elected.

Hint: It is always a good idea when changing the image of an organization with a new logo to warn the public in advance. People hate change.

Example:

Two years ago a large East Coast university decided that the seal created when the university was first founded and used on all university materials as a logo, was not being used appropriately. It had an ivy league look, and they were not ivy league. The seal appeared on t-shirts, stationery, campus signage, text book covers, etc. The university hired a large, well-known New York City advertising agency to design a new logo with a more contemporary, up-to-date look to replace the seal. The seal would be used only on official documents, diplomas, and academic publications. When the new logo appeared, it was uniformly disliked. The campus community felt the logo projected a corporate image, not an academic one, and presented an identity that made it look more like a Midwestern college.

Example:

The managing editor of an organization that publishes scholarly journals decided it was time to change the design of the journal covers. These journals, first produced in 1915, have an established reputation. The graphic designer hired to do the job suggested that the subscribers should be warned in advance, before the new designs appeared in their mailboxes. The loyal subscribers began to anticipate the new designs, and they were well received.

"Human creativity uses what is already existing and available and changes it in unpredictable ways."
—Silvano Ariet.
The Magic Synthesis, NY Basic Books, NY, 1976.

6. What are the current trends in graphic design?

The field of graphic design, like fashion design, has its own trends and styles. What is trendy one year in printed materials such as magazines, brochures, or newsletters may not be in style the next. It is important for designers to be aware of the trends so that their designs to have an up-to-date appearance, but the best designs break out of the current. Know the trends, and go beyond them!

FINDING CURRENT TRENDS IN GRAPHIC DESIGN

1. Magazines

Current periodicals are a good source for the contemporary design styles. Looking through the magazines on a newsstand will give you a good idea of the fashions in typestyles, and how type, photographs, and other illustrations are used. Look at advertisements in old magazines in the library and see if you can identify the differences between the style then and the style today.

2. Museums, galleries, and art periodicals

The graphic designer needs to keep in touch with style innovations in the fine arts since graphic design relies heavily on trends in painting, photography, printmaking, and sculpture. A former Creative Director of a large New York City corporation used to take his entire art staff to museums and galleries once a month during their lunch hour in order for them to be informed about current events in the world of the fine arts. If you do not live in a town or city that has museums and galleries, subscribe to some design periodicals.

3. Signage

Look at signs on buildings in your town. Notice signs on subways, buses, walls, and doors. Supermarket interiors and their signage used to be designed by architects. They are now being designed by graphic designers who create both an image and an atmosphere for the supermarket. Notice the colors that are used for each of the departments and throughout the store.

THE CREATIVE PROCESS

Creativity in children seems to have no boundaries. Kids have an innate creativity, relying on an intuition and a playfulness that gets stifled and suppressed as they get older and become inhibited.

Before scientists, educators, and psychologists began studying creativity, the child who was a daydreamer was looked on with disdain. However, recent studies have shown that many well-known artists were the daydreamers in their classes as children. Creative people can be found in many walks of life: business, medicine, science—not only in the arts. Creativity is an approach to life, a way of looking at things, a way of solving problems and coming up with unique solutions.

PBS produced a television series called, *The Creative Spirit*, showing people in different professions who approached their jobs and their lives in creative ways. The series described creativity as: "knocking down walls," "seeing, and seeing again," "learning to recognize happy accidents," "the freedom to make mistakes," "confronting obstacles," "singing in your own key." The inhibition of creativity was described as, a "hardening of the attitudes."

Below is a list of suggestions to help get your creative juices flowing:

1. Subscribe to design periodicals.
2. Look at different kinds of publications, magazines, books, newspapers, and newsletters.
3. Establish a library of books on graphic design.
4. Keep a reference file of design solutions you like in ads, newsletters, brochures, and logos. Look carefully at these designs and try to figure out what you like about them. Sensitize yourself to what you think is good and bad in these designs, and try to figure out why. What makes the good designs work?
5. Go to the library and look at books, both new and old.
6. Look at everything around you.

As the ideas begin to flow, be playful and experiment at your computer or at your drawing board. Even if some of your ideas seem outrageous at first, try to follow through with them. Experiment! Don't be afraid to take a risk!

The computer is a wonderful design tool, but one incapable of making design decisions. It is only as good as the person pushing the buttons.

SUGGESTED EXERCISES

The exercises in this chapter relate to looking and *seeing*, developing visual awareness and a sensitivity to the world around you and to important elements and current trends in graphic design.

1. Look at flyers on a busy bulletin board. Which ones catch your eye? Pick out the elements that make you take notice. Which ones get lost? Why?

2. Set up a file of flyers and brochures that you find appealing. At the same time, collect ones that you think need to be redesigned.

3. Begin a folder for logos and ads that you think are interesting and unique. What factors contribute to their originality?

4. Look at type in magazines and newspapers. Can you identify a trend in type use today? Notice the type used for headlines in the magazine sections of major newspapers.

5. Find old magazines in libraries. Look at the page layouts and ads. Look for similarities between old ads and the current ones.

Before attempting to design a specific printed piece understanding type is essential. The next chapter, Type as Visual Communication, introduces type as the basic ingredient in graphic design and examines its role in visual communication.

Top left: German brochure from the early 1900s produced by the graphic class of the Stettin Handwerker und Kunstgewerbeschule.

Bottom left: Old advertisement by W. S. Crawford, Ltd. for J. C. Eno, Ltd., manufacturer of health salts for constipation, indigestion, sleeplessness and other poor bodily functions. 1928.

Bottom right: Film poster Designer: Devambez, Paris, 1827.

Top: 3-D collage sculpture composed of found ads, found beauty bottles, type done in nail polish, earth, clay and plastic plants designed to educate viewers about the price of beauty. Popular image of beauty (collected from existing fashion glossies) lies between buried packages below and plastic plants above, the only vegetation that can withstand pollution.
Designer: Michael Consorte, MFA student, Pratt Insititute, 1992.

Bottom: Design for Oasis perfume—a scent designed for a high-end older women's market.
Designer: Michael Consorte, MFA student, Pratt Insititute.
Photographer: Rosemarie Kowalski, 1992.

2.
TYPE
AS VISUAL
COMMUNICATION

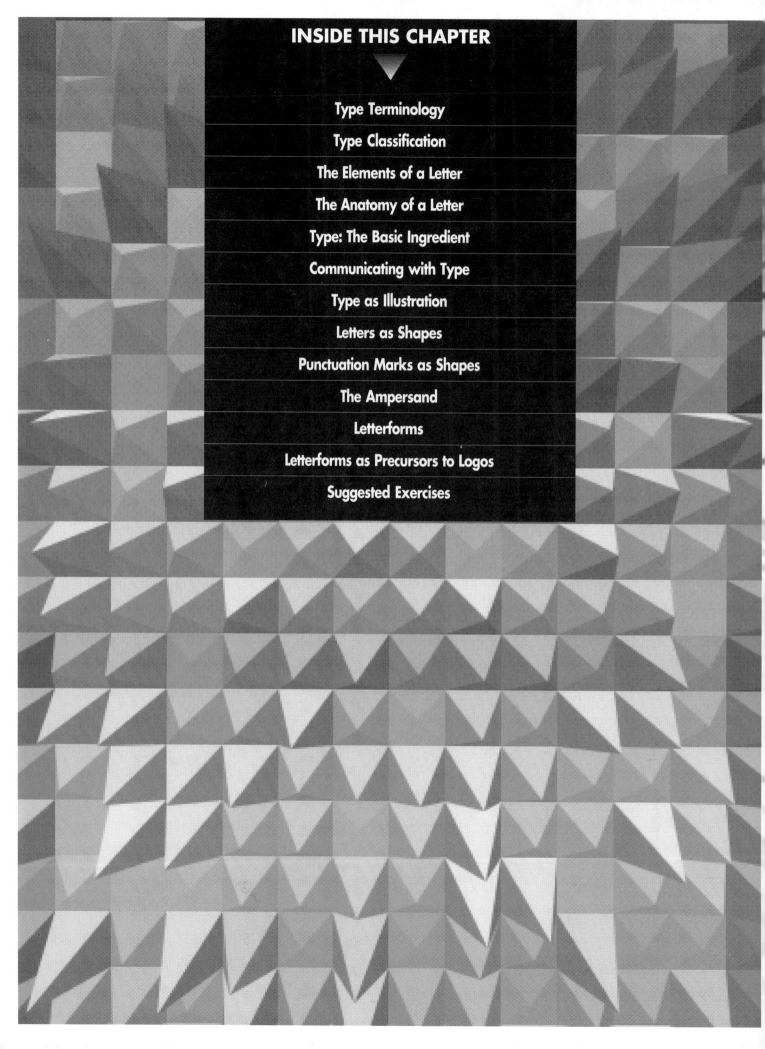

INSIDE THIS CHAPTER

2

TYPE AS VISUAL COMMUNICATION

Face created in Aldus® FreeHand with a number of different typefaces.
Illustration by George Rhoads, 1993.

Books in the Middle Ages were reproduced  by hand, laboriously copied by scribes, and valued as much as an acre of land. Only the wealthy could afford to read, while the poor remained illiterate until well after the invention of the printing press.

In 1455, Johann Gutenberg developed the letterpress, a printing process that used movable type cast from metal. The letterforms he designed were based on Gothic script modeled after the handwriting of scribes. He designed and printed the Gutenberg Bible, one of the first reproducible books. The letterpress revolutionized the printing of books, and worked so well that it established the printing system that was used for the next five hundred years.

By the 1700s, printing was a major industry. Printed materials were in high demand. Literacy increased. As the demand for reading materials grew, so did the interest in ways to make these materials more visually appealing. Printers began to develop more interesting typefaces, and different printing techniques; printers who were not skilled in lettering turned for help to craftspeople who were. Many of the typefaces created by these pioneering designers continue to be used today.

Nicholas Jenson, a successful French printer and publisher, is one of the earliest type designers on record. He developed an alphabet based on an inscription on the Trajan column

15

1950

"One of the major technological revolutions of our time revolves around the effort to diminish, if not to eliminate altogether, the use of movable types in printing. A small handsome machine called the Vari-Typer is doing its share to bring this revolution about. The Vari-Typer looks and works like a typewriter but the resemblance ends there, for it performs miracles of composition no typewriter pretends to and which only the giant Linotype can match."

—*Portfolio* magazine, 1950. When the Vari-Type machine first appeared, it was referred to as "a new revolution in the American printing industry."

1987

"Since Gutenberg, every advance in printing has served to remove the process from the direct control of the author.... But suddenly you've got a small relatively inexpensive machine on which you can write text, but also do many of the complex things that publishing today requires."

—Alvin Eisenman. "For Every Voice a Means to be Heard." Apple Computer brochure, 1987.

from second century Rome. An English engraver, William Caslon, designed his first Roman and italic typefaces in the early 18th century. During this period another Englishman, John Baskerville, who was dissatisfied with the state of printing in England and interested in letterforms, began to design typefaces and print his own books. Giambattista Bodoni, a renowned Italian type designer and printer, designed the typeface that bears his name and is still popular today. Modern typography is based on typefaces developed by these pioneers, and others from the fifteenth through the nineteenth century.

The invention of *hot type*, a machine-set type formed from molten lead cast into letterforms, evolved in the late 1800s. The term "leading" (pronounced ledding), which is still found on the type menus of some computers derives from the line or slug of lead from a Linotype machine that separated each line of type. *Cold type*, type produced through a photographic process, was introduced in 1950. This new innovation, phototypesetting, began to take over the typesetting world, and hot type began to be used less and less. Phototypesetting was faster and more efficient and provided for greater versatility in the setting and use of type.

Digital type, type electronically produced on the computer, is the most recent innovation in the type revolution, and for the first time since Gutenberg, the designer is back in the driver's seat.

TYPE TERMINOLOGY

Every field has its own jargon or vocabulary. It is important to learn the terminology in order to appear more knowledgeable when communicating with a client, another designer, or a printer.

The terms *serif* and *sans serif* are used when referring to type. Serifs are appendages, or little feet, found on the tops and bottoms of Roman letters. It is assumed that they were derived either from the chisel marks left after letters were cut into stone or from the brushstrokes used to draw the letters on the stone before cutting. Sans serif type (sans, from the French, meaning without) began to be used in the early 20th century by the de Stijl and Bauhaus designers who were interested in simplicity of form.

EARLY PRINTING

Top right: A page from the Gutenberg Bible, an example of early printing using moveable type. 1450-1455. *Courtesy of Division of Rare and Manuscript Collections. Carl A. Kroch Library, Cornell University. Ithaca, New York 14853-5302.*

Bottom left and right: Two pages from the 600 page Nuremberg Chronicle, a history of the world from the dawn of creation until the year 1493, the date of its printing. *Courtesy of Division of Rare and Manuscript Collections. Carl A. Kroch Library, Cornell University. Ithaca, New York 14853-5302.*

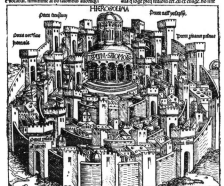

TYPE CLASSIFICATION

Caslon
CASLON

1. Roman

Roman type shows a pronounced contrast between thick and thin strokes. Serifs are added to the main strokes. Roman is the type most frequently used in text. Some of the older Roman typefaces are appropriately called Old Style.

Futura light
FUTURA LIGHT

2. Sans Serif/Gothic

Gothic letters have lines of equal weight without any flourishes or additions to the basic letter form. The term Gothic is used in reference to type without serifs.

Stuyvesant
STUYVESANT

3. Script, or Cursive, and Calligraphic

Script or Cursive type is used to simulate handwriting and calligraphy. The computer makes it possible to create an italic or oblique style and many designers use these styles rather than cursive or script because they are more readable.

Zapf Chancery
ZAPF CHANCERY

4. Gothic/Blackletter

Blackletter type was modeled after the handwriting of medieval scribes and can be found in books from that period. This type is mainly used for church materials, diplomas, and other official documents. It is elaborate, extremely difficult to read, and should be used with discretion.

Lubalin Graph
LUBALIN GRAPH

5. Square/Slab Serifs or Egyptian

Square, Slab serifs or Egyptian refer to type with heavy serifs or slabs that have uniform stroke weights. It is more effective when used in headlines than in large amounts of text.

JUNIPER
Amelia

6. Novelty, Decorative, Specialty, or Display

Specialty type began to be used in the mid 19th century, when there was a proliferation of printed materials, to attract the attention of the reader. Some of these faces are illegible when used in large amounts of text. They should be used with care because the very uniqueness of the type may call attention to itself rather than to the message to be communicated.

THE ELEMENTS OF A LETTER

Arm ▶ An upward or short horizontal stroke from a stem: L, E.

Ascender ▶ The part of a lowercase letter that extends above the normal body of the letter: b, d, f, l.

Bar ▶ The horizontal bar found in letters: A, H, e.

Baseline ▶ The bottom edge or invisible line on which type sits.

Bowl ▶ The curved line that forms an enclosed or almost enclosed negative space: P, R, d, a, c.

Counter ▶ The shape created by the enclosed space in a letter. The bowl refers to the actual line that encloses a space, and the counter refers to the space itself: e, g, o.

Descender ▶ The part of a lowercase letter that extends below the normal body of the letter: j, g, p, q, y.

Stem ▶ A full-length vertical or diagonal line or stroke: L, E.

Stress ▶ Thickening direction of a curved stroke: R, P.

Stroke ▶ The curves and stem that gives letters their basic form: w, y.

Swash ▶ A flourish that adds decoration and replaces a serif: ℛ, ℐ, 𝒩.

Tail ▶ An angled short stroke: Q, R.

x-Height ▶ The height of lowercase letters with the exclusion of ascenders and descenders. Type with a large x-height may be more readable, but it will allow for fewer characters per line and will need more space between lines. (See Chapter 6, Type Terminology and Typesetting Basics, for more information on type and readability.)

THE ANATOMY OF A LETTER

swash

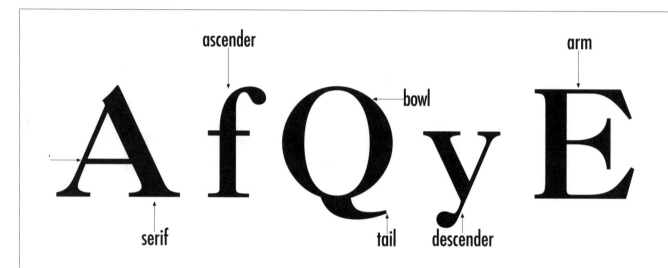

ascender

arm

bowl

A f Q y E

serif

tail

descender

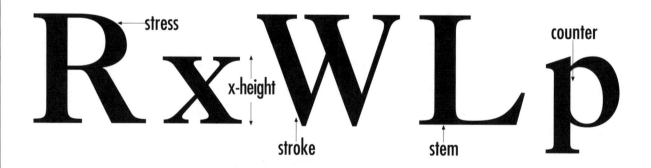

stress

counter

R x W L p

x-height

stroke

stem

THE BASELINE

the x-height of a letter

TYPE: THE BASIC INGREDIENT

When we refer to type, we are talking about the basic ingredient in visual communication, the primary element on a printed page. We are also referring to the image or personality we choose when we select a style for the letters that make up the words we use to communicate a message. The clothing you wear tells a tale about who you are and the image you are trying to convey to the people you come in contact with. You would select a different outfit to interview for a job than you would to play tennis. The clothing you wear to a job interview tells your prospective employer a great deal about who you are, and similarly, the typeface you choose for the design of a printed page sets the image for that page.

The computer can be a mixed blessing. The desktop publisher is often drawn to excesses that destroy the simplicity and confuse the layout of a page. Have you ever noticed people in a fast food, all you-can-eat restaurant? Normally moderate eaters often will fill their plates at the buffet table and go back for seconds. A similar phenomenon occurs when people first begin to use the computer. They pull down the font menu, behold a smorgasbord of fonts, and, like the diner at the buffet, fill up their page with several fonts and go back for more. Restraint must be exercised and the temptations of too many options resisted. In order to use the typefaces within easy reach, type needs to be thought of as a tool for communication, a dressing for ideas to be conveyed, and a means to mass communication. Type is one of the first things the reader sees when looking at a page. The type selected can either enhance a message, or it can confuse the reader. Type should be used as a tool to communicate the actual meaning of words (see following pages); if it is not used correctly it will communicate the wrong message.

Identity for a private Italian sailing vessel, Varcone. The letters are hand-lettered and use decorative swashes and flourishes.
Designer: Tony DiSpigna, 1992.

COMMUNICATING WITH TYPE:

Selecting appropriate typefaces & styles

On this page are the names of four different businesses. Each name is set in three different typefaces with three different layouts. Select the one typeface and design that you think is the most appropriate for each business, keeping in mind the information you have been given in the captions.

— 1

What images come to mind when you think about a bank? Which of these designs best represent what you want from a bank? Which ones are inappropriate, and which are inappropriate? Why?

First National Savings Bank

FIRST NATIONAL SAVINGS BANK

FIRST NATIONAL SAVINGS BANK

— 2

William C. Smith is a lawyer who works for large corporations. He needs to maintain a fairly conservative image. Which one of the typefaces and designs would be best for William C. Smith's image?

William C. Smith
Attorney At Law

WILLIAM C. SMITH
ATTORNEY AT LAW

William C. Smith
Attorney at Law

— 3

Two different beauty salons have the same name. The first salon caters to mature women in their late 60s to 70s who live in an expensive and upscale neighborhood in a large city, and who want hairstyles that are simple, but elegant, hairstyles that are tried and true, and conservative.

The second audience is the professional woman on-the-go, a "Thirty Something" kind of woman who is modern, stylish, and trendy.

Which of these typefaces and designs would you select for each salon?

Jennifer's Beauty Salon

JENNIFER'S BEAUTY SALON

JENNIFER'S BEAUTY SALON

— 4

Speedy Movers is a moving company that moves households of furniture for individuals and students. They do the job and do it fast. Which design and typeface do you think visually describes this business?

SPEEDY MOVERS

Speedy Movers

SPEEDY MOVERS

TYPE AS ILLUSTRATION

The samples below were executed in Aldus® FreeHand, a drawing program, and Letraset's LetraStudio®, a program which manipulates type by stretching, curving, or otherwise distorting it. This program can be used to produce illustrative text for headlines. These words were imported as graphics into PageMaker.

The typefaces used and the design of these words illustrate their meanings.

Below are two examples of printed designs that use type as illustration. The word "Wanderings" used for the title of a book, was created to simulate the Hebrew alphabet.

In the brochure at the bottom of this page, the line through the word "harassment" violates the word to illustrate what it feels like to be sexually harassed.

Top: Typeface designed for cover of Chaim Potok's *Wanderings*, a history of the Jews. Alfred A. Knopf, NY, 1978. Designer: Gun Larson designed the Hebraic-looking titles that appear throughout the book.

Bottom: Cover for brochure for students, faculty and staff about sexual harassment on campus. Designed by Publications Services, Cornell University, Ithaca, NY, 1990.

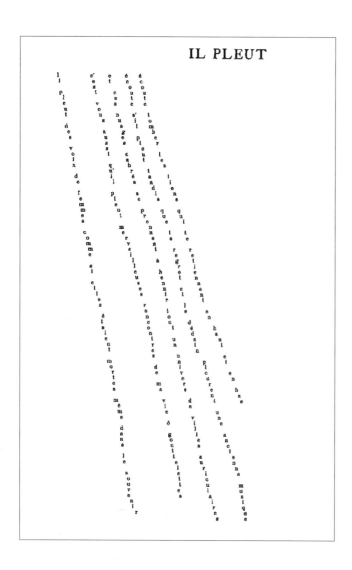

IL PLEUT

Top left: Il Pleut (It Rains) a concrete poem by French poet, Guillaume Appollinaire from Arts et Metier Graphiques, Paris, France, 1930. The words are placed vertically to illustrate the meaning of the poem.

Bottom right: Cover for a book jacket, *Psycho*. Designer: Tony Palladino, 1964 .

Robert Bloch
An Inner Sanctum Mystery

Bottom: An illustration for a book jacket. Dutton Paper Backs. 1964. Designer: Milton Glaser, 1964.

LETTERS AS SHAPES

THE LETTERFORM

Chinese philosophers referred to the essence of form in terms of empty space. Without its hollow interior, a jug is simply a lump of clay; it is the empty space inside that makes the clay into a container. Similar considerations must be taken into account when dealing with typography. The designer must think about the space inside each letter as well as the space that surrounds it.

" When printing helped to make the acceptance of the written word general, it became evident that mere legibility was not all that could be asked of letters, and that shades of thought could be projected into the shapes of the letters."

— Paul Hollister,
American Alphabets.
Harper & Brothers, New York, 1930.

In the examples below, the white letters placed in black boxes show the empty space, or the *negative space*, within each letter as well as the black space surrounding it.

—Quote below, French writer, Victor Hugo, France Et Belgique. Alpes et Pyrénées. Voyages et Excursions, Paris, 1910.

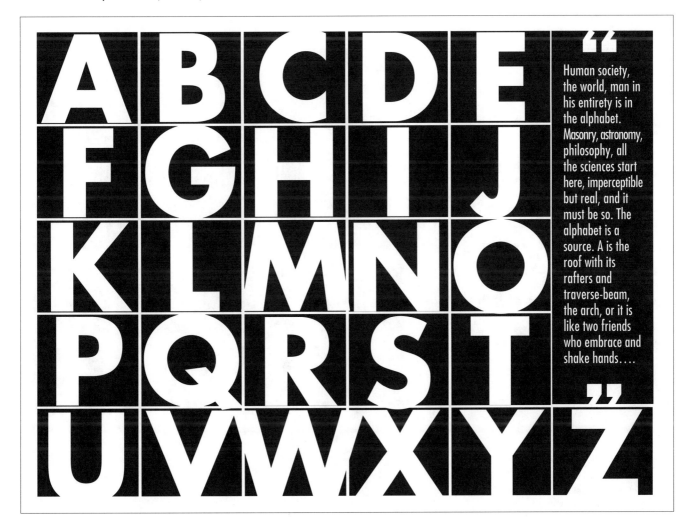

Human society, the world, man in his entirety is in the alphabet. Masonry, astronomy, philosophy, all the sciences start here, imperceptible but real, and it must be so. The alphabet is a source. A is the roof with its rafters and traverse-beam, the arch, or it is like two friends who embrace and shake hands....

PUNCTUATION MARKS AS SHAPES

Quotation marks, exclamation points and question marks assume different shapes in each type family. Punctuation marks can be used as graphic devices on a page.

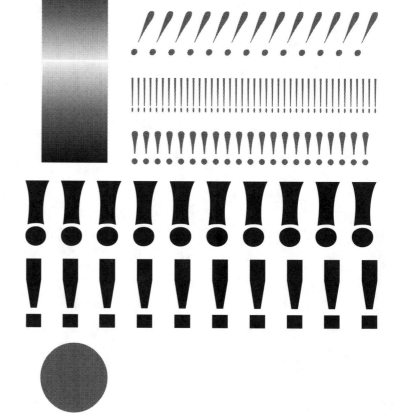

The thought balloon is from clip art in Aldus® Persuasion. The drawing of a man is from *Victorian Spot Illustrations, Alphabet & Ornaments.* Dover Publications, Inc. New York, 1982.

CASLON   BAUHAUS HEAVY   MIDDLETON   FUTURA BOLD

THE FONTS BELOW ARE THE SAME BUT ARE SET IN ALL CAPS

The shape and form of the letter A is different in each typeface. All four letters have been typeset in the same point size.

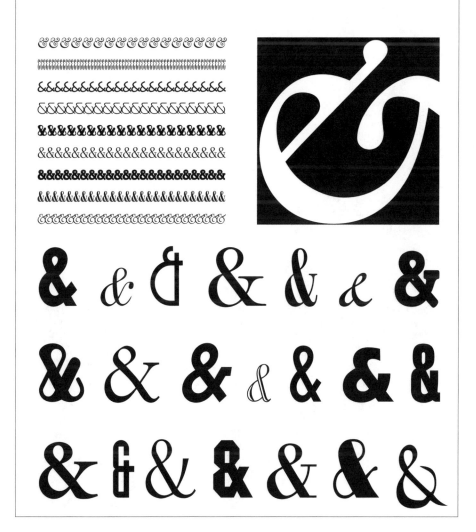

The word alphabet has been typeset using the fonts on the left to show the difference in the appearance of each word.

The typefaces of the small, repeated ampersands below from top to bottom are: Caslon 540 Italic, Arcadia, Lithos Regular, Bauhaus Light, BT Amelia, ITC Fenice Light, Italia Bold, Bodoni Poster Compressed, and University Roman.

THE AMPERSAND

The ampersand, the symbol for the word "and," comes from the Latin ET. Each font has its own ampersand. Each ampersand has a shape and style unique to its particular typeface. The ampersand can be used as a graphic element on a page, or as a significant part of a logo, as shown below.

Logo for masthead of *Upper & Lower Case* magazine. Reprinted with permission from *Upper & Lower Case, The International Journal of Type and Graphic Design;* © International Typeface Corporation. Artists: Herb Lubalin and Tom Carnase.

LETTERFORMS AND NEGATIVE SPACE

The typefaces used in these designs are Futura Bold and Eras Bold.

In the design below the A becomes the negative space in the formation of the letter R.

The designs on this page are made up of *letterforms*, two letters put together to form symbols. Placing two letters together in this way creates negative space and another shape.

The grey shapes within the letterforms on this page were put in to emphasize the negative shapes.

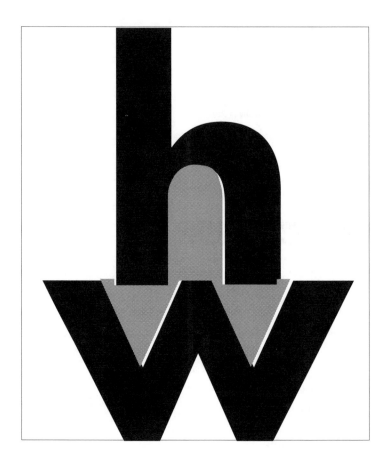

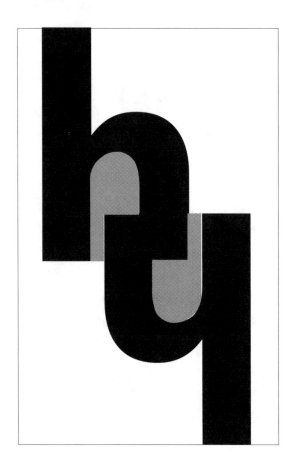

LETTERFORMS AS PRECURSORS TO DESIGNING LOGOS

Some logos are created with letterforms alone. On this page are letterforms that might be used as logos. The following chapter, Logos, Symbols, and Trademarks, discusses the designing of logos, the embodiment of graphic design, and conceptual thinking.

Typefaces used on this page: top left and right: Bodoni Poster, Black Chancery. Bottom left and right: Eras Bold, Aachen Bold.

The exercises in this chapter relate to type as a method of communicating a message visually, to perception of letters as forms and shapes, and to understanding letterforms as a precursor to designing logos.

1. Typeset your name on the computer in a drawing program using several different fonts. Which font do you think seems most appropriate as a self portrait? Using the font you selected repeat the name 3 more times and change the style of some of the letters to italics, bold, outline, shadow. Notice the pattern created by the lines of text.

2. Type can be used to illustrate words. Using a drawing program illustrate the following words using only type: shy, happy, reflection, disappearing, fearful, anxious, mirror image, sleepy, hungry. Think of other words to illustrate.

3. Typeset the initials of your name. Create a logo, an identifier for yourself by having the letters of your name form a symbol. Be aware of the negative space you are creating in the process, and think about the image your are projecting with this symbol.

THE WILD

OUTDOORS

3.
LOGOS,
SYMBOLS,
AND TRADEMARKS

INSIDE THIS CHAPTER

▼

3

LOGOS, SYMBOLS, AND TRADEMARKS

THE SYMBOL

Above: Old cattlebrands used by American cowboys in the west in the beginning of the twentieth century.

Right: 19th century printer's mark. From *Westvaco Inspirations for Printers,* Westvaco Corporation, 1926.

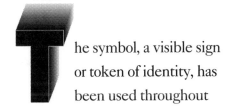

he symbol, a visible sign or token of identity, has been used throughout history as a method of communication. We think cave people scratched pictographs on the walls of caves in Altamira, Spain and Lascaux, France, to warn and inform others in the community of the presence of dangerous animals, and to convey other messages as well. Archaeologists have uncovered artifacts from ancient Greece with marks and symbols that identify the creator of the objects. Articles have been found in ancient Egyptian tombs with symbols inscribed on them, possibly the signature of the artist. In medieval society, merchants and craftspeople used marks and symbols to identify themselves in relation to their products or merchandise. Printers in the late

GEO·W·JONES

nineteenth century took great pride in their workmanship, and they used symbols as logos or signatures on each printed piece to identify the print job and the craftsmanship. At the beginning of the twentieth century, cowboys in the American West began to brand their cattle to signify ownership. They represent a pictorial language dating back to the ancient Egyptians. During the Great Depression, hobos, the professional unemployed, invented an imaginative and functional communication system, marks on walls of houses and other buildings to warn fellow hobos of danger in much the same way cave people used pictographs. Two circles and a connecting link signified handcuffs and served as a warning that local police were hostile. This sign advised others to depart quickly. Four horizontal lines on a house, meant that if wood is cut, the woman of the house would provide a meal as payment.

Graffiti on a wall in Kauserslautern, Germany.
Photographer: George Rhoads, 1989.

Graffiti, the marks made on walls, in subways, and other public places, can be considered an attempt to communicate feelings, a way of making a statement, or an attempt to establish one's existence.

SYMBOLS AND EMOTIONS

Symbols, like typestyles and colors, can evoke certain emotional responses in us. The meanings of symbols change with their usage. The original swastika dates back to prehistoric times. The Sanskrit word means "all for one" and signifies strength and fertility. This symbol was originally found on coins from ancient Crete, Pre-Colombian objects, and Navajo pottery. When Hitler's Third Reich began to use the swastika as an identity symbol, the emotional association changed. It is hard for us to look at that symbol now and see it as a benign mark. On the other hand, the symbol of the dove, used by anti-war activists during the Vietnam War in the sixties and early seventies, is associated with peace. Since symbols can have negative or positive associations, the designer, when creating a visual representation or mark, must be alert to the psychological impact and emotional response a symbol might trigger.

PICTOGRAMS

The graphic stylized symbols on this page are called *pictograms*, visual symbols that give information, pictures without words. Pictograms are graphic symbols that tell a story in a simple way.

This kind of symbol surrounds us in our daily lives. Pictograms are signs on the streets, in supermarkets, department stores, public buildings, and roads. They show us where to find telephones, restrooms, train stations, airports, and restaurants. They are a way to communicate messages without words. If you drive in a foreign country and can't speak the language, you will understand the roadside signs that warn of a sharp curve in the road or steep incline, because the signs are a universal, visual, wordless language.

Above: Street sign in Baden Baden, Germany. Photographer: Sheryl D. Sinkow, ©1993.

Right: Pictograms for a petting zoo and drive-through safari animal park. Student project. Designer: Shelly Bremmer, Rochester Institute of Technology, 1991.

WHAT IS A LOGO?

The word *logo* derives from the Greek word for language, and we think of a logo as a symbol, a sign, a modern pictograph, or pictogram, that identifies and represents an organization, business, product, or even a conference or special event. Canadians use the term "identifier" rather than logo, a better indicator of what a logo is: the embodiment of an organization that should foster instant visual identification and recognition. The logo represents a large amount of information compressed into a single visual statement.

An interesting tale is attributed to Raymond Loewy, a well-known industrial designer. He was seated next to "a lovely young lady" at a dinner party. She suddenly turned to him and asked him why he made the X drop below the line in the word Exxon. "Why ask me?" he said. "I couldn't help seeing it," she replied. "Well, that's the answer," said Mr. Loewy.

WHAT MAKES A GOOD LOGO DESIGN?

A successful logo makes an immediate impression, and it is interesting to look at. It should be immediately recognizable without explanation, and should have a uniqueness that distinguishes it from other logos. Like good wine, a successful logo should age well and be able to be used for many years. Numerous solutions exist for the designing of each logo, but simplicity is the essence of a good logo or symbol. The words "less is more" are used repeatedly by designers and those who teach graphic design. The "less is more" principle taken from the Bauhaus, should be applied when attempting a logo design.

Logo design by Shelly Bremmer, BFA student, Rochester Institute of Technology, for fictitious organization.

SYMBOL, LOGOTYPE, OR TRADEMARK?

What format will you use to represent your organization: symbol, logotype, or trademark? The important thing to keep in mind is the image you are trying to project. The format you use should reflect a strong and imaginative image. If the symbol or pictorial image is ambiguous and can be misunderstood, it has failed. Before attempting to design your logo, take a good look at other logos in magazines, newspapers, and bulletin boards. Study them carefully. The designer must work in close partnership with the client to determine the best approach to the identity design.

WHICH FORMAT WILL YOU USE?

1. Abstract symbol or pictograph

Symbols can evoke strong emotional responses. Symbols used in logos are usually stylized pictorial or abstract icons that in some way reflect the organization. Many abstract symbols have come into the marketplace since the sixties, but even more have appeared since the late '80s when desktop publishing began. The new logo software programs on the market claim that you can "create world-class logos in minutes that can be modified in an infinite number of ways." If you want to design something that is unique and will compete in the marketplace, be wary of

Logotype for Angelwood Art & Antiques, a shop that sells paintings and antiques. Designer: Marcelle Lapow Toor, 1990.

"Despite its usual long life, the best trademark needs periodic check and evaluation. What may have been a successful trademark for many years gradually takes on an old-fashioned look. It may have been satisfactory in reaching consumers a generation ago, but with the great influx of new products and new trademarks, the emphasis on modern design and the rise of a new generation of consumers, the old-fashioned trademark may symbolize an old-fashioned product—one which may remain on the shelves unnoticed."
—Harry Lapow,
"The Trademark in the Changing Market," 1955.

becoming too dependent upon these programs, because the logo you create may be indistinguishable from the dozens created by other users of these programs. A logo takes a great deal of thought. A good concept should take preference over speed.

2. Logotypes or typographic symbols

A logotype is the name of an organization, set in a typeface appropriate to that organization and is usually found without a graphic symbol. Sometimes a logotype is based on the initials of the company, as letterforms.

3. Trademarks and Descriptive Symbols

A trademark is a name, symbol or combination of the two that is used to identify the product of a business. A trademark will carry the ™ sign. This mark can be found on your computer.

QUESTIONS TO ASK BEFORE DESIGNING A LOGO

It is important to remember that designing a logo is not about making a pretty picture. The logo should always be based on a specific concept.

1. Research

What has been done by this company before? If it is a new company, what is the image the company wishes to project? If it is a redesign of an old logo, is there a way to update rather than make a radical change? The client's business and image are identified by the old logo. A drastic change might confuse the public. People have difficulty adjusting to change and often resent it. If the logo needs a drastic change, it might be a good idea to make a public fuss about the new logo, to advertise the change and call attention to the new design.

2. Who is the audience?

Answering this question will determine the general feel of the logo/logotype. Multicultural has become an important word in the '90s. The market for designers extends to countries that were formerly part of the Eastern Block. Does this logo need to cross cultural lines?

How can you represent different cultures with one symbol?

"The most significant factors currently affecting mass communications are computerization, the globalization of business, and the ecology movement. These facts will most likely determine the '90s look. The mix will include bit-mapping, computer distorted images, the layered look, recycled paper, and symbols that are understood across continental and cultural divides. But the shock of the new is always tempered by a fondness for the familiar…" Quote from designer Chris Gorman, of Chris Gorman Associates in *Graphic Design USA*.

Right: Identity for international soccer event to raise money to fight AIDS designed for Savvy Management, Inc. NYC. Designer: Tony DiSpigna, 1988.

3. Where and how will the logo be used?

If the logo is to be used in both large and small formats, displayed on trucks, and on signage, as well as on letterheads, business cards, and other printed materials, give careful consideration to how it will look in these different formats and sizes. Can the design that looks terrific large, be reduced and still maintain its integrity ? Will the design that you created small enlarge well and still retain its details and good design?

Above: Logo on a T-shirt for a shop specializing in clothing for the outdoors. Designer: Mo Viele, 1991.

4. What is the client's budget?

How will the logo eventually be reproduced? If the budget permits the use of several colors, does the client also expect to be using the logo in materials produced on a computer, and printed on a laser printer? Will the logo that looks sensational in color still look good in black and white when printed on the desktop printer?

5. Will the logo you design today hold up five to ten years from now?

Is the company growing rapidly? The best logos are the ones that have held up through the years, and updated with only minor changes. Design a logo with the future in mind.

Before designing a logo:

1. Make a list of related images on the subject that come to mind.
2. Draw pictures of some of the best images.
3. Try combining some of the above.
4. Simplify and stylize three images.
5. Try using only type and create several logotypes using a drawing program. Try creating your own letters in a drawing program and put them together as a symbol.
6. Get feedback from friends, fellow workers, roommates!

Hint: If the designs you have created do not communicate what you had in mind, go back to the computer.

Below: Two different logos for SUPERCOMPUTING conferences. The logo design in each reflects the site of each conference. Left: The site of the 1991 conference was Albuquerque and the logo has a southwestern feel. Right: The site of the 1993 conference was Portland, "the city of bridges and Mt. Hood." Designer: Mo Viele.

THE EVOLUTION OF A LOGO

The Interactive Multimedia Group (IMG) part of the Communication Department at Cornell University is a laboratory involved in interdisciplinary communication research that involves the interaction of people with computers. The state-of-the-art lab receives its funding from the National Science Foundation, Apple Computer, IBM, and a number of other organizations, and it is creating some very innovative prototypes for the field of education using the latest computer technologies. The lab needed a logo. Allan Wai, a student in the Cornell University Communication Department wanted a design project for the Fall of 1992. He contacted Professor Geri Gay, Director of IMG, when he heard she was looking for someone to design a logo. They talked about the image she wanted for the lab. After a number of discussions, Wai played with some designs and came up with the four designs below.

Below: Some ideas for logos for the Interactive Multimedia Group, Cornell University.
Designer: Allan Wai, 1992.

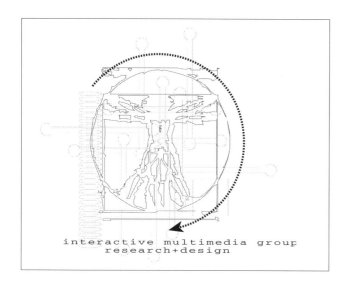

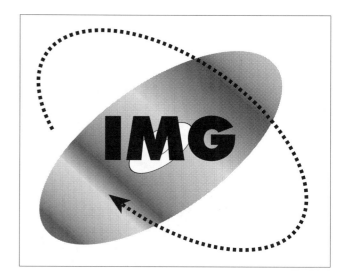

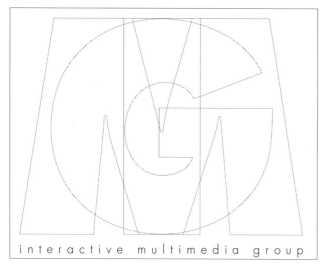

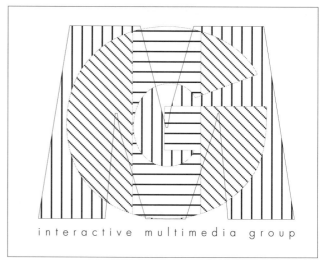

Professor Gay didn't feel that any of these designs represented the lab visually. Allan Wai graduated, and the logo design was never resolved.

In the spring of 1993 Chrissy Conant, an MFA graduate from the School of Visual Arts, was hired as Art Director for IMG. She was asked to design a logo that would be the corporate identity for the lab to be used on stationery, brochures, and other printed materials from the lab as well as for T-shirts, plaques, and any other promotional materials produced by the lab. Conant discussed the logo with Professor Gay, who now had a better idea of what she wanted. Both Conant and Gay felt that the initials IMG should be emphasized and used as a significant part of the logo and that the logo needed to visually communicate "technology and creativity."

THE STEPS IN THE DESIGN PROCESS
Step 1
Conant typeset the letters IMG in Futura Condensed Bold and felt that they looked too bare, too condensed. She used the outline function in FreeHand which enabled her to manipulate the letters as graphics. After seeing the letters together she also realized that she liked the way the letters formed a basic geometric shape, a square.

Step 2
Conant decided to dress the letters by adding texture to the background. The entire name of the organization had to be included in the logo, so she added the name using the serif typeface, Copperplate because she felt it had a current look and she liked the design of the typeface. She felt that Copperplate would work well with the sans serif Futura Condensed Bold. She wanted contrast between the IMG initials and the name spelled out. In this incarnation she felt that she had contrast in three different ways:

1. Contrast in size: the IMG initials and the size of the full name of the organization.
2. Contrast in typestyles: serif and sans serif.
3. Contrast in color: After going through shades of color she chose plain black and white, "the ultimate in contrast."

Step 3

This version shows a rectangle within a rectangle. After making this change Conant began to realize that she needed another geometric shape, a circle. She felt at this point that the logo did not visually show the interaction between people and computers or technology.

Step 4

She began to realize that she wanted the logo to visually say, "interactive and creative." Conant got the idea of using the hands from Michelangelo's *The Creation*, a painting from the Sistine Chapel "showing God creating man who is creative." She felt that it was a chichéd image but she decided to put a new twist on it for "recognition and interpretation."

Step 5

Conant scanned the hands from the painting above and traced them in Photoshop to show pronounced negative space.

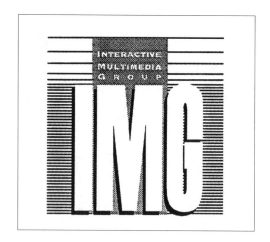

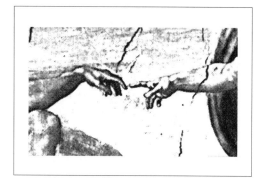

Step 6

Conant decided to incorporate the traced hands into the initials IMG, making use of the negative space. At this point she showed the design to friends and co-workers to see if her idea was getting across to others. Notice how the inside of the M is pointing down to the action.

Step 7

Here Conant has added a button in between the fingers.

Step 8
The logo completed (below)

This is where the idea for a square within a circle clicked. The button from the design above has been replaced by a mouse to incorporate the idea of technology with man as a creator.

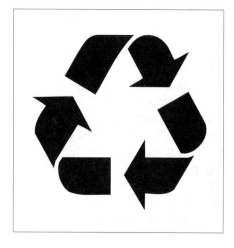

Symbol or logo to identify the use of recycled paper.

1. Look for logos on products in the supermarket. Put them into categories: symbols, letterforms, or trademarks.

2. Set up a file with logos you think are unique and unusual.

3. Contact a not-for-profit organization and ask if they need a logo designed. Most of these organizations are delighted to have design help, since they usually operate on a very low budget. Meet with the marketing or education person to get all the information you need about the organization. Design a logo based on the information they give you.

4. Design a logo for yourself using a symbol. Try to think of a symbol that best represents you.

5. Design a logotype for yourself using the letters of your name. Use a typeface you think best represents who you are.

6. Imagine that you have your own desktop publishing business. Design a logo for your business using a symbol that visually communicates the business. What images come to mind when you think of desktop publishing? Make a list of these and use them to design your logo.

4.
INFLUENCES ON CONTEMPORARY GRAPHIC DESIGN

INSIDE THIS CHAPTER

INFLUENCES ON CONTEMPORARY GRAPHIC DESIGN

GRAPHIC DESIGN ROOTS

Promotional poster for LeNali, a boutique in Corsica. Designer: Tony DiSpigna.

ontemporary graphic design has its roots in the late nineteenth, and early twentieth century. It evolved as a cross-pollination of several art movements that challenged the aesthetics of the past and is an outgrowth of a climate of rebellion against tradition, convention, and technology.

John Ruskin, an influential English critic in the latter part of the nineteenth century wrote, "Art is all one, any distinction between fine and applied art is destructive and artificial," a theme that continued into the twentieth century. William Morris, an English designer, and printer in the late 1800s, in accord with the writings of Ruskin, led the Arts and Crafts Movement, a reaction to the poor workmanship and shoddy design that came with the mechanization of the machine age. He designed typefaces based on classic faces used in early printing and renewed a spirit of pride in good craftsmanship. Morris's designs included typography and books, as well as fabrics, furniture, wallpaper, and rugs, items classified as both arts and crafts. Other designers followed in this tradition, creating both a new aesthetic and an appreciation for well-crafted design. Evidence of Morris's designs can still be found today in the form of wrapping and wallpaper.

The American architect, Frank Lloyd Wright, embraced the philosophy of the Arts and Crafts Movement. His building designs show an emphasis on the relationship between form and function. They also show his rebellion against mass production. Wright designed buildings using three-dimensional space in an abstract way, and he used bricks, concrete, wood and plaster as building materials, creating an architectural collage.

The rapid advancement of technology in the early 1900s had its effect on the art world. Fauvism, a French painting movement, led by Henri Matisse, Georges Rouault, and Raoul Dufy, shook up the art world with brash, bold, and garish colors in a rebellion against technology, while Futurism, begun in Italy by Filippo Tomasso Marinetti, used the technological advances to demonstrate sensations of movement and speed.

In Holland during World War I, the de Stijl Movement (Piet Mondrian and Theo Van Doesburg), showed painters returning to simplicity and asymmetry using geometric forms.

The Dada School began around 1916 during World War I, as a rebellion and protest against the barbarism and horrors of war. It was more a state of mind than a movement; it was a philosophical bent. Dada poets, visual artists, writers, and musicians challenged and questioned all traditional values, using elements of shock and surprise like the Fauves. Translated, the German word "dada," a word used by a child, means hobby-horse. Instead of creating order, the Dadaists created chaos and intentional disorder on the printed page using emotionally jarring words and images. They broke all rules of typography. Inspired by the collages of the Cubists, the Dadaists discovered and experimented with photomontage, a composite picture, or collage, made up of different photographic images. They altered and manipulated these images in an attempt to create a new reality. This technique is used by graphic designers today.

While the Dadaists were questioning values, Pablo Picasso, George Braque, and Juan Gris, in their Cubist period, were making paintings that were concerned with new abstract ways of looking at two-dimensional space, fragmenting familiar shapes, and objects. They created collages that were assemblages of effluvia from daily life, clippings from

Photomontage by artist Gary Lapow.

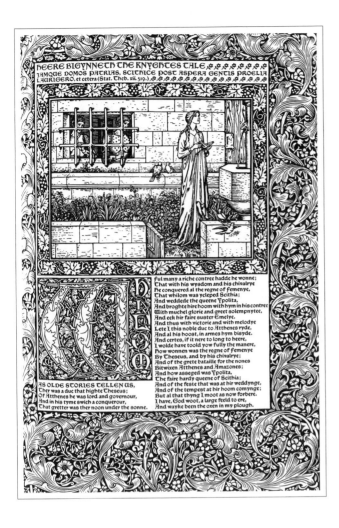

Left:

The Arts and Crafts Movement

A page from the Knight's Tale in *The Kelmscott Chaucer* designed by William Morris, 1890. *Courtesy of Division of Rare and Manuscript Collections. Carl A. Kroch Library, Cornell University. Ithaca, New York 14853-5302.*

Right bottom:

Art Deco Border

From *Spot Illustrations and Motifs.* Dover Publications, Inc. NY, 1985.

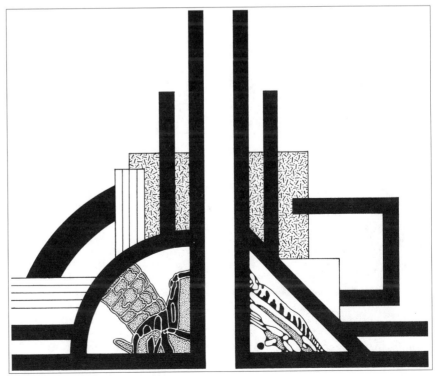

newspapers, cigarette and bottle labels, pieces of wood, and other cast-off items.

Inspired by the works of Sigmund Freud and the dream world, the Surrealists shook up the art world with paintings that delved into the world of the unconscious. The work of Surrealist painter René Magritte has had a profound influence on graphic design. Images that show a strong resemblance to his paintings appear with regularity in illustration and graphic design today.

Another important influence on contemporary graphic design was the Bauhaus School, a school of architecture and the applied arts founded by Walter Gropius in the early 1920s, as an attempt to bridge the gap between the fine and applied arts. The Bauhaus School placed equal value on all areas of arts and crafts and stressed design for design's sake. Its concern was for good design without regard for the design's ultimate purpose. The Bauhaus artists and designers were responsible for innovation in type and book design, as well as for the design of exhibitions, posters, and other publications.

Paris in the 1920's saw the beginning of the Art Deco Movement. Although the movement began in the early 1900's, Art Deco did not get its name until 1966 after a retrospective exhibition at the Musée des Arts Décoratifs of Paris of works from 1925. This movement, related to Art Nouveau, an earlier movement, represents the opposite of simplicity and shows a concern with decoration and geometric shapes. The Art Deco style began to appear in architecture and interior design (the Chrysler Building and Radio City Hall in New York City). It also began to appear in the design of packages, furniture, movie houses, borders, and typefaces. The designs were elegant and slick with interesting use of white space.

In 1933 the Bauhaus School closed, but it had created a framework for modern graphic design. In 1967, Herbert Bayer, architect and graphic designer wrote in his autobiography, "The Bauhaus movement cannot be seen as historically terminated and immutably fulfilled. It changed the world of art, design and architecture and continues, when its principles are observed, to be a creative force." At the same time the field of advertising began to take shape and become recognized. The 1960s and 1970s showed a short-lived return to Art Deco in graphic design, a style that still continues to be

The "Pan" album, a Parisian year-book. Produced by Maison Devambez, a printing house in Paris, 1827.

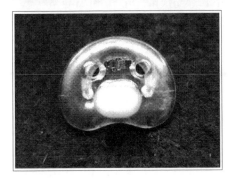

Photographs of "found faces."
Top: A child's pacifier. Middle: Lock chained to a tree.
Bottom: Doorknob on an the door of a Victorian house.
Photographer: Marcelle Lapow Toor, 1992.

embraced by graphic designers from time to time in design, architecture, and typography.

The art of the '60s and '70s, like art movements in the past, questioned previous design styles in an attempt to liberate both the printed page and life styles. Pop art prevailed with its references to graphic design and the 1980's began a new era where technology once again inserted itself. The images of the 1980s and 1990s, the Post-Modern era, show a concern for the past, a return to history. Influences derive from technology and the information age. The viewer is constantly being challenged to decipher layers of information. Many designs show a new aesthetic based on the capabilities of the computer.

An interesting thing to realize when one looks at designs from the distant or recent past is that there is really nothing new in design. All design relies on previous information and ideas. These ideas are just portrayed in different ways.

■ ■ ■

THE GESTALT PSYCHOLOGY

In 1912, while enormous experimentation and changes were taking place in the world of the arts, changes were happening in the world of psychology. Max Wertheimer, a German psychologist, published a paper on perception. Gestalt psychology, a design-related psychological movement, grew out of this paper. The Gestalt psychologists examined the way in which humans process visual images. They examined how the eye assimilates sensory information in order to form objects, and how the eye accepts suggestions of images and makes connections, as in the Rorshach test, cracks in the pavement, the man in the moon, or the found faces in the photographs on this page.

The word *Gestalt*, in relation to design, refers to vision as not only the act of seeing, but as a creative experience. The viewer of the printed page assumes an active role when looking at the page and seeks to group and organize visual material into a unified, cohesive whole. "The whole is more than the sum of its parts," was a theme of the Gestaltists. Each piece of the design puzzle relies upon the pieces around it. The printed page must be looked upon as a unified whole, the sum of all the parts, the pieces of the puzzle fitting neatly together, leaving no holes or excesses. Understanding the theories of the Gestaltists and human visual perception may help the designer achieve success in getting a message across.

In the Introduction we mentioned the significance of visual literacy and perception in relation to visual communication. The term is insinuating its way into our daily lives. In order to create successful designs, the designer must become visually literate and perceptive. It would be impossible for a person who cannot read to write a book. A person who is not visually literate has the same kind of handicap when attempting to design for the printed page. The designer needs to develop an acute awareness, and a sensitivity to images in daily life, to find out which images attract and which repel, and to develop an understanding of how we see, how a picture may communicate better than a word, and how our eyes scan and perceive information. In order to gain an understanding of this kind of perception, we must return to the early twentieth century and look at the Gestalt theories.

GESTALT THEORIES OF VISUAL PERCEPTION
1. Grouping

Our eyes have a tendency to group objects involuntarily. Painters, photographers, graphic designers, writers, and scientists learn to impose a grouping in the way they organize their materials. In *The Study of Thinking,* Jerome Bruner states, "The binding fact of mental life in child and adult alike is that there is a limited capacity for processing information. Our span, as it is called, can comprise six or seven unrelated items simultaneously. Go beyond that, and there is overload, confusion, forgetting."

2. Nearness or proximity

Optical units that are close to each other tend to be seen together because our eyes group visual elements that are in close proximity. The graphic designer should be aware of the placement of optical units on a page so that they have a relationship to each other, and are not fighting for attention on the page.

Similarity

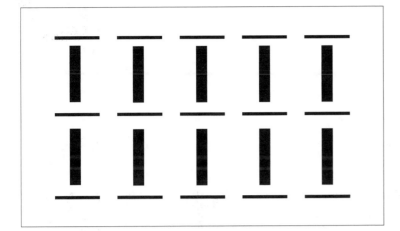

Proximity

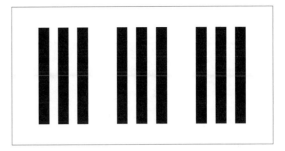

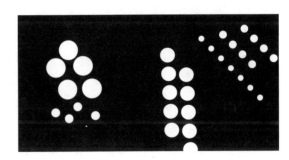

Continuity

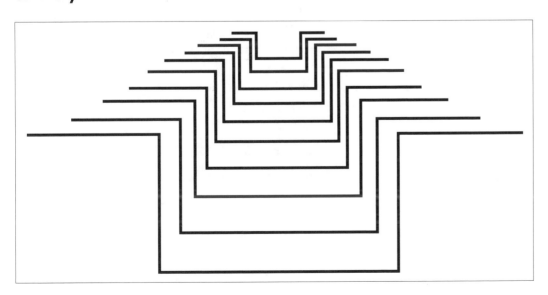

3. Similarity

While we tend to group elements that are close together, our eyes also have a tendency to group things that are similar in shape, size, color, and placement. We need similarity in order to recognize differences.

4. Continuity

Shapes, lines, or other visual elements that form a harmonious relationship, or grouping without interruption, are easily perceived by the eye and mind. The brain links them to form one cohesive image.

5. Closure

The eye has the ability to come to closure on a shape that merely suggests. Closure can create excitement because it forces the viewer to work and participate in the design, to become part of the process. The viewer should not have to work too hard or interest in the page is lost. In the example on this page, the eye connects the lines to view a pyramid or triangular shape, and though the word closure is partly obliterated, our eye still makes the connection because there is enough left of the word for comprehension.

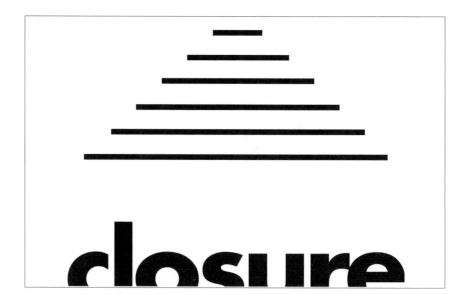

6. Figure/ground

If we refer to a page as a container, we think of a structure with two horizontal elements and two vertical elements. The addition of a mark on the blank page creates a positive space, or figure, while the

FIGURE GROUND

page itself becomes the negative space, or the ground. Figures and grounds are not seen simultaneously.

7. Negative and positive Space

Negative and positive are terms used to describe the relationship between figure and ground. Positive space is defined as that which dominates the eye. Negative space refers to the elements that are more passively displayed, the space formed when two objects are placed together, or the space left over. The designer must always consider the leftover space, the background, as sharing importance with the positive space or figure. In the examples on this page the areas become ambiguous; sometimes you see the negative space, and sometimes the positive.

8. Visual ambiguity

Our normal perception helps us establish balance or the lack of it. Visual ambiguity is like verbal ambiguity, and it occurs when the viewer must struggle to analyze elements on a page in terms of balance. If the intent of the composition is obscured, the meaning then is also obscured. Visual forms need to have clarity, harmony, or contrast, and they should relate or conflict, attract or repel. It is the designer's job to direct the viewer's focus to the important elements on the page, and to do it in a way that is obvious, not ambiguous.

9. Leveling and sharpening

Visual elements, images, or type on a page should be clear. The power of the unexpected, the surprise, takes precedence over the predictable. The opposites of harmony and stability are referred to as *leveling* and *sharpening*.

▶ Leveling uses symmetry and takes place when there is no tension on the page. In the diagrams below, the dot in the rectangle on the left has been placed dead center in the rectangle. It offers a feeling of harmony and symmetry, and lacks an element of surprise. There is no ambiguity. The eye does not need to struggle to place the dot in the center.

▶ Sharpening, the opposite of leveling, occurs when there is exaggeration and contrast, when the viewer must struggle to resolve the balance of elements, as in the middle rectangle. The dot is off center both horizontally and vertically, but we can still get a sense of balance, in an abstract way. Sharpening is an attempt to resolve ambiguity.

When designing for the printed page the designer needs to understand how we see, how to select a picture that will communicate better than a word, which images attract, which ones repel, and how our eyes scan and perceive information. With insights from the

It is not clear exactly whether the dot in the rectangle on the far right is in the center of the visual field. It is close but ambiguous in its placement.

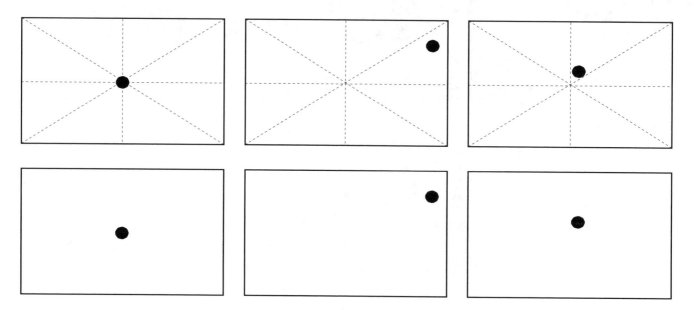

Gestaltists, the designer can create designs for the printed page that facilitate visual perception and communicate visually.

VISUAL DYNAMICS

- Perception is the key to response in graphic design.
- The eye groups information by similarity, proximity, continuity, and closure.
- Vision is a creative experience, not simply an act of seeing .
- We are able sometimes to see images that are implied, that do not exist, like in ink blots, in Rorshach tests, or in the shapes of clouds.
- Visual awareness and perception, in addition to sight, generally come through experience and previous knowledge.
- Words and groupings of words are more important to legibility than the form or shape of individual letters.

Notice how reading is impaired in the example below.

spatial relationship is an important factor in visual communication

spa tialr ela tion shi pisa nimp ort ant fac torin vis ual co mmu nic ation

ELEMENTS OF VISUAL DYNAMICS

When we look at a printed page, an ad, a magazine spread, or newspaper, all of our past experiences, cultural experiences, our emotions, even our memories, are projected onto that page, that rectangular surface, or container. We have been taught by our culture to read a page from top to bottom, left to right.

1. Balance

Balance is the essential ingredient in the success of the layout of a page. Balance in design has been compared to walking a tightrope, where the tightrope walker is constantly attempting to gain some kind of stability. It is a steadying act, with an interplay of tension and excitement that builds on the uncertainty, the threat of falling.

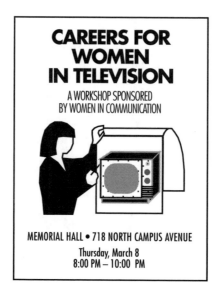 

The poster on the left uses a symmetrical design. The design in the poster on the right is asymmetrical.

When a design has balance, all the elements on a page look like they are grounded, not too heavy on the top or bottom. There are two kinds of balance, symmetrical and asymmetrical.

▶ Symmetry

Formal balance occurs when all the elements are centered on a page. Symmetrical balance has been used traditionally to organize and lay out a page. It is a good way to create a sense of stability and a lack of tension. It is easy on the eye and requires little work on the part of the viewer. There is no sharpening required. We can think of a symmetrical design as mirror images on a page, with both sides having the same and equal parts.

▶ Asymmetry

An asymmetrical design is less formal than a symmetrical

one and offers less stability, but may be more exciting to the viewer. An asymmetrical layout creates tension, requires more from the viewer, and may be unsettling but more interesting as a result. Balance can still be maintained, but it is more surprising. Gyorgy Kepes in *The Language of Vision*, states, "The living quality of an image is generated by the tension between the spatial forces: that is, by the struggle between the attraction and repulsion of the fields of these forces." Asymmetry uses balance as contrast.

2. Horizontal and Vertical

Horizontal and vertical lines stabilize us, while diagonal lines create tension and a dynamic, a contrast with the normal straight up and down. One single diagonal shape on a page will change the entire composition of a page, an effective way to create immediate interest on that page.

3. Contrast

We have all heard the phrase, "opposites attract," when referring to relationships. The theory is useful in design as well. Contrast is used to indicate differences. In *A Primer of Visual Literacy*, visual theorist Donis A. Dondis states that contrast "unbalances, shocks, stimulates, arrests attention. Without it, the mind would move towards eradicating all sensation, creating a climate of death, of nonbeing." Typographer Jan Tschichold refers to contrast as, "The single most important element in all modern design."

We use contrast in graphic design to exaggerate and emphasize, to accent, to excite and attract attention, or to dramatize. If you want to put emphasis on a large object, put a small object next to it. Contrast in design relates to differences as opposed to similarities and can be achieved with type, color, or images. When a dark image is contrasted with a light one, both images are enhanced and the design is given visual impact. Using bold typefaces with light typefaces on a page will give contrast. A black object will appear to be closer than a light object. A dark object placed in a light space will appear to be darker. Life without contrast would be very boring. A design without contrast is boring as well.

4. Rhythm

The design on a page should not be static. The designer can create an illusion of movement and rhythm on a page with the repetition of forms, shapes, type, lines, or textures.

5. Harmony

Harmony is a significant factor in the layout of a page. When a jigsaw puzzle has all its pieces in place, there is harmony. The same is true of all the elements on a page. Harmony refers to all the pieces, the elements on a page working together as a single, cohesive unit. This includes type, graphics, color, and paper.

6. Proportion

When we speak of proportion in design, we are dealing with the principle of relativity. We look at two visual elements on a page and think of them in relation to each other, in size, shape, etc. Differing proportions can affect and add contrast to a page, and they can be useful in attracting attention. Proportion also refers to the layout of a page, the relationship of the visual elements to the whole page.

TIPS TO REMEMBER

- [ ] Design principles should be a guide in the creation of a piece.
- [ ] Harmony and balance should be important considerations.
- [ ] The eye tends to group visual elements according to proximity, similarity, continuity, and closure.
- [ ] There should be no visual ambiguity in the layout of a page.
- [ ] All space on a page, both negative and positive, should be intentional.
- [ ] Consistency is essential in establishing harmony and unity in a page layout.

SUGGESTED EXERCISES

1. Look for examples of proximity, similarity, continuity, and closure in several publications.
2. Find some interesting examples of the use of negative space in logos, magazines, newsletters, and other printed materials.

5.
THE
DESIGN PROCESS

INSIDE THIS CHAPTER

5

THE DESIGN PROCESS

GRAPHIC DESIGN: A BALANCING ACT

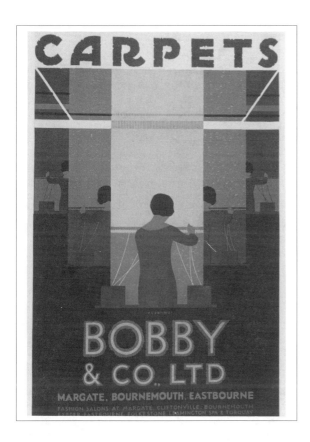

Poster from the early 1920s for Bobby & Co. Ltd, advertisers and printer. Designed by British designer, V. L. Danvers.

esigning for the printed page is a balancing act and can be compared to one performed by the trapeze artist on a high wire, or in less drastic terms, to the piecing together of a jigsaw puzzle. All the individual pieces—text, graphics, color, and paper must fit in order to form a harmonious, cohesive unit. The designer creates order out of chaos and organizes information in a hierarchy of importance, to guide the audience to the message. All of the elements discussed in previous chapters must be considered when approaching the actual design and layout of a page.

Good design is not dependent upon budget. It comes from the ability to be imaginative, to be consistent, to organize information in a creative and interesting way, and to make the pieces fit. A terrific design can be created by a good designer with a very low budget using only one color, while a poor, ineffective design using multiple colors may be made by a designer with unlimited funds. The amount of money spent on a printed piece does not determine its effectiveness or the quality of the design.

Leafing through the pages of a graphic design periodical, *Print, Communication Arts, Upper and Lowercase*, can be as inspiring and enjoyable as looking through a book of fine art. There is a very fine line between good fine art and fine graphic design. Good graphic design makes us want to look. It compels. It may be playful, shocking, surprising, witty, and intelligent. The Partnership for a Drug-Free America produced an interesting ad that appears on the back of the 1993 NYNEX Yellow Pages.

Illustrations: George Rhoads, 1993.

The ad, displayed on the facing page, shows happy kids mugging for the camera. The headline reads: "Can You Find the Drug Pusher in this Picture?" The headline is an attention grabber, and when used in conjunction with the photograph, makes a powerful statement.

We are constantly being battered and accosted by uninspired, and uninspiring, printed images that quickly become invisible and meaningless. We have learned to tune out some of the visual noise in our lives. The designer must be tuned in to this noise and to the audience. The successful design not only communicates visually, it makes direct contact with an audience. There is an implied relationship between the viewer and the printed piece. One depends upon the other. Communication today is dominated by the visual and augmented by the verbal.

GETTING IDEAS

Graphic design is a creative process, a thinking process that involves problem-solving and generating ideas. Sometimes ideas come very quickly. You have a design problem, a printed piece to create, and an idea comes to mind immediately. This is rare. Often you need to spend time mulling over the problem in your head, letting your imagination flow freely. Ideas come when they are least expected. Days after you have done a good deal of thinking about a solution, you might be relaxing in the bathtub, and suddenly the solution appears. Or you may be in a deep sleep, and awaken in a flash with a solution to the problem you have been straining to solve. A solution may even come to you while you are being held captive in your car in a traffic jam, or as your mind wanders while driving. The creative process involves intuition, accumulated knowledge, interaction with the unconscious, lots of trial, and lots of error.

Many graphic designers get inspiration from designs they have accumulated through the years. An article in the Spring, 1992 issue of *Upper and Lower Case* discusses designers and the collections they keep in their studios for inspiration and visual stimulus that include old packages and ads, interesting bottles and cans, matchbook covers, labels from old packages and fruit crates, posters, board games, rare books from used book shops, old magazines, wrapping paper, post-cards and trade cards, and wind-up toys.

This ad aimed at parents was produced by the Partnership for a Drug-Free America. The body copy reads: "We all know what drug pushers look like. We've seen them often enough on television. But the frightening thing is, a kid is more likely to be pushed into drugs by some innocent-looking schoolmate. Studies show that kids are 30 times more likely to use drugs if their friends use drugs. As a parent, how do you beat odds like that...? Know your kids' friends—and their parents. In other words, if you're in the picture, chances are a pusher won't be."

This ad is reprinted by permission from the Partnership for a Drug-Free America.

THE STEPS IN THE DESIGN PROCESS

When we talk about designing for print, we are referring to the visual images and verbal information that is to be reproduced on paper. This includes all the formats in the list at the end of this chapter.

1. Marketing Research

A portion of this task begins when the audience is defined and identified. In the heyday of the general store, the consumer had no choices. Food was sold in bulk, not in packages. There was only one kind of milk, soap, or bread. There was no competition for products, no choices, and therefore no need for advertising. Today there are endless options, and marketing research has become a significant and necessary tool. Designers often conduct research studies before beginning to design in order to make sure they have identified their audience correctly. They rely a great deal on demography, the vital statistics of population, in terms of size, distribution, and density.

Example 1:

When designing a flyer consideration must be given to how the flyer will be used. Will it be mailed or posted on a bulletin board? If it is to appear on a bulletin board bursting with dozens of other flyers, all screaming for equal attention, it is important to consider creating a design to guarantee that your flyer will be noticed. If the flyer is to be a direct-mail piece, an important consideration is whether or not it will be able to compete with the daily junk mail most people receive. You want your design to attract attention and to be read.

Example 2:

If you are designing a perfume package, you need to know where the perfume will ultimately be sold. If it is to be sold in a department store or drug store, it is a good idea to go to the particular store, or type of store, to see the other packages your package will be competing against and design a product that will stand out and be noticed. The ultimate goal is for a product to sell. Competition today is stiff. Most large design studios and advertising agencies have special departments devoted to this kind of marketing research. If you work in a small business or non-design firm, or have your own studio, you will most likely be the one to do the research.

2. The Thinking Process: Coming up with a concept

After the research has been done and the competition identified, the creative process begins. Designer Paul Rand expresses his thoughts on the creative process in *Graphic Design in America*, (Harry Abrams, Inc. 1989). "Intuition plays a very significant part in design, as it does in life. It's the initial phase of any creative work…. Animals live by instinct, and we do, too. The difference is that they don't reason. We do, and that can be a problem. You get an idea which comes intuitively. You then look at it and decide whether it's right or wrong. The important thing is not the intuition, but the decision…. Most of the time people simply latch on to trends or to freakish solutions they believe are problems, with right or wrong…. One designs for function, for usefulness, rightness, beauty."

Making lists: This can be a helpful way to define the problem and to get started.

1. List all the things that come to mind relating to the design problem at hand.

2. Think about the intended audience. Make a list of everything you associate with that audience. Is there anything special or peculiar about the audience.

3. List everything you know about the company, service, or product you are trying to promote. This list should include the advantages and benefits of this product or service. Are there particular distinctive, unique features? What would make people want this service or product?

4. List products or services that are in competition with your product. What feature is stressed in the promotional material for these products?

5. How can your product be presented in a unique way to compete with the products you have listed?

A good technique to get ideas flowing, according to Edward de Bono, a British educator and author of a number of books on problem-solving, is to list all possible solutions to a problem. Devise as many as possible in relation to the particular problem. DeBono suggests using the random input approach if you get stuck, where you select a word or object at random and apply it to the idea you have worked out to come up with a fresh solution. If that doesn't work, he suggests selecting a word at random from the dictionary for further inspiration.

Inspiration can be found in the work of other designers. Even seasoned designers get stale from time to time and need to be inspired; believe it or not, they look to other designers for ideas as well. Sometimes just looking at what others have done can be inspiring and helpful in getting your own creative juices flowing. Look at magazines, newspapers, and design periodicals that showcase exceptional graphic designs. Examine all the direct mail pieces that take up space in your mailbox. Go to the library and look at book jackets and old books. Look around you.

Remember: Whatever you see in print has been copyrighted, and it is illegal to use this material without permission from the holder of the copyright! (See Chapter 10 for copyright information.)

3. Thumbnail sketches

The thumbnail sketch is a quick sketch that indicates where the text and illustrations will go. It is a way to work out the general layout and design of a page in a small or miniature format. Designers might do twenty of these sketches, as a means of visual note-taking, jotting down ideas on paper. Most page layout programs permit you to print sixteen thumbnails on one page so that you can examine several designs together to see which ones seem most effective.

Some questions to ask as you begin this task:

▶ What is the image you wish to project?

▶ What format do you think will best suit your message and your audience?

▶ What is the size of the piece being designed?

▶ What kind of information do you plan to include?

▶ How much copy do you need ? Who will write the copy?

▶ How many graphics will you need?

▶ Will you use photographs or illustrations, charts, and graphs?

▶ Where will you get the illustrations, and/or photographs? (See Chapter 10)

▶ What other graphic devices will you use to create visual interest on the page: drop caps, dingbats, icons, borders, bullets, sidebars?

▶ Will your budget permit you to use more than one color?

▶ What kind of paper will you use?

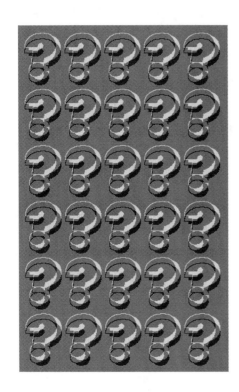

4. Rough sketches or "roughs"

After looking over the thumbnails, the designer usually selects the three best ones and blows them up to full size. These are called the rough sketches, or in the jargon, "roughs." The rough is the thumbnail enlarged, and it is used to test the ideas from the thumbnails on a larger scale. It is an opportunity to work out small problem areas that could not be worked out at the thumbnail stage. The rough may not include actual typefaces, but it may show lines to indicate the placement of the type and sketchy illustrations instead of actual photographs or drawings. The design is refined at this stage. Some of the charm of the miniature version may be lost when enlarged. Adjustments to the design will have to be made when translated from a small to large format. This stage might be eliminated when working on the computer. The designer can go right to the more finished design or comp (see below), since the type is easily accessible and does not have to be sent out to a typesetter, although some designers still prefer to use typesetters.

5. Comprehensives or "comps"

The comprehensive or "comp," is based on the rough, but is more carefully done and looks close to the finished piece. It includes all the elements, with type and graphics in place. The comprehensive is presented to the person who commissioned it for approval or suggestions for revisions.

6. The mechanical or camera-ready art

Once the rubber stamp has been put on the design, the piece must be prepared for the printer (see Chapter 10). The finished design is referred to as the "mechanical," or "camera-ready" art. This is the product that goes to the printer.

DESIGNING THE PAGE

The designer's job is to organize material in order to guide and direct the viewer through the information to be absorbed on the page. The design elements, type, and graphics must be arranged in a well-organized and orderly fashion so that the page looks easy to read, and to compel the reader to follow the information presented. The designer generally uses some kind of a system to create order and organize the elements on a page.

THE ELEMENTS OF A PAGE

1. The grid

The grid has been used by many cultures for centuries in paintings, ornamental designs, architecture, fabrics and quilts. In graphic design,

An apartment building in Coney Island in Brooklyn, New York that demonstrates the use of the grid in architecture. Photograph: Harry Lapow, 1959.

the grid is the underlying structure, the architecture for the layout of a page. The grid divides the space on a page into modular units. When a grid is used in a publication, it creates a sense of unity and a continuity for each page. It gives form and substance to the page and sets the rules that create a continuum and a flow for an entire publication. The grid is the means of organizing all the design elements. If it is not used skillfully, it can be a deterrent to exciting design and may make a page look rigid and sterile.

Page layout programs enable the desktop publisher to create grids using both guidelines and columns. The guidelines found on the computer serve the same function as the T-square and triangle used at the drawing board. They act as guides to help align all the elements when preparing the finished mechanical.

2. Columns

Most documents are set up using columns as a way to organize text and graphics. The width of a column affects its readability. If a column is too wide, the eye must strain to scan an entire line of text, thus making reading difficult. A column that is too narrow creates a strain because the eye has to advance and shift to the following line more frequently.

Type size and column width have a direct relationship to each other. If a narrow column is used, type should be small and there should be less space, or leading, between each line. If a wider column is used, type should be larger with more leading. Column width should be thought of as a way to make the reader comfortable with the text in a publication.

The white space or margins between columns is critical, and should not be too wide or too narrow. Columns placed too close together darken the page and make it look uninviting. Columns too far apart create gaps on the page and inhibit readability.

3. White space

A blank white page can be very intimidating to the inexperienced designer. Putting any mark on a virgin surface immediately alters that surface. White space on a page is often seen by the amateur designer as a hole to be filled. One of the secrets of good design is to know how to use white space intentionally. It can be a friend or an enemy. White space is a way to provide balance and breathing space on a page, and to avoid the feeling of clutter and claustrophobia that occurs when there is no place for the eye to rest. The inexperienced designer has a tendency to rid the page of all white space. It is essential to resist this urge and to know when to stop. This comes with experience, sensitivity, and careful perusal of other printed publications to see how white space is handled.

4. Gutters

In a document with several facing pages, the inner space between two pages, the margin, is called the gutter. The width of the gutter is determined by the type of binding that will be used in the final printing. The margin should be wide enough so that the text does not disappear into the gutter. If you are designing a publication that will be bound, you might want to ask your printer to suggest an appropriate margin width for the gutter.

5. Margins

The border around a page, the margin, is white space and should be used as breathing space. The size of the margin contributes to the readability, the color, and the attractiveness of the page. A large margin creates a lighter feeling on a page, while a smaller one makes the page look heavier, denser, and uninviting.

6. Focal point

When we first look at a page, our eyes are usually drawn to one area, the place that gets our immediate attention. This is the focal point. It is this point that encourages or discourages the reader's interest in the page and the rest of its contents. The focal point should not be so overpowering that it takes attention away from the rest of the composition.

Creating an effective and beautiful layout for a printed page involves making decisions and paying close attention to details.

ORGANIZING TEXT

1. Headlines

Headlines provide an introduction to the text, and they serve to captivate and intrigue. A catchy slogan will get attention. Headlines should be short, informative and to the point, so they can be read quickly. The typeface used should contrast with the type used in the body text for contrast and to create color on the page.

To give emphasis and contrast in headlines:

- Type for the headline should be larger than the body copy.
- If the same typeface is used for both headlines and text, the headlines should be a larger size and set in all caps .
- Use a different typeface for the headline and body text. If the text is in a serif face use a sans serif face for the head lines.
- Use **bold** type for emphasis.
- If the headline is very long, type set in upper and lowercase will be easier to read.
- Limit headlines to two or three lines, if possible.
- If the headline is short, you may want use all caps for emphasis.
- Headlines with one or two lines can be centered and will still be readable. If a headline has more than two lines and is centered, it becomes more difficult to read. Flush left is a better choice of alignment for long headlines.

2. Subheads

Subheads lead the reader into the text by providing a transition from the headline to the text. They can add visual interest to the page, and they help the reader identify the information that follows.

To give emphasis and contrast with subheads:

- They should be larger than body copy and smaller than headlines.
- They should be placed physically close to the body text they introduce, with more room above them than below.
- They can be the same typeface as the headlines to show their relationship to the headlines.
- If the headlines are in all caps, you might want to make the subheads upper and lower case, for contrast.
- Subheads can be centered, flush left or flush right, depending on how they fit with the headline and the body copy.
- Rules can be placed under subheads for emphasis and to make them stand out.
- All the subheads should be consistent throughout a publication.

3. Style sheets and templates

Most page layout programs enable the designer to set up a style sheet to define all the text in an entire publication. Once you learn how to use a style sheet in your page layout program, your text will be consistent throughout your publication. You can define the typeface for the body text, headlines, subheads, and captions to include all the desired features for your page: leading, caps or upper and lower case, tracking, style, and color for each style. If you have set up a style sheet, and you decide that you want to change all the headlines from Helvetica to Futura, you can redefine the styles, and every headline throughout the entire publication will automatically change to Futura. This is a great time-saver in a long publication, or one that is produced on a regular basis, like a newsletter.

The computer is a wonderful tool for setting up a format or a template for a publication that is produced on a regular basis. The template makes the job of designing and producing the publication a simpler task than starting from scratch each time. It also provides for consistency within each subsequent publication.

Page layout programs enable the desktop publisher to set up a template so that the design of a periodical publication will be consistent with each issue. The front page and subsequent pages of a newsletter or magazine can be set up permanently to define clearly the nameplate, masthead and all the other necessary information that will appear in each issue (see Chapter 8). Once a style sheet has been set up and a template designed, a person other than the designer can produce the newsletter or other periodical each month.

4. Header or running head

A header is a heading found at the top of a page in a book, a magazine, a newsletter, or other publication that has several pages. The header may identify the publication, the chapter title, or page number. It helps guide the reader quickly to important information and can be set up in the master pages of a document so that this information will automatically appear on all the desired pages.

5. Footer or running foot

A footer may contain the same information as a header but is located at the bottom of the page. In this book, a footer is used on the page on the left-hand side to identify the title of the book and page number. Another footer on the right-hand page gives the title of the chapter and page number.

6. Jumpline

When text is continued on another page, a jumpline is used to indicate the page with the continued information. The jumpline eliminates confusion when an article begins on one page and continues on another page within the publication. It guides the reader to the remainder of the article or text.

7. Caption

When a photograph or illustration appears in a publication, the reader wants information about it. Have you ever watched people at an art exhibition? They read the titles for clues about the picture and its creator. Studies show that people read captions more than any other part of a publication. Captions should give the reader important information about a photograph or an illustration. They should be in a smaller typeface, placed near the piece they identify, with white space between. Captions can be centered, or aligned on either side of the illustration, and they should fit within the boundaries of the illustration. They should be informative but silent, not the main focus of the page.

8. Nameplate

The nameplate refers to the logotype on the cover of a publication (newsletter, magazine) that identifies the title of that publication. It appears on every issue. The nameplate should be identifiable and distinctive and should appear in the same way, and in the same place, in each issue.

9. Masthead

The masthead contains the nameplate, plus other important editorial information that may include the name of the organization or owner of the publication, staff, volume number of the issue, and date of the publication.

10. Pull-quote

A pull-quote is a quote that is extracted, or pulled, from a story or article to get the reader's attention. It gives the reader a piece of information that is found in the story. It is used as an attention-getting device and adds graphic interest to a page. The pull-quote is often set in larger type and may have enlarged quotation marks.

11. Sidebar

The sidebar is the smaller, related story alongside the main story in a magazine or newspaper. It often appears in a shaded box.

SELECTING THE APPROPRIATE FORMAT

In Chapter 1, under Defining the Problem, we talked about identifying the audience, coming up with an objective, and finally using this information to determine the format for your printed piece. Below is a list of different kinds of printed materials that can be used to convey your message.

MATERIALS THAT INFORM

Newsletters
Brochures
Manuals
Catalogs
Fact Sheets
Menus
Articles
Magazines
Reports
Marketing Plans
Directories
Booklets
Flyers
Posters

MATERIALS FOR BUSINESS

Letterheads
Business Cards
Envelopes
Office Memos
Invoices
Labels
Note pads

RESPONSE VEHICLES

Direct Mail
Invitations
Questionnaires
Order Forms
Surveys

MATERIALS THAT PERSUADE

Advertisements
Posters
Flyers
Invitations
Calendars
Brochures
Proposals
Postcards
Prospectuses
Direct Mail
Handbills
Speciality Items: pens, mugs, note pads, T-shirts, watches, pads, post-cards

Newsletters

The newsletter is a periodical publication, an informational piece aimed at a particular audience with common interests. Newsletters have proliferated since the advent of desktop publishing. There are newsletters for every possible kind of special interest group from financial experts to train buffs to people interested in the environment, to solid waste management.

Manuals

A manual is used as a reference and usually is found in the form of a booklet or single sheet. The information presented is factual and instructional.

Catalogs

Catalogs are direct mail pieces that get into many homes and attempt to sell items from fancy clothing to kitchen equipment. They range in design from the simple to the slick.

Brochures

The brochure is a vehicle for a business or an organization to describe and promote its activities or products. It is also a way to disseminate information about public health issues or a special event. Brochures come in different sizes, 8½" x 11" or 8½" x 14," and they may be self-mailers or fit into a legal size envelope. If there is more information, the brochure might be 11"x 17" folded and stapled like a booklet.

Advertisements

An advertisement attempts to persuade and promote. An ad may take many forms and shapes. It may appear as a flyer or a poster, or even a brochure. When we think of ads, we normally think of the ads we see in magazines, newspapers, and commercials on TV. Ads can also be found on public transportation, in the yellow pages, theater booklets, and even in yearbooks. The main function of an advertisement is to persuade an audience to buy a particular product or service.

Posters and flyers

The main purpose of a poster or a flyer is to inform a varied audience about a particular event or exhibition. There is a minimum of information or copy on the piece.

Business Materials

All the materials for a business, letterhead, business card, envelopes invoices, and memos should look like they belong to the same organization. They should be consistent in design and reflect the image of the organization.

■ Letterheads & envelopes

The letterhead contains the name of the organization, the logo, address, and telephone and fax numbers. It sets the identity and image for the organization.

The envelope matches the letterhead and usually looks like a reduced version in terms of the placement of logo and address. Telephone and fax numbers are left off the envelope.

■ Business cards

Like the letterhead, the business card also sets the image for an organization, and can serve as an advertisement for a business. Business cards are given to prospective clients and should create an impression. All the information on the business card should be legible and reproduce well.

Direct Mail

Some of the printed materials discussed on this page and the previous page are considered direct mail pieces. Direct mail is one of the main and most successful modes of advertising today. These are the printed pieces that clutter up your mailbox. Catalogs, announcements, flyers, personalized letters, and some newsletters target a very specific, selected audience and are more effective in reaching a targeted audience than other forms of advertisements. Businesses buy mailing lists from consumer profiles that identify consumers according to age, income, special interests, number of children, gender, etc. You may have noticed that after you fill out a warranty card for a product, you begin to receive catalogs for related products. The rate of success for direct mail is pretty high. There is no middleman for the product. Direct mail often has a response mechanism, an order form or questionnaire, so the manufacturer knows very quickly if the advertising is working.

SOME PROMOTIONAL MATERIALS

Top left: Watch for ACM SIGGRAPH (Association for Computing Machinery Special Interest Group in Graphics) conference, 1993. The conference logo is the face of the watch. Designer: Mo Viele.

Top right: Mug sold at SUPERCOMPUTING '91 conference, Albuquerque, NM. Designer: Mo Viele.

Bottom left: Promotional note card with SIGGRAPH logo. Designer: Mo Viele.

Bottom right: Mouse pad sold at SIGGRAPH's 1993 conference with the conference logo in color. Designer: Mo Viele.

DESIGNING FOR THE PRINTED PAGE

Armed with the knowledge and the skills in using the current software and hardware, it is possible to produce many kinds of publications on the desktop. Do-it-yourself publishing has become the wave of the future, and the publications produced run the gamut from off the laser printer to the copy machine, to the more elaborate four-color production by a traditional printer.

There are no absolute rules when designing for print, but knowledge of the basic building blocks of graphic design as discussed in previous chapters is essential. The designer today must be a visual communicator in search of a creative solution to a problem, with an understanding of advertising, marketing strategy, and editorial thinking. The designer must struggle with the balance of interplay between the visual and verbal.

The computer is a wonderful, accessible, and useful tool for creating a variety of printed materials. It is only a tool, however, and, like the camera, it will work best in the hands of the person with knowledge of the entire graphic design process. Thinking before designing and coming up with a concept or idea, is the most important part of the process. Planning ahead with a clear idea of the purpose, the message, and the concept of the piece to be designed is the beginning of the path to creating successful publications. After some practice and experience, you will develop an aesthetic sense and a sense of style. In the same way that each person has an individual style of dress, and furnishing one's dwelling, each designer has an individual design style that comes from within, and is influenced by a lifetime of observing. Images that we have seen through the years are stored in our subconscious. The cells in our brain are like documents stored on the hard drives of our computers. Sometimes we forget that these documents exist, but they are there. The mind works in a similar way. Like the computer's hard drive, the mind is a great storage facility, and it will store images that have made some impression. We are influenced by all we see around us. When it comes to actually designing a printed piece, we call upon that unconscious part of our minds. Images may appear in our own designs without an awareness of origin. The style that develops as our own evolves from past experience, knowledge of the design process, and awareness of the visual images surrounding us.

THE ROLE OF THE DESIGNER

Simplicity is a good way to dispense information in an organized fashion to a mass society almost deafened and blinded by too many words and images. In an article from *The New York Times Magazine*, March 6, 1977, designer Rudolph deHarak talks about design and the extraordinary amount of data for people to absorb and how the designer should "synthesize information" to convey it efficiently and economically, in order to reduce the problem to its essentials.

A GOOD LAYOUT:

- ☞ Will stop the viewer
- ☞ Will hold the viewer's attention and encourage further reading of the printed piece
- ☞ Shows a successful marriage of type and graphics
- ☞ Is well organized
- ☞ Shows an understanding of the audience
- ☞ Shows a good grasp of the basic elements of design
- ☞ Communicates a message to the selected audience
- ☞ Has a clear concept
- ☞ Reduces the problem to its essentials

Before designing a printed piece think of yourself as a reader and consumer of magazines, newsletters, newspapers, brochures, ads, and flyers. As a reader, you are an expert. You know what you look for and like in the printed materials you buy and receive through the mail. You know which commercials you actually enjoy watching on TV and which you turn off quickly. Rely on that inherent sense to guide you in designing for others. Before designing any publication, think about your own experiences as a consumer, and use them.

In the chapters that follow you will learn about type as the basic ingredient in graphic design. You will discover what questions to ask before designing a specific publication for print, the pitfalls to avoid, questions to ask concerning the use of illustrations, how to develop a critical eye when creating your publication, and how to create printed pieces with a purpose.

6.
TYPE TERMINOLOGY AND TYPESETTING BASICS

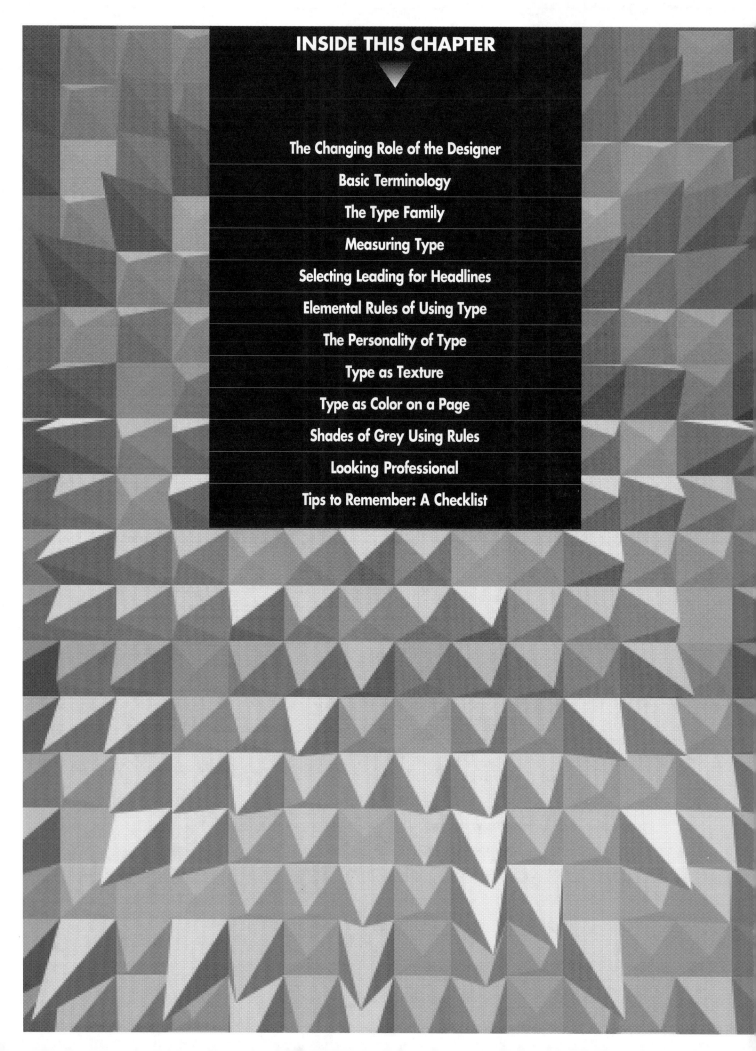

INSIDE THIS CHAPTER

6

TYPE TERMINOLOGY AND TYPESETTING BASICS

THE CHANGING ROLE OF THE DESIGNER

Ad designed by French printers, Draeger Fréres. *Westvaco Inspirations for Printers,* Westvaco Corporation, 1926.

The following chapters examine the designing of specific materials for print: informational, editorial, and advertising materials. Before designing any pieces for print it is essential to have an understanding of type and its significance on the printed page.

The role of the graphic designer has changed since desktop publishing began. Today's designer, in addition to knowing how to design, must be proficient on the computer, must know a multitude of software programs, and must be able to perform a task not required of designers in the past, the task of typesetting. The designer who is skillful on the computer, and who knows typesetting and the basics of graphic design has control and power over the entire design process with an extremely powerful design tool.

Typography, the arrangement and selection of faces of type, sizes, and spacing on the printed page, is the fundamental building block of visual communication. The printed page needs to be both inviting and readable, and since type is a basic element, the designer must understand and appreciate the nuances of typesetting, the differences in typefaces, the personalities of the many available typefaces, and the use of type for the printed piece to look professional and speak to the reader.

This chapter is about typesetting, becoming familiar with type terminology, and learning to use type with a professional eye and with a sensitivity to the page being designed. Developing an appreciation of typefaces can be compared to becoming a connoisseur of good wine.

Caslon 540 Roman font
ABCDEFGHIJKLMN
OPQRSTUVWXYZ
abcdefghijklmnopqrstuvwxyz
1234567890," "?

or

Caslon 3 Roman bold
ABCDEFGHIJKLMN
OPQRSTUVWXYZ
abcdefghijklmnopqrstuvwxyz
1234567890," "?

"Type is one of the most eloquent means of expression in every epoch of style. Next to architecture, it gives the most characteristic portrait of a period and the most severe testimony of a nation's intellectual status."

"Type is one of the most eloquent means of expression in every epoch of style. Next to architecture, it gives the most characteristic portrait of a period and the most severe testimony of a nation's intellectual status."

"Type is one of the most eloquent means of expression in every epoch of style. Next to architecture, it gives the most characteristic portrait of a period and the most severe testimony of a nation's intellectual status."

"Type is one of the most eloquent means of expression in every epoch of style. Next to architecture, it gives the most characteristic portrait of a period and the most severe testimony of a nation's intellectual status."

—Peter Behrens.

BASIC TERMINOLOGY
Font
A font is all the letters, punctuation marks, and numerals in the same point size in a particular type style.

Typeface
We talk about typefaces in terms of a family of letters using the same design motif, but varying in style, width, weight, and texture. The term "face" originates from the days of metal type where the surface of the letters were raised and the face of the letter receiving the ink came into contact with the printing surface.

▶ BODONI
ABCDEFGHIJKLMNOPQRSTUVWXYZ
abcdefghijklmnopqrstuvwxyz
1234567890," "?
ABCDEFGHIJKLMNOPQRSTUVWXYZ
abcdefghijklmnopqrstuvwxyz
1234567890," "?

▶ BAUHAUS
ABCDEFGHIJKLMNOPQRSTUVWXYZ
abcdefghijklmnopqrstuvwxyz
1234567890," "?
ABCDEFGHIJKLMNOPQRSTUVWXYZ
abcdefghijklmnopqrstuvwxyz
1234567890," "?

▶ FUTURA
ABCDEFGHIJKLMNOPQRSTUVWXYZ
abcdefghijklmnopqrstuvwxyz
1234567890," "?
ABCDEFGHIJKLMNOPQRSTUVWXYZ
abcdefghijklmnopqrstuvwxyz
1234567890," "?

▶ Univers Ultra Condensed
ABCDEFGHIJKLMNOPQRSTUVWXYZ
abcdefghijklmnopqrstuvwxyz
1234567890," "?
ABCDEFGHIJKLMNOPQRSTUVWXYZ
abcdefghijklmnopqrstuvwxyz
1234567890," "?

"Type is one of the most eloquent means of expression in every epoch of style. Next to architecture, it gives the most characteristic portrait of a period and the most severe testimony of a nation's intellectual status."

▶ TIMES
ABCDEFGHIJKLMNOPQRSTUVWXYZ
abcdefghijklmnopqrstuvwxyz
1234567890,""?
ABCDEFGHIJKLMNOPQRSTUVWXYZ
abcdefghijklmnopqrstuvwxyz
1234567890," "?

"Type is one of the most eloquent means of expression in every epoch of style. Next to architecture, it gives the most characteristic portrait of a period and the most severe testimony of a nation's intellectual status."

▶ ERAS LIGHT
ABCDEFGHIJKLMNOPQRSTUVWXYZ
abcdefghijklmnopqrstuvwxyz
1234567890,""?
ABCDEFGHIJKLMNOPQRSTUVWXYZ
abcdefghijklmnopqrstuvwxyz
1234567890," "?

"Type is one of the most eloquent means of expression in every epoch of style. Next to architecture, it gives the most characteristic portrait of a period and the most severe testimony of a nation's intellectual status."

▶ BERNHARD MODERN BT
ABCDEFGHIJKLMNOPQRSTUVWXYZ
abcdefghijklmnopqrstuvwxyz
1234567890,""?
ABCDEFGHIJKLMNOPQRSTUVWXYZ
abcdefghijklmnopqrstuvwxyz
1234567890," "?

"Type is one of the most eloquent means of expression in every epoch of style. Next to architecture, it gives the most characteristic portrait of a period and the most severe testimony of a nation's intellectual status."

▶ ITC FENICE LIGHT
ABCDEFGHIJKLMNOPQRSTUVWXYZ
abcdefghijklmnopqrstuvwxyz
1234567890,""?
ABCDEFGHIJKLMNOPQRSTUVWXYZ
abcdefghijklmnopqrstuvwxyz
1234567890," "?

"Type is one of the most eloquent means of expression in every epoch of style. Next to architecture, it gives the most characteristic portrait of a period and the most severe testimony of a nation's intellectual status."

▶ LILITH LIGHT
ABCDEFGHIJKLMNOPQRSTUVWXYZ
abcdefghijklmnopqrstuvwxyz
1234567890,""?
ABCDEFGHIJKLMNOPQRSTUVWXYZ
abcdefghijklmnopqrstuvwxyz
1234567890," "?

"Type is one of the most eloquent means of expression in every epoch of style. Next to architecture, it gives the most characteristic portrait of a period and the most severe testimony of a nation's intellectual status."

▶ Industria Solid
ABCDEFGHIJHLMNOPQRSTUVWXYZ
abcdefghijklmnopqrstuvwxyz
1234567890,""?

Typographic design using different members of the Helvetica family.

HELVETICA LIGHT
ABCDEFGHIJKLMNOPQRSTUVWXYZ
abcdefghijklmnopqrstuvwxyz

HELVETICA
ABCDEFGHIJKLMNOPQRSTUVWXYZ
abcdefghijklmnopqrstuvwxy

HELVETICA CONDENSED LIGHT
ABCDEFGHIJKLMNOPQRSTUVWXYZ
abcdefghijklmnopqrstuvwxyz

HELVETICA CONDENSED BOLD
ABCDEFGHIJKLMNOPQRSTUVWXYZ
abcdefghijklmnopqrstuvwxyz

HELVETICA COMPRESSED
ABCDEFGHIJKLMNOPQRSTUVWXYZ
abcdefghijklmnopqrstuvwxyz

HELVETICA EXTRA COMPRESSED
ABCDEFGHIJKLMNOPQRSTUVWXYZ
abcdefghijklmnopqrstuvwxyz

HELVETICA ULTRA COMPRESSED
ABCDEFGHIJKLMNOPQRSTUVWXYZ
abcdefghijklmnopqrstuvwxyz

HELVETICA BLACK
ABCDEFGHIJKLMNOPQRSTUVWXYZ
abcdefghijklmnopqrstuvwxyz

The Type Family

Each single typeface has variations that include different widths, weights, italics, and styles.

SOME MEMBERS OF THE HELVETICA FAMILY

Helvetica Light

Helvetica Light Oblique

Helvetica

Helvetica Italic

Helvetica Condensed Light

Helvetica Compressed

Helvetica Extra Compressed

Helvetica Extra Compressed Italic

Helvetica Ultra Compressed

Helvetica Ultra Compressed Italic

Helvetica Black

TYPE SIZES IN POINTS

8
10
11
12
14
18
24
30
36
48
60
72
90
98

MEASURING TYPE

1. Size

■ Points

We refer to type in points. Seventy two points equal an inch. The white space between words and lines of type, the width of spaces, the thickness of lines are all measured in points. Type that is 36 points is approximately ½ inch in height.

■ Picas

The term pica is used to indicate 12 points of space. A pica is made up of 12 points. There are 6 picas to an inch. Line lengths are measured in picas.

2. Width

Type width can be altered horizontally on the computer by expanding or condensing it in a page composition program or a drawing program. Typefaces with thick and thin strokes will not condense well, whereas type with lines of equal weight will.

FUTURA BOLD CONDENSED 70%
FUTURA BOLD NORMAL WIDTH 100%
FUTURA BOLD EXPANDED 130%

---

3. Weight

The weight of type relates to the lightness or heaviness of the strokes. Characters can have different weights or density depending on the typeface and the style used. The weights may be referred to as light, medium, bold, black, extra bold, or ultra black.

FENICE LIGHT

FENICE REGULAR

FENICE BOLD

FENICE ULTRA

Minus leading
10/9

"The type of the future will surely more and more strip away the historic style elements of the past, yet without descending to a geometric abstract form of letters. For the optical requirements remain the same so long as the letter images are still received by the human eye and not exclusively by an electronic reading machine."

10/10

"The type of the future will surely more and more strip away the historic style elements of the past, yet without descending to a geometric abstract form of letters. For the optical requirements remain the same so long as the letter images are still received by the human eye and not exclusively by an electronic reading machine."

Auto leading
10/Auto

"The type of the future will surely more and more strip away the historic style elements of the past, yet without descending to a geometric abstract form of letters. For the optical requirements remain the same so long as the letter images are still received by the human eye and not exclusively by an electronic reading machine."

Open leading
10/20

"The type of the future will surely more and more strip away the historic style elements of the past, yet without descending to a geometric abstract form of letters. For the optical requirements remain the same so long as the letter images are still received by the human eye and not exclusively by an electronic

4. Style

The type menu on the computer has several style options: plain, bold, italic, underline, outline, shadow, and reverse. You can use the same typeface but change the style in order to get a different effect.

NORMAL
BOLD
ITALIC
<u>UNDERLINE</u>
~~STRIKE THROUGH~~
OUTLINE
SHADOW
REVERSE

5. Leading

Leading (pronounced "ledding"), refers to the amount of spacing between lines, and, like type, is measured in points. Leading should always be one or two points larger than the type size or 20 percent of the point size or auto leading on the computer. If the type is 10 point, the leading would be 2 points (10/12). When you are using all caps the auto leading might seem a little excessive so it is best to adjust it to less than 120 percent, or less than the point size.

6. Kerning

The computer cannot always be relied upon to provide spacing between individual letters that is visually pleasing. Some letters need to be moved closer together manually in order for them to look more evenly spaced. Kerning, done manually in either a page layout program or drawing program, can either eliminate spacing between two letters, or add spaces where needed. Kerning should be done with a magnified view of the page (400%) so that you can see very clearly what you are doing. The example below shows the letters that need to be kerned.

You need to kern certain letter pairs to eliminate awkward spacing

SELECTING LEADING FOR HEADLINES

This is a headline set in 36pt type with auto leading.

The leading in this headline is set in 30 point type with auto leading.

This is a headline that is set in 36pt type with minus leading.

The leading in this headline has been adjusted to 34 points, or minus leading, so that there is tighter spacing between the lines. The lines have a better relationship to each other than the one above.

THIS HEADLINE IN SET IN ALL CAPS 36 PT WITH

The leading between these line is right for a headline with all caps.

THE ELEMENTAL RULES OF USING TYPE

1. Legibility and readability

Legibility is the most fundamental aspect of typography. Fonts that have exaggerated thick and thin strokes reduce legibility. Type with extra thin strokes sometimes gets lost on a page.

Type is to be read, and it should always be readable!

Belwe condensed	▶	**Type should always be readable!**
Bauhaus Light	▶	Type should always be readable!
Caslon Roman	▶	Type should always be readable!
Industria	▶	Type should always be readable!
Black Chancery	▶	Type should always be readable!

Example:

The text below has been set in different typefaces using 10 point type and auto leading. Each typeface takes up a different amount of space. Some of the typefaces are more readable than others.

The quote is from Hermann Zapf.

2. Type size and readability

When text type is too large or too small it becomes difficult to read. Type for text should be set in a range of 10 to 12 points depending on the x-height. Different typefaces set in the same point size may appear to be larger or smaller according to their x-height. To fit a large amount of copy into a small space, select a typeface that is small, medium weight, with a large x-height.

Bernhard Fashion BT

"The type of the future will surely more and more strip away the historic style elements of the past, yet without descending to a geometric abstract form of letters."

Caslon 3 Roman

"The type of the future will surely more and more strip away the historic style elements of the past, yet without descending to a geometric abstract form of letters."

Palatino

"The type of the future will surely more and more strip away the historic style elements of the past, yet without descending to a geometric abstract form of letters."

Lubalin Graph Demi

"The type of the future will surely more and more strip away the historic style elements of the past, yet without descending to a geometric abstract form of letters."

Caslon 540 Roman

"The type of the future will surely more and more strip away the historic style elements of the past, yet without descending to a geometric abstract form of letters."

Fenice Regular

"The type of the future will surely more and more strip away the historic style elements of the past, yet without descending to a geometric abstract form of letters."

Industria

"The type of the future will surely more and more strip away the historic style elements of the past, yet without descending to a geometric abstract form of letters."

Eras Medium

"The type of the future will surely more and more strip away the historic style elements of the past, yet without descending to a geometric abstract form of letters."

The quote below has been set in Caslon 540 Roman, a serif typeface:

"Typography has one plain duty before it and that is to convey information in writing No argument or consideration can absolve typography from this duty. A printed work which cannot be read becomes a product without purpose."

The quote below has been set in Futura Light, a sans serif typeface:

"Typography has one plain duty before it and that is to convey information in writing. No argument or consideration can absolve typography from this duty. A printed work which cannot be read becomes a product without purpose."

—Emil Ruder,
Adobe Font & Function, 1988.

3. Serif vs. sans serif

Serif type is often used for text or body copy because it is easier to read than sans serif. The serifs help your eyes with the horizontal flow. Serif typefaces are more formal than sans serif ones. Most books use serif typefaces.

4. Caps vs. upper & lowercase

Words set in uppercase and lowercase have a distinctive outline enabling the reader to recognize the words and read them quickly.

"Typography has one plain duty before it and that is to convey information in writing. No argument or consideration can absolve typography from this duty. A printed work which cannot be read becomes a product without purpose."

5. All Caps

Words that are set in all uppercase letters have an even horizontal outline which makes reading more difficult than type set in upper and lowercase letters. It is more difficult to distinguish between the words typeset in all caps in the quote below. Notice the strain on your eyes as you read.

"TYPOGRAPHY HAS ONE PLAIN DUTY BEFORE IT AND THAT IS TO CONVEY INFORMATION IN WRITING. NO ARGUMENT OR CONSIDERATION CAN ABSOLVE TYPOGRAPHY FROM THIS DUTY. A PRINTED WORK WHICH CANNOT BE READ BECOMES A PRODUCT WITHOUT PURPOSE."

No tracking

"Art is a human activity having for its purpose the transmission to others of the highest and best feelings to which men have risen."

Very loose tracking

"Art is a human activity having for its purpose the transmission to others of the highest and best feelings to which men have risen."

Loose tracking

"Art is a human activity having for its purpose the transmission to others of the highest and best feelings to which men have risen."

Normal tracking

"Art is a human activity having for its purpose the transmission to others of the highest and best feelings to which men have risen."

Tight tracking

"Art is a human activity having for its purpose the transmission to others of the highest and best feelings to which men have risen."

Very tight tracking

"Art is a human activity having for its purpose the transmission to others of the highest and best feelings to which men have risen."

—Count Lyof Nikolayevitch Tolstoi,
What is Art? 1898.

6. Letterspacing/tracking

The track function on the type menu enables you to adjust the spacing between letters in a line of type. When letterspacing is at its best, the text has an even typographic color, which enhances readability and makes communication more appealing. The tighter the letterspacing, the darker the line of type. Display type can be set tighter than text type which usually requires more space for maximum readability. Proper letterspacing depends on many factors: the typeface you select, the line spacing, the amount of copy, type weight and size, plus the nature of the design.

No tracking
Very loose tracking
Loose tracking
Normal tracking
Tight tracking
Very tight tracking

7. Line length and readability

Our eyes scan a line of text, or at least several words at a time. We do not read individual words. If a line of text is too long, it tires our eyes and makes it difficult to locate the beginning of the line that follows. If a line is too short, sentence structure might be disrupted, and the eye must change lines too often. Sans serif faces should be typeset in shorter lines than serif typefaces for maximum readability. Typefaces like Bodoni Poster below, have strong contrasts, thick and thin lines, a picket fence look and they should have a shorter line length or they will tire the eye.

"Art is a human activity having for its purpose the transmission to others of the highest and best feelings to which men have risen."

Flush left/ragged right

"He who first shortened the labor of copyists by device of movable types was disbanding hired armies, and cashiering most kings and Senates, and creating a whole new Democratic world: he had the Art of printing."

Centered

"He who first shortened the labor of copyists by device of movable types was disbanding hired armies, and cashiering most kings and Senates, and creating a whole new Democratic world: he had the Art of printing."

Flush right

"He who first shortened the labor of copyists by device of movable types was disbanding hired armies, and cashiering most kings and Senates, and creating a whole new Democratic world: he had the Art of printing."

Justified

"He who first shortened the labor of copyists by device of movable types was disbanding hired armies, and cashiering most kings and Senates, and creating a whole new Democratic world: he had the Art of printing."

Bodoni Poster is a dramatic typeface. A little goes a long way. It can be very effective when used in headlines, or other small amounts of text, but should not be used for large amounts of body copy.

8. Italics

Italics, or slanted type, slows down reading when there is a lot of text. It is good to use italicized type for emphasis when trying to make a few words stand out from the rest of the text. If you are unsure about whether or not to use italics, use them sparingly to provide *emphasis*. The quote below is from Thomas Carlyle, *Sartor Resartus*, 1834.

"He who first shortened the labor of copyists by device of movable types was disbanding hired armies, and cashiering most kings and Senates, and creating a whole new Democratic world: he had the Art of printing."

9. Text alignment

Alignment on the computer refers to how a block of type is set up: flush left, flush right, centered, justified, or force justified. The alignment used should be well-planned, with readability as the main concern.

■ Align left or flush left, ragged right

This refers to lines of type evenly lined up on the left while the text on the right side is uneven or ragged. Type set flush left is frequently used for informal, easy to read text, and allows for even word spacing.

■ Align center or centered text

Text should be centered only in small amounts, one or two lines, otherwise it becomes unreadable.

■ Align right or flush right, ragged left

Lines of type that evenly lined up on the right, while the left side is uneven or ragged is referred to as flush right. This alignment is not good for long lines of text, or body copy, since we are not accustomed to reading from right to left, but can be used effectively for display type, headlines and captions.

■ Justified text

Justified text is text that is aligned on both left and right sides. When text is justified it takes up less space than text using other alignments, but undesirable white spaces often appear since the computer has to force the words and letters to fit within a column. If you justify text, typesetting tricks and adjustments must be used in order to fill in the gaps.

■ Force justified text

Force justifying text puts spaces between characters and spreads out words and letters. This alignment can be used effectively for one word, or a short line of text, to expand it evenly across a column. It is a good technique to use for fitting one line of text, or one word under another word.

Example below.

GRAPHIC DESIGN ON THE DESKTOP
A GUIDE FOR THE BEGINNING DESIGNER

10. Word spacing

Improper word spacing can create gaps or "rivers" of white space in the text that slows down reading and changes the color of the text. This kind of white space is not favorable to good design.

Improper word spacing creates gaps and causes rivers to form in the text, and makes reading more difficult.

RULES OR LINES

Hairline rule

---

5 point rule

---

1 point rule

---

2 point rule

---

4 point rule

---

6 point rule

---

8 point rule

---

12 point rule

Dotted rules, 1 point

11. Hyphenation

Page layout programs give you control over the number of successive hyphens. Too many hyphens in a row can be disruptive to the reader. Hyphenation is necessary if you justify text. Unjustified paragraphs will look neater if attention is paid to hyphenation.

12. Rules or lines

Lines or rules, as they are called, like type, are measured by point size. Horizontal rules are used to separate elements to provide a visual barrier. Since lines are so easy to draw on the computer, inexperienced designers tend to use them without discrimination. The questions to ask before putting in a rule is, "Is this really necessary? Does the rule help the design?" If you cannot justify using lines or rules, leave them out.

13. Widows and orphans

A widow is defined as a single word on a line by itself at the end of a paragraph. Widows make the text harder to read and look awkward. An orphan is the last word or line of a paragraph that sits alone at the top of a column of text. Most page layout programs allow you to adjust the text to eliminate these or text can be edited to eliminate the widows and orphans.

Widow

"He who first shortened the labor of copyists by device of movable types was disbanding hired armies, and cashiering most kings and Senates, and creating a whole new Democratic world: he had the art Art of printing."

Orphan

individuality.

"He who first shortened the labor of copyists by device of movable types was disbanding hired armies, and cashiering most kings and Senates, and creating a whole new Democratic world: he had the Art of printing."

"He who first shortened the labor of copyists by device of movable types was disbanding hired armies, and cashiering most kings and Senates, and creating a whole new Democratic world: he had the Art of printing."

"He who first shortened the labor of copyists by device of movable types was disbanding hired armies, and cashiering most kings and Senates, and creating a whole new Democratic world: he had the Art of printing."

"He who first shortened the labor of copyists by device of movable types was disbanding hired armies, and cashiering most kings and Senates, and creating a whole new Democratic world: he had the Art of printing."

14. Reversed text

When we speak of reversed text, or a reversal, we are referring to white type on a colored or black background. Type set this way is more difficult to read, but more dramatic, and commands attention. If you use a reversal, the typeface should be bold and large enough to read. Bold sans serif faces work better when reversed than serif faces with thin strokes. Note the difference in readability in the samples of reversed type on this page. The typeface on the top of the screened box on the left is Lubalin Graph, a slab serif face. Caslon 540 Roman, a serif face, is the typeface in the middle, and sans serif, Eras Bold, is the one on the bottom.

REVERSED TEXT

REVERSED TEXT

▲ The typeface at the top of the box is Futura Bold, a sans serif face. The one underneath it is Caslon 540 Roman.

▼ The typeface in the box below is Futura Bold Oblique.

REVERSED TYPE IS EFFECTIVE WHEN SET IN A BOLD TYPEFACE IN A FEW LINES RATHER THAN ENTIRE PARAGRAPHS. IT IS ALSO MORE READABLE!

THE PERSONALITY OF TYPE

Each typeface has a distinct personality. Type should be selected for its appropriateness to your design, message and audience. Typefaces can be elegant, bold, informal, friendly, stylish. Some should only be used for headlines. The typefaces below have unique styles and personalities.

Black Chancery is a font with elegance. It is good for formal wear. A little goes a long way!

Bauhaus Heavy with its bold round letters has an Art Nouveau look.

BREMEN IS AN INTERESTING SPECIALTY TYPE-FACE THAT SHOULD BE USED SPARINGLY.

Bodoni Poster used in headlines is elegant and makes a dramatic statement!

Caslon Roman has good readability and is frequently used for body copy in books.

Futura is a classic from the twenties. It is an old favorite of designers.

LITHOS IS PLAYFUL, AND INFORMAL AND COMES ONLY IN ALL CAPS.

MACHINE IS A NO NONSENSE, BOLD, ALL CAPS TYPEFACE. IT IS GOOD FOR HEADLINES IN ADS & BOOK TITLES.

TYPE AS TEXTURE

We can look at lines of black type as creating color on a page. There are several ways to create a gray effect on a page. Type set in a light typeface, or with a great deal of leading, has a gray appearance.

Type set with tight leading looks denser and appears to be blacker. A mixture of thick and thin typefaces will help change the color of a page. Different weights and widths of Helvetica and Futura have been used in the samples below.

FUTURA BOLD AND FUTURA LIGHT

RHYTHMRHYTHM**RHYTHM**RHYTHM**RHYTHM**RHYTHM
RHYTHMRHYTHM**RHYTHM**RHYTHM**RHYTHM**RHYTHM
RHYTHMRHYTHM**RHYTHM**RHYTHM**RHYTHM**RHYTHM
RHYTHMRHYTHM**RHYTHM**RHYTHM**RHYTHM**RHYTHM
RHYTHMRHYTHM**RHYTHM**RHYTHM**RHYTHM**RHYTHM
RHYTHMRHYTHM**RHYTHM**RHYTHM**RHYTHM**RHYTHM
RHYTHMRHYTHM**RHYTHM**RHYTHM**RHYTHM**RHYTHM
RHYTHMRHYTHM**RHYTHM**RHYTHM**RHYTHM**RHYTHM
RHYTHMRHYTHM**RHYTHM**RHYTHM**RHYTHM**RHYTHM
RHYTHMRHYTHM**RHYTHM**RHYTHM**RHYTHM**RHYTHM
RHYTHMRHYTHM**RHYTHM**RHYTHM**RHYTHM**RHYTHM
RHYTHMRHYTHM**RHYTHM**RHYTHM**RHYTHM**RHYTHM
RHYTHMRHYTHM**RHYTHM**RHYTHM**RHYTHM**RHYTHM
RHYTHMRHYTHM**RHYTHM**RHYTHM**RHYTHM**RHYTHM
RHYTHMRHYTHM**RHYTHM**RHYTHM**RHYTHM**RHYTHM
RHYTHMRHYTHM**RHYTHM**RHYTHM**RHYTHM**RHYTHM
RHYTHMRHYTHM**RHYTHM**RHYTHM**RHYTHM**RHYTHM
RHYTHMRHYTHM**RHYTHM**RHYTHM**RHYTHM**RHYTHM
RHYTHMRHYTHM**RHYTHM**RHYTHM**RHYTHM**RHYTHM
RHYTHMRHYTHM**RHYTHM**RHYTHM**RHYTHM**RHYTHM
RHYTHMRHYTHM**RHYTHM**RHYTHM**RHYTHM**RHYTHM
RHYTHMRHYTHM**RHYTHM**RHYTHM**RHYTHM**RHYTHM
RHYTHMRHYTHM**RHYTHM**RHYTHM**RHYTHM**RHYTHM
RHYTHMRHYTHM**RHYTHM**RHYTHM**RHYTHM**RHYTHM
RHYTHMRHYTHM**RHYTHM**RHYTHM**RHYTHM**RHYTHM

HELVETICA BLACK, LIGHT AND EXTRA COMPRESSED

TEXTURETexture**TEXTURE****TEXTURE**Texture**TEXTURE****TEXTURE**
TEXTURETexture**TEXTURE****TEXTURE**Texture**TEXTURE****TEXTURE**
TEXTURETexture**TEXTURE****TEXTURE**Texture**TEXTURE****TEXTURE**
TEXTURETexture**TEXTURE****TEXTURE**Texture**TEXTURE****TEXTURE**
TEXTURETexture**TEXTURE****TEXTURE**Texture**TEXTURE****TEXTURE**
TEXTURETexture**TEXTURE****TEXTURE**Texture**TEXTURE****TEXTURE**
TEXTURETexture**TEXTURE****TEXTURE**Texture**TEXTURE****TEXTURE**
TEXTURETexture**TEXTURE****TEXTURE**Texture**TEXTURE****TEXTURE**
TEXTURETexture**TEXTURE****TEXTURE**Texture**TEXTURE****TEXTURE**
TEXTURETexture**TEXTURE****TEXTURE**Texture**TEXTURE****TEXTURE**
TEXTURETexture**TEXTURE****TEXTURE**Texture**TEXTURE****TEXTURE**
TEXTURETexture**TEXTURE****TEXTURE**Texture**TEXTURE****TEXTURE**
TEXTURETexture**TEXTURE****TEXTURE**Texture**TEXTURE****TEXTURE**
TEXTURETexture**TEXTURE****TEXTURE**Texture**TEXTURE****TEXTURE**
TEXTURETexture**TEXTURE****TEXTURE**Texture**TEXTURE****TEXTURE**
TEXTURETexture**TEXTURE****TEXTURE**Texture**TEXTURE****TEXTURE**
TEXTURETexture**TEXTURE****TEXTURE**Texture**TEXTURE****TEXTURE**
TEXTURETexture**TEXTURE****TEXTURE**Texture**TEXTURE****TEXTURE**
TEXTURETexture**TEXTURE****TEXTURE**Texture**TEXTURE****TEXTURE**
TEXTURETexture**TEXTURE****TEXTURE**Texture**TEXTURE****TEXTURE**
TEXTURETexture**TEXTURE****TEXTURE**Texture**TEXTURE****TEXTURE**
TEXTURETexture**TEXTURE****TEXTURE**Texture**TEXTURE****TEXTURE**
TEXTURETexture**TEXTURE****TEXTURE**Texture**TEXTURE****TEXTURE**
TEXTURETexture**TEXTURE****TEXTURE**Texture**TEXTURE****TEXTURE**
TEXTURETexture**TEXTURE****TEXTURE**Texture**TEXTURE****TEXTURE**

TYPE AS COLOR ON A PAGE

Black is the basic color in typography. Using different sizes, thicknesses, styles, and spacing of type will create an extensive scale of gray tones. This quote by the well-known graphic designer, Bradbury Thompson, has been set in several different typefaces all in the same size and leading to show the difference in color in each when used in a body of text. Some of these text blocks are dense, giving a very black appearance, while others tend to create a grayness within the text block.

The text blocks below have all been typeset in 10 point type with 15 point leading.

"Type is a thing of constant interest….It is sometimes a serious and useful tool, employed to deliver a message, sell a specific article or give life to an idea."
▶ Futura Light

"Type is a thing of constant interest….It is sometimes a serious and useful tool, employed to deliver a message, sell a specific article or give life to an idea."
▶ Bauhaus Light

"Type is a thing of constant interest. It is sometimes a serious and useful tool, employed to deliver a message, sell a specific article or give life to an idea."
▶ Lilith Light

"Type is a thing of constant interest ….It is sometimes a serious and useful tool, employed to deliver a message, sell a specific article or give life to an idea."
▶ University Roman

"Type is a thing of constant interest….It is sometimes a serious and useful tool, employed to deliver amessage, sell a specific article or give life to an idea."
▶ Industria Solid

"Type is a thing of constant interest….It is sometimes a serious and useful tool, employed to deliver a message, sell a specific article or give life to an idea."
▶ Bernhard Modern BT

"Type is a thing of constant interest...It is sometimes a serious and useful tool, employed to deliver a message, sell a specific article or give life to an idea."
▶ Middleton

"Type is a thing of constant interest…It is sometimes a serious and useful tool, employed to deliver a message, sell a specific article or give life to an idea."
▶ Helvetica Ultra Compressed

"Type is a thing of constant interest….It is sometimes a serious and useful tool, employed to deliver a message, sell a specific article or give life to an idea."
▶ Stuyvesant BT

"Type is a thing of constant interest….It is sometimes a serious and useful tool, employed to deliver amessage, sell a specific article or give life to an idea."
▶ Belwe Condensed

"Type is a thing of constant interest….It is sometimes a serious and useful tool, employed to deliver a message, sell a specific article or give life to an idea."
▶ Futura Bold

"TYPE IS A THING OF CONSTANT INTEREST….IT IS SOMETIMES A SERIOUS AND USEFUL TOOL, EMPLOYED TO DELIVER A MESSAGE, SELL A SPECIFIC ARTICLE OR GIVE LIFE TO AN IDEA.
▶ MACHINE

"Type is a thing of constant interest….It is sometimes a serious and useful tool, employed to deliver a message, sell a specific article or give life to an idea."
▶ Univers Ultra Condensed

"Type is a thing of constant interest….It is sometimes a serious and useful tool, employed to deliver a message, sell a specific article or give life to an idea."
▶ Bodoni Poster

"Type is a thing of constant interest….It is sometimes a serious and useful tool, employed to deliver a message, sell a specific article or give life to an idea."
▶ Eras Bold

"Type is a thing of constant interest….It is sometimes a serious and useful tool, employed to deliver a message, sell a specific article or give life to an idea."
▶ Lubalin Graph

"Type is a thing of constant interest…. It is sometimes a serious and useful tool, employed to deliver a message, sell a specific article or give life to an idea."
▶ Playbill

SHADES OF GRAY USING RULES

Type is not the only way to create a gray effect on a page. Rules and other typographic ornamentations will accomplish the same task.

The samples below demonstrate how different thicknesses of rules, like type, will give the illusion of shades of gray.

HAIRLINE   .5 POINTS   1 POINT   1.5 POINTS   2 POINTS

DOTTED LINES

DOTTED LINES

DOTTED LINES WITH ARROWS

MORE SHADES OF GRAY

This page shows other ways to create tones of gray. A small quantity of black overpowers white. In some instances it almost removes the white.

Patterns can be created using type, arrows, and boxes and can be used when designing logos. The examples below show some of these patterns.

HAIRLINE   .5 POINT   1 POINT   2 POINT

	MACINTOSH	PC
™	Option - 2	
£	Option - 3	Alt - 0163
¢	Option - 4	Alt - 0162
∞	Option - 5	
§	Option - 6	Ctrl - Shift - M
¶	Option - 7	Ctrl - Shift - 7
•	Option - 8	Ctrl - Shift - 8
fi	Option - Shift - 5	
fl	Option - Shift - 6	
¢	Option - $	
®	Option - r	Ctrl - Shift - g
©	Option - g	Ctrl - Shift - o
÷	Option - /	
√	Option - v	
é	Option - e then letter	Alt - 0233
ü	Option - u then letter	Alt - 0252
î	Option - i then letter	
ñ	Option - n then letter	Alt - 0241
ç	Option - c	Alt - 0231
Ç	Option - Shift-C	Alt - 0199
¿	Option - Shift-/	Alt - 0191
¡	Option - 1	Alt - 0161
"	Option - [	Ctrl - Shift -]
"	Option - Shift - [	Ctrl - Shift - [
'	Option -]	Ctrl - [
'	Option - Shift -]	Ctrl -]
° Degree	Option - Shift - 8]	Alt - 0186
— En	Option - hyphen	Ctrl - =
—— Em	Option - Shift - hyphen	Ctrl - Shift - =
… Ellipsis	Option - ;	

FINDING SPECIAL CHARACTERS ON THE KEYBOARD

Both the Macintosh and the PC have special built-in characters, symbols for trademarks, copyright signs, register marks, and accent marks. These can be found on the Macintosh by using Key Caps on the Apple menu. You will get a window with a keyboard display. All your fonts can be found under the Key Caps menu. You can scroll to the typeface you are using, and the keyboard will change to reflect that typeface. If you hold down the Option key and Option + Shift keys, you will see a display of all the characters and symbols for that typeface.

The PC does not have on-screen Key Caps. On the left is a list of keyboard commands for special characters in PageMaker. The PC key characters change with each software program.

ZAPF DINGBATS

The Zapf dingbat typeface offers interesting and useful characters to provide extra embellishments to your designs. They can be used as bullets, or as graphics for emphasis, or as decoration for your printed page.

You are here ⇒

❖ **Dingbats make good bullets for listing things**

❦ **Dingbats make good bullets for listing things**

❧ **Dingbats make good bullets for listing things**

☞ **Dingbats make good bullets for listing things**

LOOKING PROFESSIONAL

Most of us are familiar with computer keyboards because we used typewriters. We learned rules when we learned to type, and we followed these rules religiously: putting two spaces after a period, underlining book titles or words for emphasis, using two dashes for a hyphen, etc. When we transfer these rules to the computer, the result is a telltale design that says *unprofessional* and *amateurish*.

The old rules of typing must be cast off, and new rules, the rules of typesetting, learned and followed with the same religiosity. The typewriter is quite different from the computer because each character or letter takes up the same amount of space. Each character on the computer is spaced proportionally. Some letters require more space than others, some require less. A "w" for example, takes up more space than an "i;" an "m" takes up more space than a "t."

1. Bitmapped or jagged fonts

Your computer, Macintosh or PC, comes with its own built-in fonts. Some fonts will print out looking bitmapped (jagged) on the laser printer because they were initially designed for the computer monitor. The fonts with city or country names such as Monaco, Geneva, Chicago, London, New York have equivalents that are not bitmapped. Instead of using Geneva, Monaco, or Chicago use Helvetica, unless a bitmapped, computer effect is what you want.

Hint: If you want your letters to be smooth, and without jagged edges, do not use any fonts with city or country names.

2. Apostrophes

The computer keyboard, like the typewriter, has an apostrophe that looks like this ('). If you look at professional publications, you will see an apostrophe that looks like this ('). Check the diagram of special characters to find the key character for the curved apostrophe.

3. Boxed text

When you place text in a box, white space should be left as a border on all sides, otherwise it will look crowded, uninviting to read and unprofessional.

•	Regular bullet
■	Regular box
□	Open box
❑	Zapf Dingbats
✳	Zapf Dingbats
▲	Zapf Dingbats
▼	Zapf Dingbats
❖	Zapf Dingbats
✳	Zapf Dingbats
●◗	Zapf Dingbats
☛	Zapf Dingbats
❋	Zapf Dingbats
✔	Zapf Dingbats
✎	Zapf Dingbats
✚	Zapf Dingbats
✺	Zapf Dingbats
✳	Zapf Dingbats
✧	Zapf Dingbats
✈	Zapf Dingbats
➠	Zapf Dingbats
➟	Zapf Dingbats
➡	Zapf Dingbats
→	Zapf Dingbats
➢	Zapf Dingbats
➘	Zapf Dingbats
➥	Zapf Dingbats
➤➤	Zapf Dingbats
➹	Zapf Dingbats
➤➤	Zapf Dingbats
⇒	Zapf Dingbats
➢	Zapf Dingbats
✦	Zapf Dingbats

> Text in a box without enough white space around it is very difficult to read. It appears too crowded and is not inviting to read.

> Text in a box with white space around it is easier and much more inviting to read.

4. Bullets

Bullets are graphic symbols that are used for listing items. When we used the typewriter, we used a dash or an asterisk instead of a bullet. Normal bullets (•) can be found on your computer, or you can create your own bullets using the box tool, or use graphic symbols found in Zapf Dingbats as demonstrated on the left. Check the Key Caps or the typeface, Zapf Dingbats, to see what other possibilities exist for decorative bullets.

5. Captions

Captions identifying illustrations should be set in a different, and smaller typeface from body copy. White space should be left between the caption and illustration.

6. Dashes: en dashes, em dashes, and hyphens

Instead of two hyphens for a dash (--), typesetters use en (–) and em (—) dashes.

■ A regular dash is used to either break a word at the end of a line, or after certain words. It serves as a hyphen:
up-to-the-minute

■ An en dash (–) is the width of the letter (n), and is used to indicate a duration of time:
Between the hours 9:00 – 10:00 PM
From 2 – 6 years of age
January – June

■ An em dash is the width of the letter m, and is double the width of an en dash. An em dash is used instead of a semi-colon or parentheses to separate thoughts, or to further explain something:

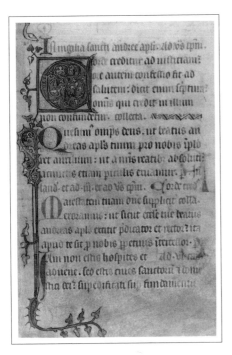

Top: Large initial capital letter from the Kelmscott Chaucer illustrated by William Morris, 1896.

Bottom: Large initial capital letter from an illuminated manuscript. Date unknown.

Credit for both manuscripts: Division of Rare and Manuscript Collections, Carl A. Kroch Library. Cornell University, Ithaca, NY 14853-5302.

" Most graphic designers do free work on occasion, and a few do it pro bono in its literal meaning—for the public good."

—Steven Heller, *Print* magazine, October, 1992.

7. Ellipsis

An ellipsis, three dots to indicate that something has been removed, is an actual character on the computer and should be used instead of three periods.

Three periods (...)

An ellipsis (…)

To type an ellipsis:

MAC: Option-;   PC: Alt.-193

When you use the key character for the ellipsis, the computer puts in three thin equal spaces between each period that look more professional than three periods.

8. Large initial caps

■ *Drop caps* are large initial letters that drop into the body of a paragraph. They should always line up with the baseline of one of the lines of text.

■ *Raised caps* rise above the body and sit on the first line of text in a paragraph. Large initial caps are used to create graphic interest on a page, and to attract attention. They were originally used in illuminated manuscripts to signify the beginning of a new paragraph.

9. Mixing typefaces

Too many typefaces on a page deters readability and creates confusion. Avoid the "ransom note" look, and use only two typefaces or different styles (bold, outline, etc.) within a typeface when designing a printed piece. If you use two different typefaces, it is best to use one serif face and one sans serif face. Don't mix two serif faces or two sans serif faces.

In the example on the next page, the words Graphic Images are typeset in bold Caslon Roman, a serif face. The words underneath are set in Futura Condensed Light, a sans serif face that provides a contrast in color. The text in both lines has been force justified in order to fit the two lines within a block and create a neat rectangle. This is a good technique to use for a masthead of a newsletter.

GRAPHIC IMAGES

A MONTHLY NEWSLETTER FOR THE GRAPHIC DESIGN PROFESSIONAL

10. Smart quotes, or curved quotation marks

When we used the typewriter we used the inch (") mark to indicate quotes. It was the closest we could get to quotation marks. Typesetters use "smart" quotes. Notice the difference between the two.

11. Spacing after a period

Typing rules dictated two spaces after a period because typewriter spacing, unlike the computer, was not proportional. When you are wordprocessing on the computer, you only need to put one space after a period. If you forget this rule, you can make global changes in your page layout program.

12. Underlining words

When we used the typewriter, we used the underline function on the keyboard to emphasize something or to indicate the title of a book. It is unnecessary to use the underline function on the computer because we can *italicize* the words we want to emphasize. Underlining words makes them more difficult to read.

<u>Underlining looks unprofessional, and makes for difficult reading because it cuts into some of the descenders and puts the line too close to the type!</u>

Instead of underlining, use italics!

Or, if you want to emphasize a word with a line under it, draw the line instead of using the underline function.

<u>Be professional, with your line!</u>

TIPS TO REMEMBER: A CHECKLIST

- ☐ The typeface(s) you use reinforce(s) your message.
- ☐ Use the appropriate dashes, en, em and hyphens.
- ☐ Use an ellipsis… rather than three periods...
- ☐ Use novelty typefaces for headlines and special effects, and not for body copy.
- ☐ Eliminate all rivers or gaps in the text.
- ☐ Increase the leading along with increasing the width of a line.
- ☐ Follow each period with only *one* space.
- ☐ Use all caps in headlines alone and not in large amounts of body copy.
- ☐ Allow a sufficient border of white space on all sides for text in a box.
- ☐ Include margins wide enough to allow for breathing space on the page.
- ☐ Use italics rather than the underline function for emphasis.
- ☐ Use "smart" quotes and smart apostrophes, rather than the inch and foot key.
- ☐ Line up drop caps with a line of text.

SUGGESTED EXERCISES

The exercises in this chapter relate to developing an awareness and a sensitivity to type and typesetting tricks.

1. Typeset the word "reverse" in white in several different fonts, both serif and sans serif, and place them in a black box. Which typeface works best when reversed?

2. Search through magazines and pay attention to interesting use of leading and word spacing in headlines.

3. Set up a file of magazine articles that use type in an interesting way in terms of:

    Leading

    Word spacing

    Kerning in headlines

4. Notice signage in supermarkets and other public places. See if you can recognize the typefaces. Are they serif or sans serif?

Which do you see most often?

5. Look for examples of type in publications that seem to be inappropriate to the message being communicated.

6. Look for examples of widows and orphans in printed materials.

7. Look for mistakes most commonly made in newsletters, brochures, and other published materials that put up a red flag that says "amateur."

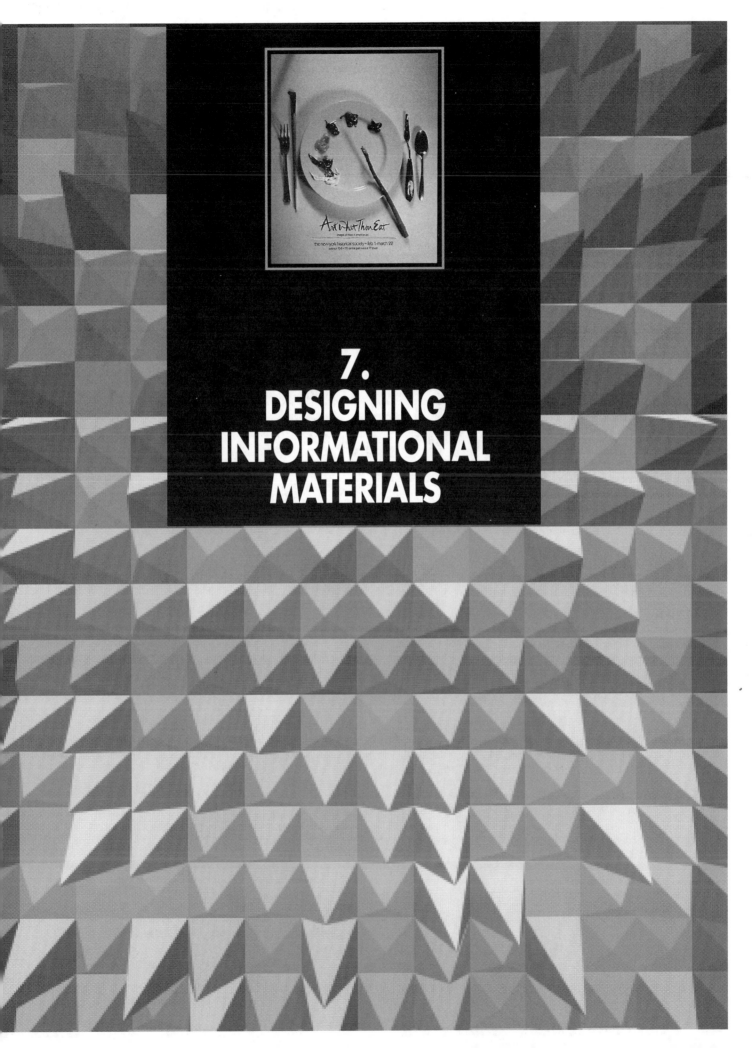

7.
DESIGNING
INFORMATIONAL
MATERIALS

INSIDE THIS CHAPTER

▼

DESIGNING INFORMATIONAL MATERIALS:
Flyers, Posters, and Brochures

Poster for a lecture on typographic/letterform design by Tony DiSpigna. Designer: Tony DiSpigna, 1990.

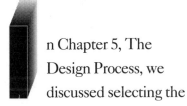

n Chapter 5, The Design Process, we discussed selecting the appropriate format for each printed piece to be designed. Flyers, posters, and brochures fit into the category of materials that inform. They also fit into the category of materials that persuade. In this chapter we will discuss designing flyers, posters, and brochures as informational materials.

FLYERS

The purpose of a flyer is to convey information within a limited time span. The flyer may announce an event or advertise a product or service. It is an inexpensive form of advertising. The flyer should give the whole picture of the event or the product it is promoting. Since it has a short life span and is usually thrown away after the date of the event it announces, it must make a fast impression and attract the attention of the intended audience. The successful flyer hung on a bulletin board is a good vehicle for advertising because it will reach a large number of people at once. A flyer should present information in a typeface that is readable, with information in a hierarchy based on the upside down pyramid principle used in a newspaper article: who, what, when, where, why, and how. It should have large headlines, a small amount of text, and some visual, a photograph or illustration that will catch the eye of the viewer. Standard sizes for flyers are 8 ½" x 11", 8 ½" x 14" or 11" x 17".

POSTERS

A poster is similar in function to the flyer. It is also a printed piece that informs and announces an event. The

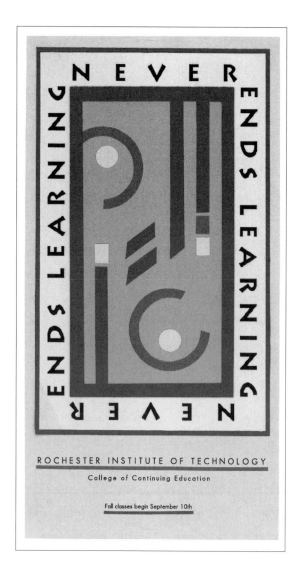

ROCHESTER INSTITUTE OF TECHNOLOGY

College of Continuing Education

Fall classes begin September 10th

"The poster, almost by definition, is designated for public spaces, for the street."

—David Kinzle,
Graphic Design in America. Harry N. Abrams, Inc, 1989.

Left: Poster for RIT designed by Shelly Bremmer, student at Rochester Institute of Technology, 1992.

Right: Poster, "Art What Thou Eat," for an exhibition of images of food in American art. The New York Historical Society. Designer: Michael Consorte, 1993.

poster for an art exhibition may be quite elaborate and expensive to produce. If the poster is used to announce an art exhibition, and is a beautiful object in itself, its function changes from informative to decorative, and unlike the flyer it may be kept and hung on a wall.

A poster should communicate in a direct way to attract attention. The impact of the poster must be established at first glance. The poster or flyer should have only a small amount of text that can be read quickly. The poster, like an ad, must stop, interest, and enlist the viewer to take action: visit an exhibition or participate in a seminar.

Some Basic Considerations Before Designing a Poster
1. What exactly do you wish to communicate?

You should have a clear idea of what you want to say to your audience. Think about every aspect of the information you have to present. Isolate the most important factor— or factors—that you need to convey your message.

2. Will your graphic (photograph or illustration) convey the appropriate message to your audience?

The main idea should be presented with a graphic, a visual image or type. The image should not be ambiguous or the idea will be misinterpreted. Whether you decide to use humor, drama, or an abstract image, your idea should be conveyed quickly and accurately.

3. Are the typefaces and typestyles appropriate to the effectiveness of the piece?

The same typeface in different typestyles and sizes can be used in order to help emphasize and stress important information. Type sizes and styles (bold, italics, outline, etc.) should be varied depending upon the information to be stressed. A catchy headline in bold type will attract immediate attention.

4. Does your copy get to the point?

Is the verbal information set up in a hierarchy of importance? Have you presented subsequent information logically and in relation to type size and position? Does your copy, and your layout, lead the audience from one piece of information to the next in order of importance? If the information presented becomes confusing, the audience is lost, and the poster is ineffective and useless.

5. Does this poster make you want to look twice?

Will people look at this poster more than once? Would you want to hang this poster or flyer on the wall in your house? Does this poster have a spark of imagination that makes it unique and intriguing? If the design is imaginative, people will not only look at the design, but will want to own it.

There are no laws, no real rules, when designing a poster. The successful poster design is based on imagination and presentation of information. The most important aspect in designing a flyer or poster is that it be noticed.

TIPS TO REMEMBER: A CHECKLIST

- ☐ The poster is compelling.
- ☐ The headline is bold, readable, and an attention-grabber.
- ☐ The poster will stand out among other posters if it is to be displayed on a bulletin board.
- ☐ The message is communicated clearly.
- ☐ The typefaces are appropriate to the audience and are easy to read.
- ☐ The graphic (photograph or illustration) is unambiguous and appropriate to the message and audience.
- ☐ The poster has a clear focal point.

SUGGESTED EXERCISES

1. Look at posters on a bulletin board in a public building. Which ones stand out from the rest? Why?
2. Design a flyer for a local organization that will appear on a bulletin board. Look at the other flyers on the board and see if you can design one that will stand out in the crowd.

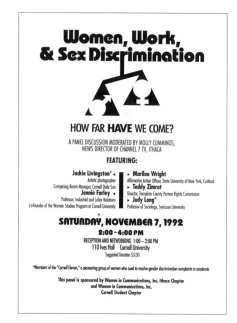

Flyer for a conference, "Women, Work & Sex Discrimination." The logo was designed for the conference. Designer: Marcelle Lapow Toor, 1992.

DESIGNING FOR PRINT
DESIGNING BROCHURES

A brochure is a printed piece the purpose of which is disseminating information, or advertising a service or a product. The design of a brochure calls upon the understanding of the basic principles of advertising, copyrighting, page layout, and production. Like other kinds of promotional materials, the brochure needs a concept, a theme, to tie it together. Brochures may range in design from a simple one-color, three-panel on plain, white stock produced on a laser printer, to a more elaborate four-or five-color design printed on special glossy or expensive flecked recycled stock.

Brochures come in different sizes and shapes. The most common is the three-panel, 8½" x 11", or the four-panel, 8½" x 14". Some brochures use a newsletter format, 11" x 17" folded once, because they must include more information than will fit on the standard sizes. Brochures are informational, and they are used as vehicles for self-promotion, college recruitment, and ads for products. They are good ways to inform a certain audience about conferences and other events, or they can be purely educational and inform the public about health-related or similar public issues. They may be direct mail pieces, self-mailers, that use one, two, three, four or five column grids in their design.

QUESTIONS TO ASK BEFORE DESIGNING A BROCHURE:

1. What is the objective of this brochure?
2. Who is the audience? If there is more than one audience, you may want to think about designing several brochures.
3. How will the customer benefit from this product or service?
4. What information will be contained in the text?
5. Who will write the copy?
6. What is the message?
7. What format will be most appropriate to the message, the amount of information you need to include, and the audience?
8. Will you use a graphic on the cover to attract attention, or do you plan to use a bold, attention-getting headline?

KEEPING IT CONSISTENT

When designing a brochure—or any other printed piece—consistency, and simplicity are the keys to a successful design. Headlines

Brochure announcing the rules for SuperQuest 1991, a competition for problem-solving on the supercomputer aimed at high school students and teachers, sponsored by The Cornell Theory Center, IBM Corporation, Cornell University and the National Science Foundation. Designer: Mo Viele, 1991.

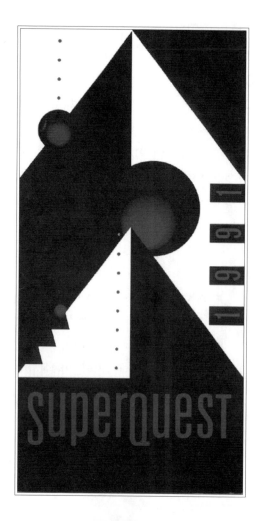

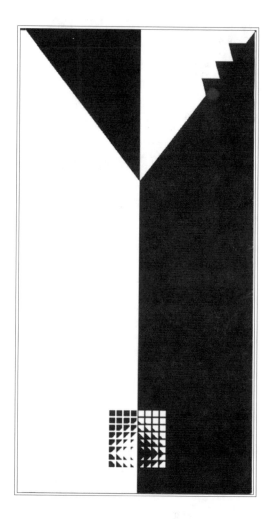

Top left and right: Front and back cover of a program brochure for the SuperQuest banquet for students who won a supercomputing contest sponsored by the Theory Center at Cornell University, IBM and the National Science Foundation, 1991.

Bottom: The inside of the brochure.
Designer: Mo Viele.

and subheads should be consistent within the piece and should provide contrast with the body copy. If two typefaces, sans serif and serif are used, they should look good together.

FOLDING THE BROCHURE

The mechanics of folding the brochure are part of the design process. Margins and panels need to be set up to allow for the folds, with the text in mind. In a three-panel, three column brochure with half-inch margins, the spacing between the columns should be one inch, or twice the amount of the margin. It is essential before designing a brochure to make up a dummy, or mock-up, so that you know the information that will be contained in each panel. The dummy will help you decide how to lay out the panels and will make it easy for you to experiment with the folds. There are several different kinds of folds: gate folds, book folds, and concertina folds. Discuss these with your printer.

> *Hint: Before designing an oversize brochure that does not fit the dimensions described above, consult the post office about their specifications for first class mail: sizes, proportions, and their relationship to mailing costs.*

The diagram below shows a dummy for a three-panel, two-fold brochure with indications for column guides. The dotted lines represent the folds.

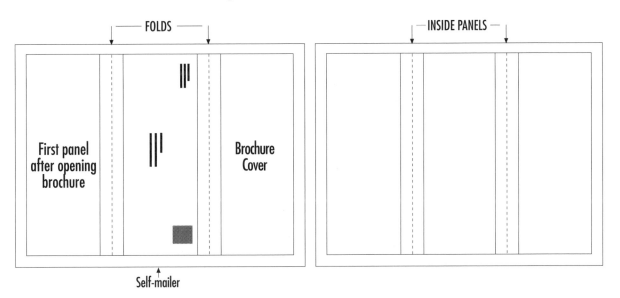

FOLDING
THE
BROCHURE

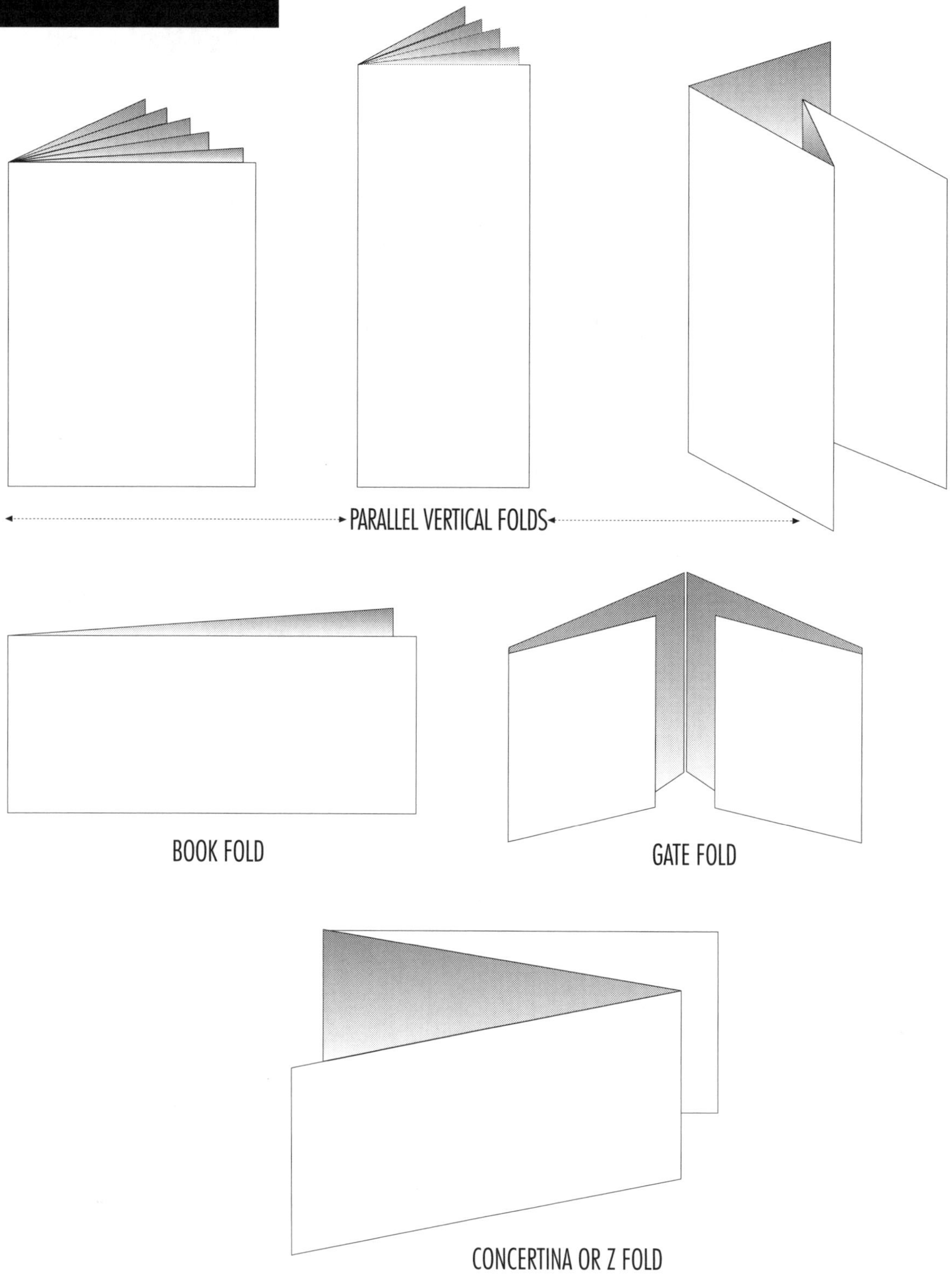

PARALLEL VERTICAL FOLDS

BOOK FOLD

GATE FOLD

CONCERTINA OR Z FOLD

DESIGNING FOR PRINT:

A BROCHURE DESIGN FOR REUNING & SONS VIOLINS

Designer: Phil Wilson.
Copywriter: Ed McKeown.
Photographer: Dede Hatch,
1992.

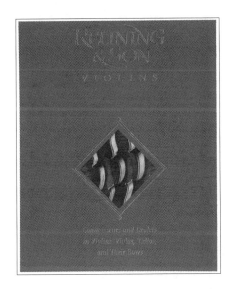

THE PROBLEM:

To design a brochure for Reuning & Sons, a business that makes handcrafted violins, violas, and cellos that would show "old-world standards for craftsmanship and service…with a contemporary understanding of the needs of serious musicians."

THE SOLUTION:

This elegant brochure in booklet form serves as a tour of the studio where the instruments are constructed by hand. Scanned designs and handwritten music from old books were used as tinted backdrops on the page to give the piece an "old-world" feel. In order to reinforce and carrry through the classic tradition of Western culture, the designer has used the golden mean of proportion for the size of the brochure (8" x 9 ¾") based on the Fibonacci series (see glossary). The strong photographs, duotones, (see Chapter 12), have a richness against the paler, decorative background and pick up the background color. The brochure conveys an "old world" feeling in a contemporary setting.

The diamond-shaped cut-out on the cover lets the photograph of the violins peek through and appear first as an interesting and intriguing pattern. The cover is burgundy with gold type. The rest of the booklet uses the same colors with screened backgrounds.

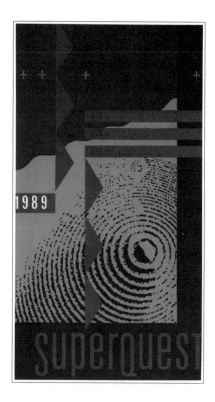

Top left: Brochure for SuperQuest, a program that brings high school students interested in science together with scientists from college campuses as a "challenge to the potential of high school students and teachers." Designer: Mo Viele, 1989.

Top right: Call for participation brochure for "SUPERCOMPUTING '91" held in Albuquerque, New Mexico. The cover and the logo have the feel of the Southwest. Designer: Mo Viele.

Bottom right: Brochure for SuperQuest, for a supercomputing competition aimed at high school students and sponsored by the Theory Center, Cornell University, IBM, and the National Science Foundation. Designer: Mo Viele, 1990.

Update: Hip Dysplasia in Dogs

JAMES A. BAKER INSTITUTE for Animal Health

College of Veterinary Medicine • Cornell University

Top and bottom: A brochure in the form of a narrow booklet for the James A Baker Institute for Animal Health, College of Veterinary Medicine, Cornell University, called, Update Hip Dysplasia in Dogs. The brochure uses very appealing, heart-warming photographs. Photographers: C. H. Brown (cover photo); Charles Harrington (inside photographs); Designer: Phil Wilson, 1993.

HIP DYSPLASIA, *an abnormal formation of the hip joint, occurs in many mammals. It is a serious medical problem for both humans and dogs, although it is far more prevalent in dogs.*

In contrast to a one to two percent incidence in humans, canine hip dysplasia can occur in 50 percent or more of some of the larger breeds of dogs. Unlike human hip dysplasia, the canine condition is not detectable at birth, although it can be identified within the first year of life. It affects dogs and bitches equally. The information that follows is intended only to familiarize dog owners with some of the characteristics of hip dysplasia. A veterinarian should be consulted for specific advice.

Who is affected?

Hip dysplasia is prevalent in the large breeds of dogs. It is particularly common in breeds such as the Bernese Mountain Dog, Bloodhound, Boxer, Brittany Spaniel, Chesapeake Bay Retriever, English Setter, English Springer Spaniel, Golden Retriever, Gordon Setter, German Shepherd Dog, Labrador Retriever, Old English Sheepdog, Standard Poodle, Rottweiler, St. Bernard, Welsh Springer Spaniel, and the Welsh Corgi.* Mixed breeds are also subject to hip dysplasia. Not even the toy breeds are spared, although incidence is lower in small dogs. Large dogs that have a relatively low incidence of hip dysplasia include the Borzoi, Doberman Pinscher, Great Dane, Greyhound, Irish Wolfhound, and Siberian Husky.

What are the signs of hip dysplasia?

Hip dysplasia usually begins to manifest itself through decreased activity with varying degrees of joint pain. Often these signs are first observed between the ages of four months and one year. Young dogs may have a swaying

*Frequency of hip dysplasia by breed was taken from a table in *Cornell University College of Veterinary Medicine Animal Health Newsletter*, volume 11 number 2, April 1993.

and unsteady gait. They may draw their hind legs forward, placing more weight on their forelimbs. Afflicted dogs often run with both hind legs moving together in a gait that has been described as "bunny hopping."

As the disease progresses, a dog may have difficulty rising after sitting or lying down. Stairs become difficult to climb, and the dog may whimper or snap when an affected joint is manipulated. The disease is progressive and often crippling, but some dogs experience little discomfort despite severe abnormalities in their joints. In most cases, pain limits movement of the joint. Running and intense activity aggravate the condition and can reveal signs of disease in dogs that otherwise appear normal.

How is it diagnosed?

Although observation of a dog's gait can arouse suspicion of hip dysplasia, the diagnosis can be established only by X-ray examination. The dog is first anesthetized

TIPS TO REMEMBER: A CHECKLIST
Look at the brochure as if you were on the receiving end.

☐ The information is organized in a hierarchical order of importance.

☐ The information has been presented in a simple, clear way.

☐ The facing pages work well together.

☐ The facing panels work together in terms of design and information presented.

☐ There a good sense of balance on the page.

☐ The illustrations or photographs work well with the text and enhance the page; they do not overwhelm the information.

☐ The paper selected enhances the design of the brochure and allows for easy folding.

Right: Brochure cover for the Summer Session of the International Agriculture Program, Cornell University. Designer: Mo Viele, 1988.

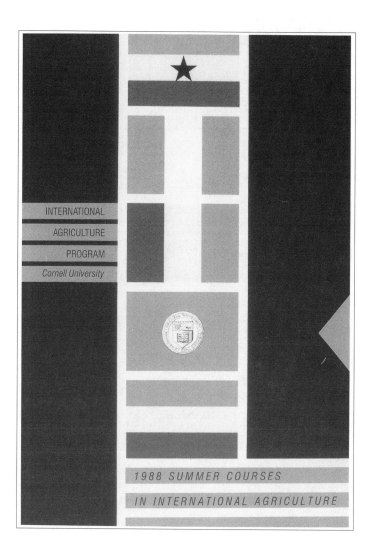

INTERNATIONAL

AGRICULTURE

PROGRAM

Cornell University

1988 SUMMER COURSES

IN INTERNATIONAL AGRICULTURE

GRADUATE SCHOOL OF BUSINESS
INDIANA UNIVERSITY

THE
NEW
MBA
1993-94

The
next
step
you
take...

8.
DESIGNING EDITORIAL
MATERIALS

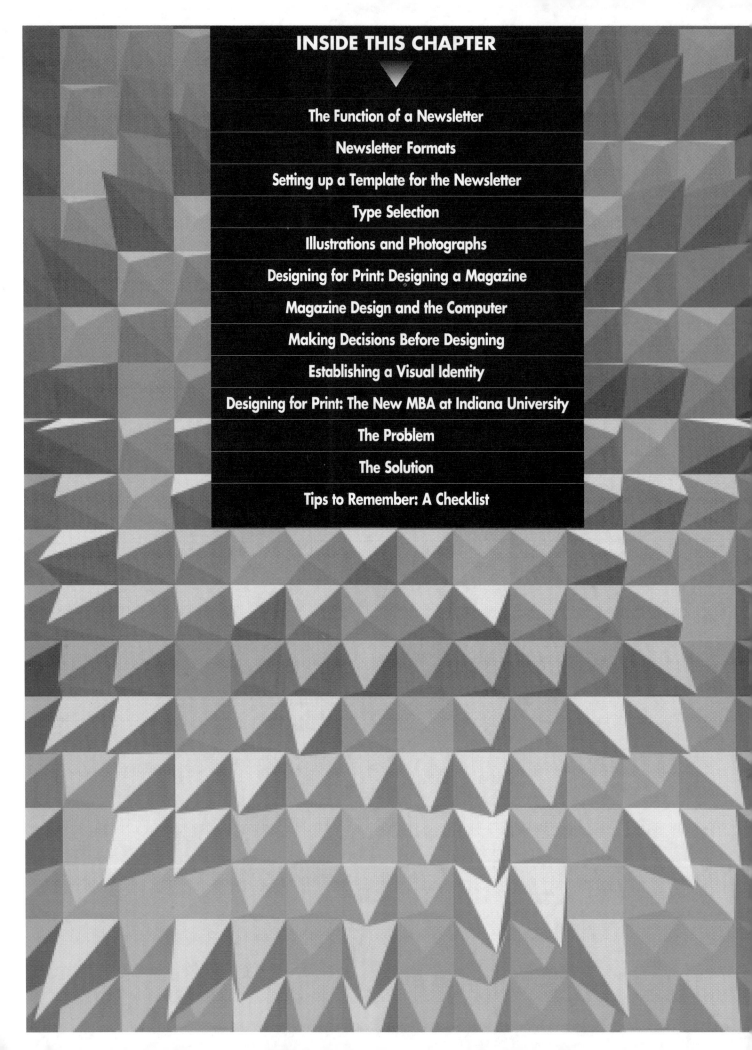

INSIDE THIS CHAPTER

8

EDITORIAL DESIGN: Newsletters and Magazines

NEWSLETTERS: THE BEGINNINGS

Newsletter for the Johnson School of Management, Cornell University.
Designer: Phil Wilson, 1992.

The newsletter, a periodical like a magazine, is produced on a regular basis and fits into the category of editorial design. The newsletter in America, the predecessor to the newspaper, dates back to the Colonial period—a time before telephones, TV, and magazines. It was the main vehicle to disseminate news of local interest to the public and was originally presented in the form of a personal letter. The newsletter has once again become a significant presence in our society and the most popular means of communicating information in the United States today. It is a way to reach and inform a specific audience with common interests about events, stories, or news items of particular interest. Since desktop publishing systems appeared on the market in the mid-1980s, thousands of newsletters have been produced. Often the job of designing and producing a newsletter is performed as an extra task by a person in an organization, a secretary, editor, administrative assistant, or assistant director. Unless the newsletter is an elaborate affair with its own regular staff of writers, editors, and designers, it is not unusual for the person who designs and produces the newsletter to serve as writer and editor as well.

The newsletter is an excellent advertising medium since it can be informative while it sells. Like any other periodical, it should have an editorial focus based on the audience it serves. The sophistication of a newsletter design relates directly to the audience and the purpose of the publication.

Newsletters can be used to provide gossip or relevant

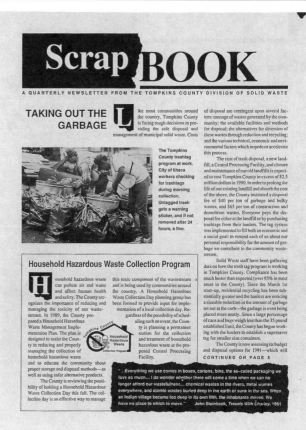

Top left and right : Newsletter for the Tompkins County Solid Waste Division. The newsletter uses interesting drop caps that resemble torn pieces of paper to give the feeling of paper that has been recycled. Page numbers are done in the same manner. Designer: Mo Viele, 1990.

Bottom left and right: Newsletter used as a promotional direct mail piece for a printer, Whitman Communications Group. Designer: Dana R. Walkup, 1991.

information to employees in a large corporation; as a way to keep up with university alumni; a promotion tool for a company to disseminate information on their latest innovations, or as a way of fund-raising for a not-for-profit charitable organization, like a library, or the American Red Cross.

THE FUNCTION OF A NEWSLETTER

1. A newsletter or business report sponsored by an organization as an in-house communication with information about the members of the organization.
2. A letter that advocates some kind of action on the part of the reader by a charitable or political organization.
3. A newsletter produced by an organization as a public relations advertising tool.
4. A newsletter that is subscription-based and gives information of a specific nature to a designated audience of subscribers.

NEWSLETTER FORMATS:

1. The letter, the old traditional format.

This is the traditional old format, in the form of a personal subscription letter. The *Kiplinger Washington Letter* reaches over 500,000 people and has been around for many years. It began as a letter and is still produced in letter format.

Newsletters produced in the 8½" x 11" letter format often look like they have been produced on a typewriter.

2. The small magazine format, or magaletter.

This popular 8 ½" x 11" format imitates a magazine in style and presentation, and may run the gamut from inexpensively-produced on the desktop and duplicated at a copy center, to slick, expensively-produced, with full-color illustrations or photographs and printed on glossy paper. Some colleges and universities use the magaletter as a promotion vehicle to entice prospective students.

Some mail order catalog companies use this format to give the impression of a newsletter. They might include some piece of interesting information relating to the product they are selling. It is a good promotional tool.

MASTHEADS

The masthead on a newsletter or magazine contains important information: the logo or logotype, the volume number, the date, and other information that is repeated with each subsequent edition. Below are some different mastheads for the same audience.

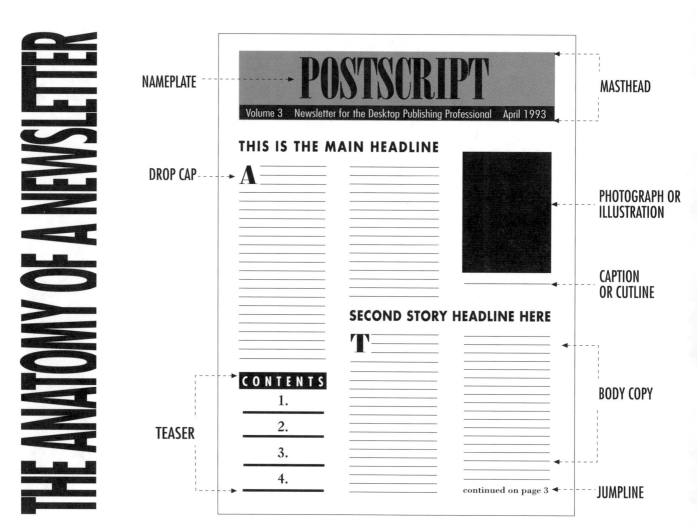

3. Newspaper or tabloid format

This 11" x 17" format resembles a tabloid newspaper and is often produced on good quality paper. This larger format allows for the presentation of more information and is often used by museums.

SETTING UP A TEMPLATE FOR THE NEWSLETTER

Every periodical has some constants that are present in each issue. In newsletters, newspapers, and magazines, the constants are the masthead and nameplate, typography, folios, and table of contents. If a template is set up on the computer, the task of producing each subsequent issue is simplified. The template or pattern provides the structure and foundation for the newsletter. A template is like a pattern for sewing a dress. Once you have the pattern, you can produce several similar dresses in different colors or fabrics, or you can alter the style slightly. A template for a publication can be used like the pattern for a dress. Once the pattern is designed and a grid set up, all subsequent issues will have a consistent look with slight changes in each issue. After the template is designed, the newsletter can be produced by anyone in the organization who knows desktop publishing and has been taught to use the template.

The twelve questions to ask before designing a newsletter:

1. What is the ultimate function of this newsletter?
2. Who is the audience?
3. What kind of information will this newsletter contain?
4. How many issues will there be?
5. How will this newsletter be distributed; will it be a self-mailer, or will it be distributed in another way?
6. What format and size will the newsletter be? The size of the newsletter should be appropriate to the audience and the amount of information to be presented.
7. Who will produce and design it?
8. Who will print it?
9. How will it be printed?
10. What kind of paper will it be printed on?
11. What is the budget?
12. Will it be printed in one color or several?

Some important considerations:

- The front page is the first thing the viewer sees. It should have instant appeal and recognition.
- The newsletter should have an established format that remains constant in subsequent issues.
- The newsletter should have its own strong identity.
- Each issue should have a familiarity. Readers should be able to locate regular columns quickly, but each issue should contain something new and unexpected.

The balance of the familiar and the new can be done with visual images that include:

- The use of logos or icons to identify different kinds of articles.
- Exciting cover designs.
- Interesting treatment of feature stories.
- Large initial capital letters by themselves or in boxes.
- The use of shaped text.
- Housekeeping details: (mastheads, content listings, letters, calendars, etc.).
- Folios (page numbers) presented in a unique way.

Basic items that will appear in each issue:

- Masthead, including nameplate logo, volume number, identification of ownership, date, etc.
- Table of contents or teaser on the front page
- Folios (page numbers)
- Reviews
- News sections (sections should have a recognizable style and be consistent in the page position from one issue to the next)
- Features
- Advertisements
- Credits
- Graphics: photographs, illustrations, charts, and graphs
- Captions
- Jumplines
- Return address if newsletter is a self-mailer

Items that add visual interest:

- ☞ Drop caps or bold initial caps
- ☞ Dingbats or small graphic symbols
- ☞ Photographs or illustrations, charts, and diagrams
- ☞ Shaded boxes
- ☞ Boxes with shadows
- ☞ Lines or rules
- ☞ Icons for page numbers
- ☞ Icons to identify articles
- ☞ Pull quotes
- ☞ Enlarged lead paragraphs
- ☞ End marks
- ☞ Special type
- ☞ Reversed type
- ☞ Frames for photographs or illustrations
- ☞ Contrast in type
- ☞ Interesting column configurations
- ☞ Unique teaser
- ☞ Enlarged numbers as visuals

Your newsletter needs some visual interest!

ORGANIZING THE NEWSLETTER

Five questions to ask yourself:

1. Is there a newsletter design you've seen that you like?
2. What part of the design appeals to you ? Why?
3. What will Page One contain? Masthead, one or two articles, photographs, table of contents box?
4. What will Page Two and Page Three contain, etc.?
5. If the newsletter has been published before, how will readers feel about a design change? Should the new design be different or would it be better to "clean up" the present design?

Making design decisions for the structure of the pages:

1. How can you make the newsletter look appealing and readable?
2. Will the design be casual, open, friendly, or does the editorial content stress a more formal, serious design?

3. How many columns do you want for each page: two, three, or four columns per page?

4. What kind of column configuration will you use: two, three, four columns?

5. Will the text be justified or flush left?

6. How wide do the margins need to be to provide sufficient white space and breathing room on the page?

7. How much white space should there be between columns?

8. Does your budget allow for illustrations or photographs or will you rely on type and other graphic devices (dingbats, bullets, rules, boxes) for visual interest?

Hint: It's a good idea to think about some interesting column configurations when setting up your design. Experiment with 2, 3, 4 column grids with columns of unequal widths. What is the best configuration for both column width and readability?

The newsletters below show the use of a three column grid on the left and a two column grid on the right. Each one presents a slightly different image.

CONTAINER GARDENING

N Lorem ipsum dolor sir consectetuer adipiscin, tincidunt ut laoreet dolo diam nonummy nibh euismond aliquam erat volutpat. Ut wisi enim ad minim veniam, quis nostrud exerci tation ullamcorp suscipit lobortis nisl ut aliquip ea commodo consequat. Duis autem vel eum iriure dolor in hendrerit in vulputate velit esse molestie consequat, ve illum dolore eu feugait nulla facilisi. Lorem ipsum dolor sir amet, consectetuer adipiscing elit, sed diam nonummy nibh euismond tincidunt ut laoreet dolore mag aliquam erat volutpat. Ut wisi enim ad minim veniam, quis nostrud exerci tation ullamcorp ea commodo consequat. Duis autem vel eum iriure dolor in hendrerit in vulputate velit esse molestie consequat, ve illum dolore eu feugait nulla facilisi.

Lorem ipsum dolor sir amet, consectetuer adipiscing elit, se diam nonummy nibh euismond tincidunt ut laoreet dolore mag aliquam erat volutpat. Ut wisi enim ad minim veniam, quis nostrud exerci tation ullamcorp suscipit lobortis nisl ut aliquip ea commodo consequat. Duis autem vel eum iriure dolor in hendrerit in vulputate velit esse molestie consequat, ve illum dolore eu feugait nulla facilisi. Lorem ipsum dolor sir amet, consectetuer adipiscing elit, se diam nonummy nibh euismond aliquam erat volutpat. Ut wisi ea commodo consequat.

Duis autem vel illum dolore veniam exceri tation magna

MADE IN THE SHADE

D lipsum dolor sir amet, consectetuer adipisscing diam nonummy nibh eu tincidunt ut laoreet dolore mag aliquam erat volutpat. Ut wisi enim ad minim veniam, quis nostrud exerci tation ullamcorp suscipit lobortis nisl ut aliquip ea commodo consequat.

Lorem ipsum dolor sir amet, consectetuer adipiscing elit, se diam nonummy nibh euismond tincidunt ut laoreet dolore mag aliquam erat volutpat. Ut wisi enim ad minim veniam, quis nostrud exerci tation ullamcorp suscipit lobortis nisl ut aliquip ea commodo consequat. Duis autem vel eum iriure dolor in hendrerit in vulputate velit ess molestie consequat, ve illum dolore eu feugait nulla facilisi. Lorem ipsum dolor sir amet, diam nonummy nibh euismond aliquam erat volutpat.

CONTENTS

Vel illum dolore tation magna

Continued on page 2

SEPTEMBER 23, 1996 · VOL. 64

CONTENTS ••••

CONTAINER GARDENING

N Lorem ipsum dolor sir consectetuer adipiscin, liber tempor sol tincidunt ut laoreet dolodiam nonummy nibh eleifend option euismondaliquam erat volutpat. Ut wisi dignissm qui et iusto enim ad minim veniam, quis nostrud exerci tation ulla dolore te feug mcorp suscipit lobortis nisl ut aliquip ea commodo con nulla dolor sit sequat. Duis autem vel eum iriure dolor in hendrerit in amiet euismond vulputate velit esse molestie consequat, ve illum dolore aliquip vel ill eu feugait nulla facilisi.
• Enim ad minim veniam, quis nostrud exerci tation ulla dolore te feug mcorp suscipit lobortis nisl ut aliquip ea commodo con nulla dolor sit sequat. Duis autem vel eum iriure dolor in hendrerit in amiet euismond vulputate velit esse molestie consequat, ve illum dolore aliquip vel ill eu feugait nulla facilisi. Enim ad minim veniam, quis nostrud exerci tat

Duis autem vel illum dolore veniam exceri ation magna

D Lorem ipsum dolor sir consectetuer adipiscin, liber tempor sol tincidunt ut laoreet dolodiam nonummy nibh eleifend option euismondaliquam erat volutpat. Ut wisi dignissm qui et iusto enim ad minim veniam, quis nostrud exerci tation ulla dolore te feug mcorp suscipit lobortis nisl ut aliquip ea commodo con nulla dolor sit sequat. Duis autem vel eum iriure dolor in hendrerit in amiet euismond vulputate velit esse molestie consequat, ve illum dolore aliquip vel ill eu feugait nulla facilisi.

Continued on page 2

TYPE SELECTION

Questions to ask before selecting typefaces:

1. Which typefaces will be most readable?
2. Do you want the headlines to be a serif or sans serif face, bold, all caps or upper and lower case?
3. Is the typeface you selected appropriate for your audience?
4. Is the typeface modern and stylish, or will it give the newsletter an old-fashioned look?
5. Which typeface will you use for the body copy, a serif or sans serif face? (It is usually a good idea to stick with one headline typeface throughout a newsletter varying it in style and size for subheads.)
6. Is the typeface readable and appropriate for the audience?
7. Does the typeface selected for the headlines and subheads work well with the body copy typeface?

ILLUSTRATIONS AND PHOTOGRAPHS

Six questions to ask:

1. Is an illustration needed to add visual interest to the page?
2. Will the illustration style (photograph, line drawing, clip art, collage) complement the overall style of the newsletter?
3. Can you afford illustrations or photographs?
   If the newsletter is serious and formal, a cartoon would be an inappropriate illustration. If you cannot afford to hire an illustrator and you cannot draw, do not use illustrations; do interesting things with type.
4. Does this newsletter need charts, diagrams, or tables?
5. Can you create your own charts and graphs on the computer?
6. Can you substitute tables or text for graphs and charts?

Hint: You can create your own graphs with special software programs (see Software Bibliography).

TIPS TO REMEMBER: A CHECKLIST

☐ The masthead contains all the necessary information.
☐ The nameplate is easily recognizable and distinctive.
☐ The front page looks inviting and easy to read.
☐ The headlines are distinguishable from the body text.

- [ ] Each article is easy to identify.
- [ ] The newsletter has a distinctive identity.
- [ ] The body copy typeface is inviting and easy to read.
- [ ] One typeface has been used throughout, or one face has been used for headlines and subheads and one for body copy.
- [ ] The illustrations relate to the publication and the audience.
- [ ] There is enough white space on each page.
- [ ] There enough white space between columns.
- [ ] The text has been proofread and all typos eliminated.

SUGGESTED EXERCISES

1. Start a collection of newsletters that you find interesting.
2. Find a poorly-designed newsletter. Evaluate the design problem. What makes the design unappealing?
3. Create two new nameplates and mastheads for the newsletter that improve on the old design.
4. Change the column configurations and the headlines.
5. Try making changes to the design of the front page of the newsletter. Try to give it a different image, one that will appeal to each of the following audiences: teachers, business people, teenagers, college students.
6. Contact a non-profit organization and offer to redesign their current newsletter.

DESIGNING FOR PRINT:

MAGAZINE DESIGN

MAGAZINE DESIGN AND THE COMPUTER

The magazine came into being as one of the many outgrowths of the Industrial Revolution and the development of photographic reproduction and automated printing. Early magazines were produced as journals with political or literary themes, and, like medieval manuscripts, they were too expensive for general circulation. They were published exclusively for the very wealthy. This is no longer the case.

The magazine racks in the supermarkets, book stores, and newsstands reveal the wide sampling of consumer magazines being produced today for a variety of audiences. Magazines exist for almost every special interest group: music, model building, cars, sports, sewing, art, etc. There are magazines for the consumer over fifty *(Modern Maturity)*, magazines for kids seventeen and under *(Seventeen, Humpty Dumpty)*, and magazines that are gender-specific *(Vogue, Ms., GQ)*. The present range of magazines and magazine design is vast.

Magazine design has undergone severe changes since TV became its competition. In the past, magazines were read from cover to cover. Today's reader has little time to read, and a short attention span. In an attempt to persuade consumers to buy magazines, graphic designers use techniques like large photographs of celebrities and teasers on the cover to seduce the potential reader.

Although they both fall into the category of periodicals, and involve editorial design, most newsletters today are most likely produced by amateurs on their desktops. Major magazines still have art directors, designers, copywriters, editors, and marketing people working together to produce a publication—people who have been trained for their tasks. Since the arrival of the personal computer, some editors are now producing the magazines they were originally hired to edit. A few years ago, the editor of a journal for a major East Coast university was told that since she had a computer and desktop publishing software on her desk, she would be responsible for the design and production of the magazine in addition to the editing. This is not an isolated or unusual situation.

Magazines run the gamut from the inexpensive, in-house designed and produced publication to the slick, elaborately designed, multicolored magazine. Magazines may be produced for a specialized audience in a particular trade, or for a more generalized one.

ANNUAL REPORTS

Annual reports are magazines produced for the purpose of providing financial information to stockholders in a publicly-held corporation or to people who have an interest in the progress of an organization.

Top left: Annual report from Ben & Jerry's Homemade, Inc., producers of ice-cream in unique flavor combinations. The design is playful, happy and friendly in a horizontal 11" x 8 ½" format and is printed on 100% recycled paper with 50% post-consumer waste. This annual report has a different feel from the corporate-looking one below.

Top right: Contents page of the annual report.
Designers: Sarah Forbes and Edgar Stewart, 1992.

Bottom right: 1990-1991 Annual report for Cornell University's School of Industrial and Labor Relations. The annual report is sent to corporations that contribute money to aid in the research conducted at the school. The look of the annual report is fairly formal and corporate.

Bottom left: An inside two-page spread from the report.
Designer: Marcelle Lapow Toor, 1991.

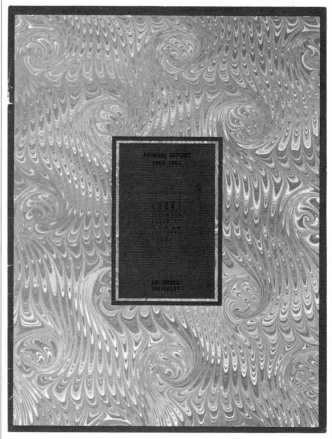

The design of a magazine should reflect the editorial goal and the interest group being served. *Modern Maturity* magazine, whose audience is people over fifty, would not sustain its audience if it had the look and feel of some of the new wave music magazines with small type and lines of intersecting text. On the other hand, the music magazines would alienate their readership if the designs were conservative. Each magazine needs its own identity or personality which is geared to the reader it is attempting to reach.

Magazines are luxury items. While the general public will buy newspapers, readers do not look on magazines in the same way. Magazines have a great deal of competition for their audiences, and whenever that kind of competition exists, design becomes an extremely important factor. People buy books and magazines because they are attracted to the covers.

TYPES OF MAGAZINES

1. Consumer magazines

Consumer magazines come under the category of frivolous items that readers buy because the reader is interested in the subject matter. *(Spy, Vogue, The New Yorker, Time, Newsweek, Spin, Art News)*

2. Trade magazines

Trade publications or journals (graphic design, desktop publishing, medical) have a built-in readership because they offer professional or occupational information: the doctor who wants to keep in touch with the latest medical developments must read medical journals, the desktop publisher who needs to know about new software and hardware in order to keep up with technological advances must read publications on the subject, and the scientist who wants to keep up with the latest developments in science needs to read scientific periodicals. *(New England Journal of Medicine, Publish, Print, Scientific American)*

3. House organs

House organs, or public relations magazines, are produced for a select readership, people who have bought products from that company or business. *(Aldus Magazine, Font & Function, Upper & Lowercase)*

4. Subscription

Subscription-only magazines cannot be purchased at the corner newsstand. They are sold only through subscriptions. *(Modern Maturity, Smithsonian, National Geographic)*

When we talk about magazine design, most people think of the popular magazines mentioned above, those slick publications found on newsstands. Many magazines are being produced by desktop publishers or people like the editor at the university. If you have never attempted to design a magazine before, the task may seem overwhelming.

Where do you begin?

Careful planning and organization is the first step in designing a magazine. The designer's initial task is to create a roadmap, a pattern or plan for the design and layout of the magazine similar to the preparation and organization of a newsletter.

MAKING DECISIONS BEFORE DESIGNING
Important factors to consider before designing a magazine:

1. What is the purpose or function of the magazine?
2. What is the nature of the audience: age, gender, income?
3. What kind of personality or image will the magazine have? Will it be conservative, sophisticated, or playful?
4. Where will the magazine be sold or dispensed?
5. What other magazines will be competing with yours?
6. What kind of circulation do you expect?
7. If the magazine is to be a periodical, how often will it be produced?
8. How much color will you use?
9. How will the magazines's appearance/image reflect the reader?
10. What size will the magazine be?
11. What kinds of illustrations will you use?
12. What will the regular features be like?

13. Will the stories open with a two-page spread?

14. What amount of space will be allocated to advertisements, editorial articles, and departments in each issue?

ESTABLISHING A VISUAL IDENTITY

Magazine readers like the familiarity of the magazines they purchase. They like to be able to locate their magazines quickly on the rack. In previous chapters we discussed negative reactions to change. Readers hate design changes in their magazines, which is why the more established magazines stick pretty closely to the original format. *The New Yorker* magazine has had a long life, about fifty years in the same format. It recently changed ownership and is undergoing a makeover in design, a change that demonstrates it is going after a new audience. In a September 29, 1992 article in the *New York Times*, critic Walter Goodman wrote a review of the new look:

> "The table of contents (three words that no longer appear) is much changed. It is a lot busier and noisier, with boldface capitals to classify the merchandise....Now, this is a significant change, not just because it replaces a placid table of contents with a cluttered one, but because it descends to a hard sell of the sort that the New Yorker always shunned, not to say disdained."

1. The cover

Faces, not places, sell magazines. Many consumer magazines feature photographs of famous people on their covers. Industry analysts calculate that Cher's face on a cover will sell any magazine. The cover of a magazine is like the front window of a store: it makes people want to enter. It invites. Established magazines like *Smithsonian* and *National Geographic* do not have to experiment graphically with their covers because they have loyal subscribers. Many magazines are still looking for those loyal subscribers. Covers can make a magazine easily identifiable.

2. Table of contents

Some magazines contain a great deal of information and demand a large table of contents, perhaps two pages, with pictures. If the persuasive cover has resulted in a purchase, the reader then turns to the table of contents page to find out where to read about Cher. This is where the reader browses the content and decides how much time to spend with the magazine.

Gone are the days of the one-column, black-and-white table of contents. Since the competition between magazines is so keen, today's contents pages are mini-magazines, sometimes featuring annotated pictures and pullouts. The underlying message here is that there is so much important information in this issue that you have to know about it before you turn another page.

3. Departments

A magazine department can be anything from a letters-to-the-editor section to opinions, photo essays, or reviews. Readers get used to seeing the same departments each month, and they usually have their favorites.

4. Features

The features section of a magazine is a showcase for the editorial backbone of the magazine, as well as for art and graphics. Art directors are allowed to experiment with how the words look on the page. The *New York Times*, which is a fairly conservative newspaper, has altered the look of the Sunday magazine section with the use of imaginative typography for the headlines of each article that illustrates the content of the article.

5. Illustration and photography

Illustrations and photographs create a focal point on a page and attract the reader who does not have much time to read all the

Right: Two-page spread from *Inland Architect* magazine. (Inland Architect), 1993.

articles. In an information age, where color images are invasive, black-and-white photography stands out and is being used in magazines with big photographs that bleed off the page and little text. A two-page spread will often have one page with a full page photograph or illustration and little or no text.

6. Typography

The typefaces and typestyles should fit with the editorial message and the profile of the audience. The typefaces and the sizes used should be appropriate to the editorial message. Type can be used in an illustrative way to create visual interest on a page where there are no illustrations.

7. Advertising

Except in rare instances, magazines usually depend upon ads to remain in business. A fine balance must be worked out in the design of the magazine so that readers do not see ads only. The design of the ads and the editorial content must work together in an interesting visual way.

DESIGNING FOR PRINT:

THE NEW M.B.A. PROGRAM AT INDIANA UNIVERSITY

Marketing: Cynthia McFarland, McFarland & Associates.
Designer: Phil Wilson.
Photographer: Patrick Bennett, 1993

Opposite page:
Top left: Cover of the magazine with a photograph of feet that visually reinforces the words, "The next step you take…"

Top right: The table of contents called "Finding your way around this book." The table of contents maintains the editorial concept carried throughout the entire magazine stressing before, during, after—now and then.

Bottom: A two-page spread in the Before section with the clocks as icons for "3 a.m. thoughts."

THE PROBLEM

To introduce a new Master of Business Administration (MBA) program at the Graduate School of Business at Indiana University.

THE SOLUTION

Cynthia McFarland, of Cynthia McFarland & Associates, a specialist in marketing research and strategy, Phil Wilson, a graphic designer, and Patrick Bennett, a photographer, were hired by Indiana University to come up with a marketing strategy and a printed piece with photographs that would introduce and promote a new MBA program for the Graduate School of Business.

Most MBA candidates are men and women who have been in the workforce for a number of years. Returning to school is often a big decision and a difficult one to make—one that may account for many sleepless nights. McFarland and Wilson developed a concept for a magazine that would address the fears of the person making that difficult decision.

The copy on the first page, entitled BEFORE reads, "A few 3 a.m. thoughts about going for the new MBA," and speaks to the person awakening in the night haunted by the thoughts of a drastic life change, going from a working person to a student. It continues, alleviating these fears by introducing the prospective candidate to a team of students who have "lived and breathed" the new MBA. These students discuss the program from their points of view and talk about the team concept that the program stresses. The clock is used throughout the BEFORE section as an icon to demonstrate time passing for the person lying awake contemplating this decision.

Wilson used New Century Schoolbook condensed for the body copy and broke it up with strong colorful and appealing photographs of students, professors, views of the campus and attractive views of the town, Bloomington. The overall feel of this piece is welcoming, unintimidating, inviting and reassuring. The magazine also serves as a visit to the campus and town.

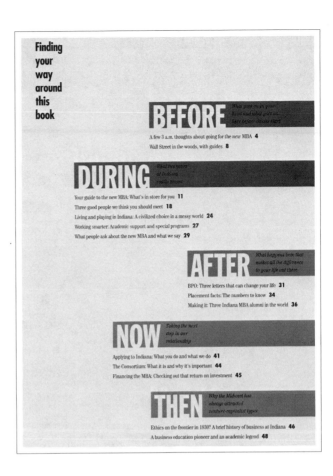

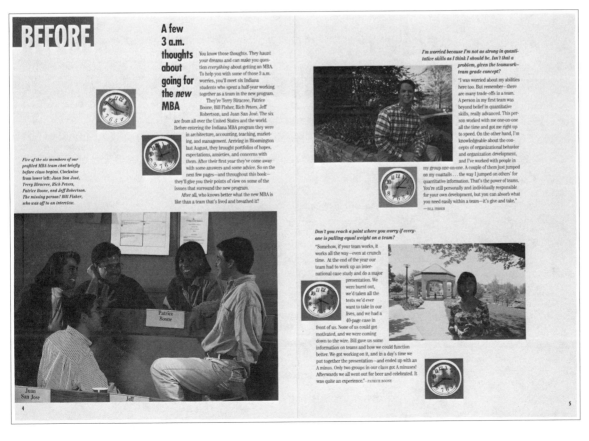

TIPS TO REMEMBER: A CHECKLIST

- ☐ The magazine has a distinctive personality.
- ☐ The magazine is consistent in editorial and visual content.
- ☐ The feature stories have their own identification with some kind of graphic treatment: drop caps, icons, logos.
- ☐ The typography is appropriate and will appeal to the audience.
- ☐ All the visual elements work together and do not fight each other for attention.
- ☐ The large initial caps line up with a line of type.
- ☐ All the elements are lined up with the margins or columns.
- ☐ Each issue is visually fresh and intriguing.
- ☐ Each illustration or photograph has a caption.
- ☐ The caption is distinguishable from the body copy.
- ☐ The layout is uncluttered.
- ☐ The illustrations in a two-page spread have been placed so that the crease will not ruin the effect.
- ☐ The ads fit well with the design in appearance and placement.
- ☐ White space has been used well.
- ☐ The column configuration lends itself to easy reading.
- ☐ There a good balance of text and graphics.
- ☐ The magazine is inviting to look at and to read.

SUGGESTED EXERCISES

1. Look at magazines on a rack of a newsstand or in a bookstore to get an idea of the many types of magazines and design styles.
2. What kinds of visual devices do these magazines use that interest you? What changes would you make?
3. Study the magazines you receive in the mail. What aspects of the design do you find interesting?
4. Design a two-page magazine spread using illustrations from a magazine. Think about how the two pages can fit together in an interesting way.
5. Create headlines for your spread in a drawing program, and use a typeface to illustrate the article.
6. Experiment with drop caps and other large initial capitals.
7. Experiment with different column configurations.

9.
DESIGNING ADS &
BUSINESS MATERIALS

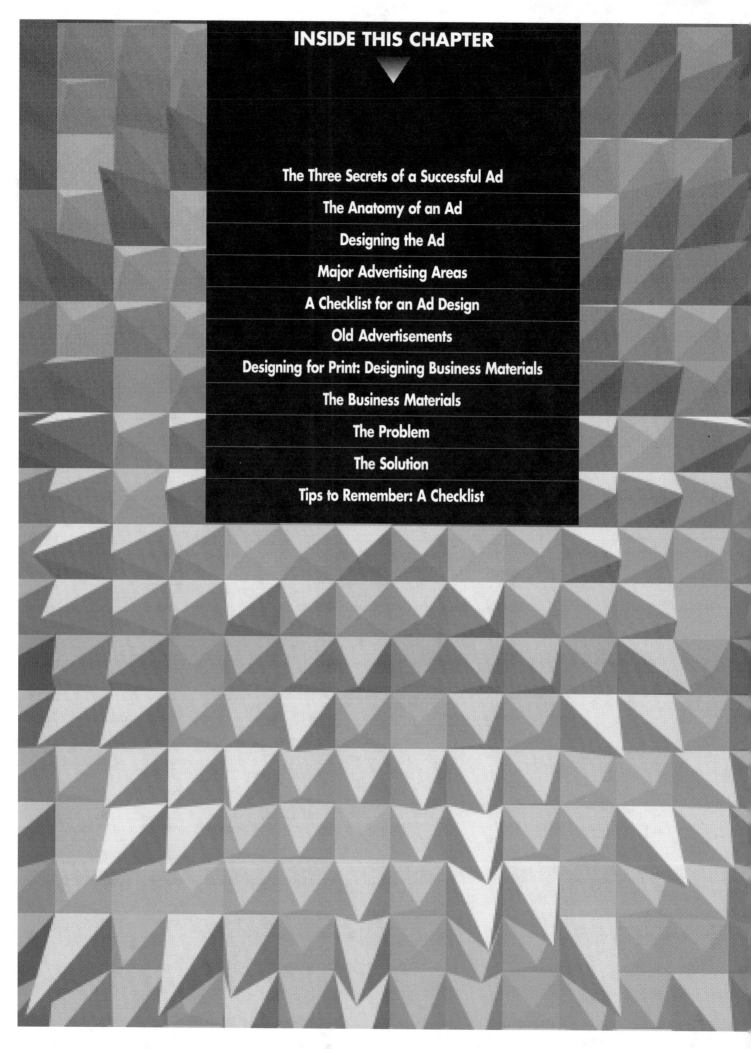

INSIDE THIS CHAPTER

ADVERTISING DESIGN

DESIGNING ADS AND BUSINESS MATERIALS

Old ad for Lever Brothers. *Goods and Merchandise: A Cornucopia of 19th Century Cuts.* William Rowe. Dover Publications, 1982.

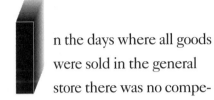

In the days where all goods were sold in the general store there was no competition for products. Manufacturing and commerce increased during the Industrial Revolution creating a need for workers who were able to read and write. As more people began to read, the need for reading materials increased, and newspapers and magazines were created to satisfy that need. An increase in products meant that consumers were needed to purchase these products, and newspapers and magazines became the way to reach the people who would buy the products. Advertising agencies grew out of a need to purchase space for advertising in newspapers and magazines. The agencies purchased space wholesale and sold it to their clients at retail prices.

The main purpose of an ad is to persuade and to stimulate the consumer to act, to purchase a particular product, or, in a political advertisement, to cast a vote for a political candidate. Advertising attempts to change the perception of a product and tries to convince the consumer that the product has desirable qualities. An ad sells an attitude and a lifestyle. It is a way to compete with similar products on the market. The success of an ad campaign is how well it communicates a message, creates an image, and sells a product or service.

An ad may appear in any number of formats: posters, brochures, TV commercials, direct mail, point of purchase displays, billboards, magazines, newsletters, and newspapers. Ads also appear on public transportation.

The computer has made it possible for the desktop publisher, working alone without the usual advertising team of copywriters, designers, illustrators, and marketing people, to create quick ads for newspapers and magazines that are camera-ready, direct from the laser printer.

Questions to ask before designing an ad:

1. Who is the audience?
2. What is the nature of the product?
3. Where will the ad appear?
4. What is the purpose of the ad?
5. What is the budget? (The budget will determine the size of the ad.)
6. Have you done some marketing research to find out:
   The competition for this product?
   Consumer needs and desires?

THE THREE SECRETS OF A SUCCESSFUL AD

1. Attract attention in its overall design
2. Communicate through a unified arrangement of elements
3. Persuade through the interaction of strong and appropriate copy and layout

A good ad should:

STOP!
INTEREST!
SELL!

ANATOMY OF AN AD

1. The space for the ad.

Unless the ad will appear in the form of a flyer that will be hung in public places, the amount of space, size, and proportion purchased in the newspaper or magazine will affect the design of the ad and the cost. Newspapers and magazines sell space in terms of height and width, or numbers of columns. The publication selected for an ad should be appropriate for the consumer of the product. The placement of the ad, right or left side of the page, front or back of the publication, the size, and the design will have an effect on the success of the ad in reaching an audience.

2. Typography

An advertisement should have a limited amount of text, a headline, and some brief, to-the-point body copy. The headline may be the main attraction if there is no illustration or photograph. If this is the case, it should be an attention-getter and cleverly written so the viewer will be interested and read the rest of the copy.

3. Photography or illustration

Often the focal point of an ad is an interesting or unusual photograph or illustration. Viewers will remember a powerful photograph and associate it with a product.

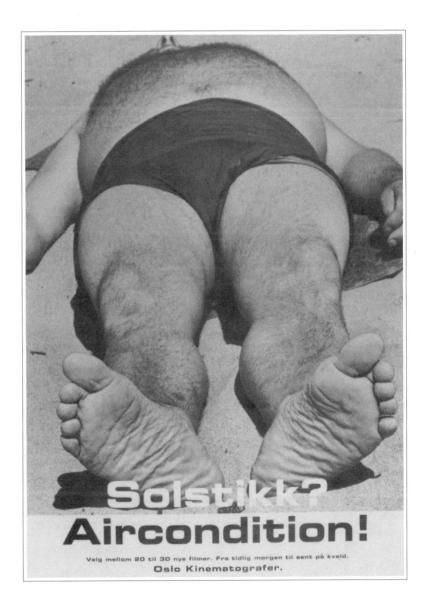

Ad for Oslo Norway Cinema. The ad reads: "Sunstroke? Air-conditioning! Choose between 20 and 30 new movies from early morning until late night." Designed by New Deal DDB Needham Advertising Agency, Oslo Norway, 1993. Photograph by Harry Lapow from *Coney Island Beach People,* Dover Publications, 1978.

4. Color

Since we are accustomed to seeing many colorful visual images daily, black and white photography is being used in some ads, including TV commercials, as a contrast to color, and an attention-getter. The client's budget for the job will determine the amount of color to be used.

Ten questions to ask before designing an ad:

1. How will the ad arrest the reader's attention?
2. What will make the reader want to look at, and read, the ad?
3. Does the ad have a strong focal point?
4. Is the headline a grabber ?
5. Is the ad based on a concept related to the selling premise?
6. Does the ad have campaign potential?

    Unique page personality?

    Distinctive in its category?

    Visual or verbal equity maintained from ad to ad?

7. Does the ad create a positive feeling about the product and the advertiser?
8. Does the ad insult the viewer's intelligence?
9. Does the ad appeal to the audience it is aimed at?
10. Does the ad entice the reader to buy the product?

DESIGNING THE AD

Things to consider and questions to ask:

1. The Layout and design

Is the ad arranged for easy reading?

Is the headline clear and readable?

Is the body text easy to follow and easily digestible?

Is the ad pleasing to the eye?

2. The Illustrations

Will the illustration or photograph intrigue and involve the reader?

Does the illustration dramatize visually?

Can the reader identify with the picture?

Does the image show the benefit of the product clearly?

3. The Headline

Does the headline work together with the illustration to stop, intrigue, and involve the reader?

Does the headline offer a benefit relevant to selling the idea?

Is the viewer surprised and involved through the headline?

Does the headline encourage the reading of the body copy?

4. The Text

Does the text persuade and lead the reader?

Does the text have clear, concise prose?

Does it carry the reader from interest to conviction?

Does the copy close the argument with a call for action?

MAJOR ADVERTISING AREAS:

1. **Television**
2. **Newspapers, newsletters, or magazines**
3. **Direct mail**

1. Television

Advertising on TV is very expensive. Marketing research plays an important role to help find out the peak viewing hours for the audience the ad intends to reach. Research will help define a personality profile of the viewer. The ads can be geared to the interests of the viewing audience.

Ads from an anti-smoking ad campaign. Michigan Department of Health. Copywriter: Marcie Brogan. Creative Director: Bonnie Folster. Designer: Jaime Perry, 1992.

2. Newspapers, newsletters, or magazines

Newspapers and magazines carry both regional and national ads and are seen by many people.

3. Direct Mail, 1st & 3rd class mail

In direct mail the advertiser acts as publisher and produces a flyer, brochure, catalog, or newsletter, rather than renting space. The advertiser buys a select mailing list keyed to a particular audience, and sends the publication directly to that specialized audience.

Advantages of direct mail:

- A mailing list will reach a specialized audience known to have a definite interest in the product.
- The direct mail piece doesn't have to compete for attention with other ads on a printed page.
- The piece can be flexible in format: catalog, letter or flyer.

Disadvantages:

- Some people resent receiving junk mail.
- Direct mail requires the participation and cooperation of the recipient.
- The risk that the piece will be thrown in the trash without ever being read.

A CHECKLIST FOR AN AD DESIGN:

- ☐ The ad appeals to the identified audience.
- ☐ The ad attracts immediate attention.
- ☐ The ad has a good, clear focal point and a good illustration.
- ☐ The typography treatment is appropriate to the audience.
- ☐ The headline is an attention-grabber.

SUGGESTED EXERCISES

1. Find some simple ads in your local newspaper. Redesign them while asking the questions in this section regarding headlines, typefaces, illustrations, etc.

2. Think about yourself as a product. Create an ad that will market you as a product (the ultimate ad). What are the things you want to stress? What typeface seems appropriate?

3. Study headlines in ads you find appealing. Start an ad collection for further study.

TO FIND YOURSELF, TRY THERAPY. TO FIND SOMEONE ELSE, TRY LORI OLSON.

Got a case involving a missing person? Call Lori Olson, 338-3394. She'll help you keep your sanity.

LORI OLSON
Private Investigator

Would you like a nice pair of speakers?

We could say a lot about all the birds we carry. But our wide selection speaks for itself.

The Pet Gallery
2403 S. Wrightsville Ave, Nags Head, 441-1852

Top left: Ad for Lori Olson, Private Investigator.
Design: Bozell, Minneapolis.
Creative Director: Bert Gardner, 1992.

Right top and bottom: Ads for The Pet Gallery.
Art Director: Sean Riley.
Copywriter: Raymond McKinney.
The Martin Agency, 1992.

We have a horrible gift selection.

We're sure to have the perfect gift for every oddball on your list.

The Pet Gallery
2403 S. Wrightsville Ave, Nags Head, 441-1852

OLD ADVERTISEMENTS

The early 20th century ads on these page were found on plaques hung on a wall in Carmel, California.

Photographer: Marcelle Lapow Toor, 1993.

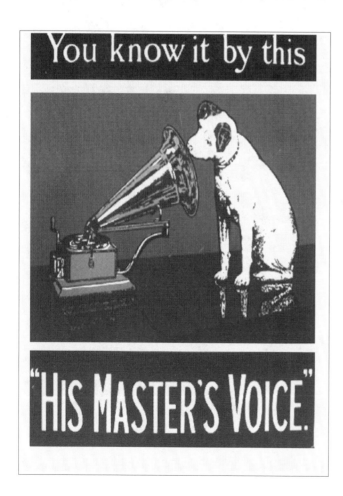

DESIGNING FOR PRINT:
BUSINESS MATERIALS

Every business has some basic materials that are used daily. These materials include the letterhead, the envelope, business card, invoices, and note or memo pads. Some other materials that might be produced by a business or organization are: newsletters, business reports, and annual reports.

THE BUSINESS MATERIALS
1. The letterhead

The letterhead should set up an appropriate image for an organization or business. It should be considered an advertisement for the organization.

In a business or organization, the letter has several functions: to commit thoughts to paper, to record ideas, or to make a permanent record of ideas or proposals. The design of the letterhead must take into consideration its main purpose, a forum for the message. The size of the typeface, and the typeface itself convey a message that should be related to the identity of the organization.

Items that appear on the letterhead:

1. The name of the organization or business
2. The logo or logotype
3. Mailing address
4. Telephone number
5. Facsimile or telex number
6. The names of the board of directors in large corporations might be listed on the letterhead.

If a great deal of information is to appear on the letterhead, the design must be carefully thought out, the typeface selected small enough, yet readable, with enough space left to write the letter.

Placing the logo or logotype

The logo or logotype should not overwhelm the page, but should be in a prominent place since it is the identifier for the organization. Logos can be centered, flush left, flush right, or vertically along the side of the page. The letterhead design may be symmetrical or asymmetrical depending on the organization's image.

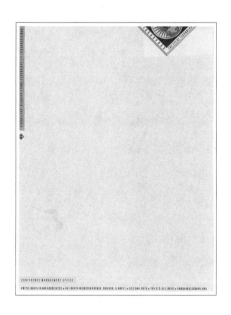

Letterhead for ACM (Association for Computing Machinery, Special Interest Group in Graphics) SIGGRAPH. Designer: Mo Viele, 1993

Placing the addresses, telephone, and fax numbers

Since a letter is a response vehicle, the address, telephone and fax numbers should be complete and easy to locate on the letterhead. The zip code needs to be included with the address, and the area code should be part of the telephone number. The placement of this information should be consistent with the placement of the logo. If the logo is centered, the address might be placed below it. If the logo is placed asymmetrically, the placement of the address can help maintain the balance of the page.

2.   The envelope

Consistency is important in business materials. The letterhead, the envelope, and the business card should all look they belong together. Business envelopes are approximately 9½" x 4".

The items that appear on the envelope:

1.   The logo
2.   The name of the business
3.   The business address, street or post office box number, city, state, and zip

The type with all the information on the envelope should not be more than 10 or 12 points, depending on the typeface used. Telephone and fax numbers should not be on the envelope.

3.   The business card

All the above materials, the letterhead, the envelope and the business card, are a family unit. They should have a family resemblance, a consistency. Together they set the image and identity for the business or organization. Business cards are usually 2" x 3½" and designed for either a horizontal or vertical format. Some organizations have business cards that are folded to 2" x 3½" to include more information on the inside.

The items that should appear on the business card:

The business card should make an impression on the person receiving it. It can be a good advertisement for your organization.

Business card for SIGGRAPH with designer's name.
Designer: Mo Viele, 1993

THE PROBLEM

To design a new identity for the Chessy System, a barbershop quartet based in Chesapeake, Ohio, named after the Chesapeake railroad whose nickname is the Chessy System. The members of the quartet wanted a design that was modern, upscale, more sophisticated and professional in appearance than the original.

THE SOLUTION

The new design uses an old line drawing of a train to give more sophistication to the materials and an "old world" look normally associated with barbershop quartets, while the typefaces, Bodoni Poster Compressed and Futura Condensed, give the design a contemporary look, a combination of the old and the new.

Top: The original business card.

Bottom right and left: The new letterhead, envelope, and business card. Designer: Marcelle Lapow Toor, 1993.

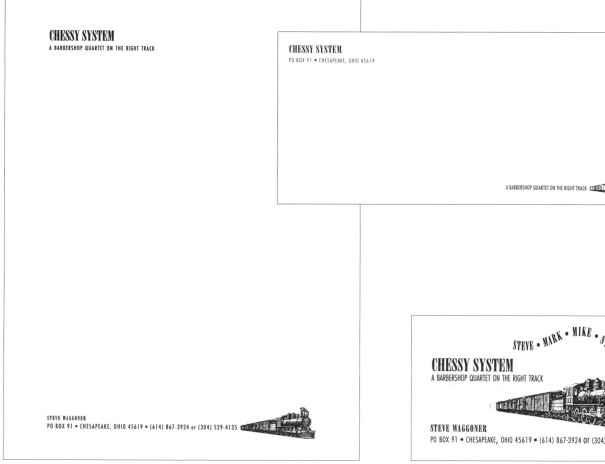

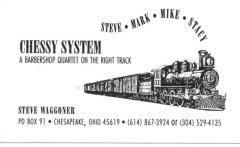

The business card is a miniature version of the letterhead and must contain a great deal of information in relation to its size that includes:

1. The logo
2. The name of the business
3. The address, street or post office box number, city, state and zip code
4. Telephone, telex, and/or fax numbers
5. The name and title of the individual, salesperson, vice president, to contact

TIPS TO REMEMBER: A CHECKLIST

☐ The materials, letterhead, envelope, and business card, look like they belong together.

☐ The materials contain all the necessary information and are distinctive.

☐ The materials adequately represent your organization's image.

☐ The letterhead allows sufficient room for a letter.

Business materials for Art/Science Studio/Lab, a lab and studio that offers custom photographic services. Designer: Marcelle Lapow Toor, 1993.

SUGGESTED EXERCISES

1. Design business materials including: a logo, letterhead, envelope, and business card for a desktop publishing business.
2. Look closely at the business materials you receive in the mail at home and at work. What image do you get of an individual organization from these materials? Which ones give the wrong impression based on what you know about the organization?

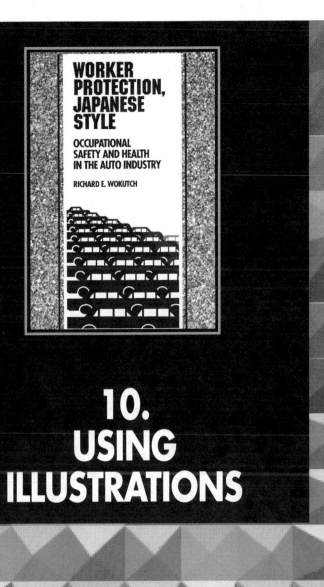

10.
USING
ILLUSTRATIONS

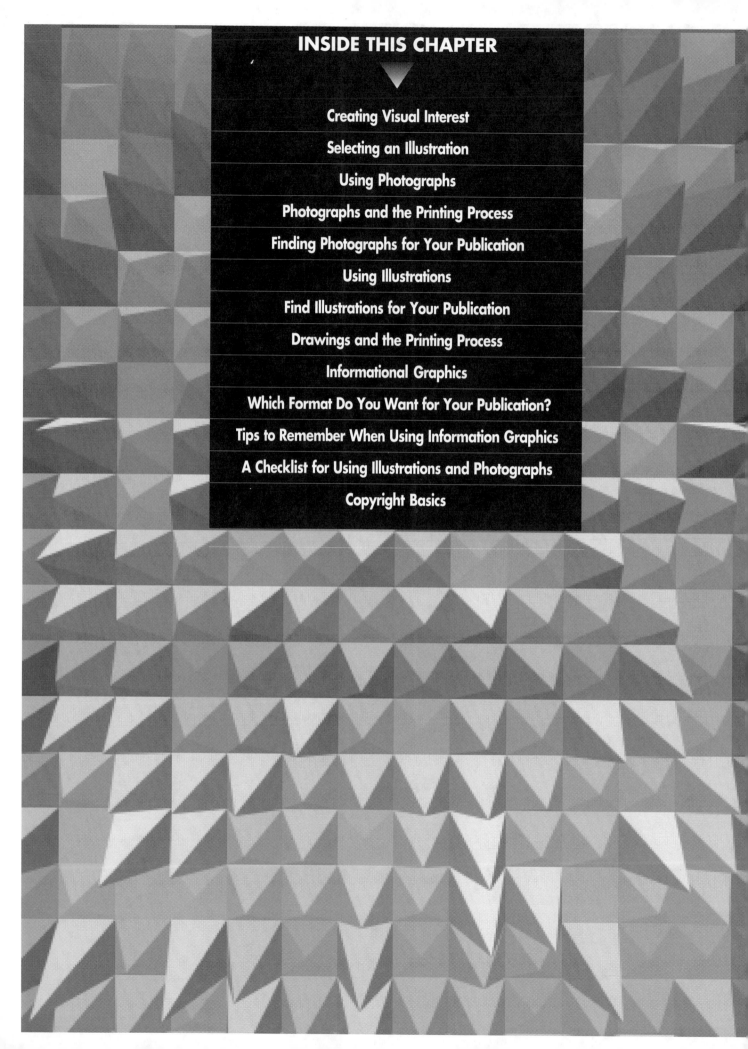

10

USING ILLUSTRATIONS

CREATING VISUAL INTEREST

Photograph taken on the beach in Coney Island. Photographer: Harry Lapow, © 1978.

We are all familiar with the old Chinese proverb, "one picture is worth more than ten thousand words." In previous chapters we talked about the use of graphic devices, large initial capital letters, bullets, dingbats, rules, and logos to add some visual interest to a page. Those devices are helpful in dressing up a page, but do not serve to grab the attention of the viewer. Newspapers and television give us massive doses of information. Our world is a more visual place than it was in the past, and the reader today responds more to pictures than to words. Photographs and other illustrations are extremely important in enhancing and communicating the message of the printed page.

An illustration—photograph, drawing, map, chart, or graph—is an integral element in any printed piece, and it is one of the main pieces that must fit with the overall layout. Visual images will attract attention, add a sense of reality to a publication, establish a mood, involve our emotions—and entertain in the process. Some events can be described better with a picture than with words. A photograph showing the devastation from a forest fire, or survivors of a hurricane in front of their storm-ravaged houses, will make a stronger statement and involve our emotions more than words alone. Printed materials that lack an illustration must have a powerful verbal message in order to make an impression on today's audience. The choice of a graphic image is directly related to the audience, the printed piece, and the kind of message to be communicated. The quality of the image has the same importance as its appropriateness.

SELECTING AN ILLUSTRATION

What kind of illustration should you use? Photographs, drawings, charts, or graphs?

Before making a decision about the kind of illustration you want to use in your printed piece, there are some questions you need to ask:

1. What kind of budget do you have?

2. Who is your audience?

3. What kind of graphic will be most appropriate and appeal to this audience?

   If your audience is children who watch a great deal of TV, a cartoon might be the best way to get their attention. But if the audience is the young professional concerned with appearance, a photograph might be more appropriate.

4. What kind of art will appeal to this audience and get a response? Do some marketing research to determine the interests of your audience.

5. What kind of graphic image will reproduce well, given the printing process and the paper you will be using?

   If you are producing the entire publication on the computer for reproduction on a copying machine and intend to use scanned photographs, you need to know that the photographs will not appear as sharp as if the printer makes a halftone. If your publication is not printed on glossy or smooth paper, the photographs will not reproduce as well as you might like.

6. What is the content of the message?

   If you are designing a magazine spread for a short story, an illustration might have a better "feel" than a photograph, since the story does not need realism. If you are designing a brochure for a human service organization, photographs of people would be more effective. If you have data to explain the information in your newsletter article, a chart or graph would be a better choice. Information is easier to grasp when enhanced visually.

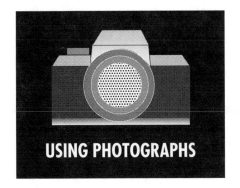

USING PHOTOGRAPHS

THE PHOTOGRAPH

In an article on photography from a journal dated 1861, Jaben Hughes, an English critic wrote, "Hitherto photography has been principally content with representing Truth." He goes on to encourage photographers to produce pictures "whose aim is not merely to amuse, but to instruct, purify, and ennoble."

Research has proven that photographs are the first, second, and third items that a reader looks at in the newspaper. The average person believes that photography represents the truth. Due to their ability to engage the viewer, photographs in a publication can be an extremely powerful communication tool; an effective way to document and inform the reader of a particular event. Newspapers use photographs because they are reporting real events and a successful two-page photographic spread should tell an entire story without the need for any words, or very few.

A good photograph should:

- Be unambiguous
- Tell a story
- Appeal to the intended audience
- Attract attention
- Be a strong sharp image
- Engage the interest of the viewer
- Be cropped well
- Be placed on the page using principles of design and visual perception
- Be sharp and crisp for reproduction

Hint: Cropping (cutting) the extraneous parts of a photograph can change the meaning and the impact that it makes on the viewer.

The quality of the photograph is important if you want your design to look professional. In order to reproduce well, a photograph should be sharp with good contrast. A photograph printed on glossy paper stock will reproduce best. The size, placement, composition, and cropping of the photograph contribute to the effectiveness of its impact.

Some thoughts on using photographs for your publication:
1. Size

A tiny photograph obviously will not have the impact of a larger one. A photograph contains information. The area with the information should be as large as you can possibly afford in terms of space and the other elements that exist on the page.

2. Cropping

There are two schools of photographers, those who believe in cropping (cutting off portions of a photograph), and those who are purists and try to frame the picture before they shoot. When using a photograph for a design layout, cropping is essential. You want a strong image in order to grab the attention of your viewer. In order to make a powerful statement, photographs need to be edited just like words. Cropping a photograph can turn a weak image into a stronger, more effective one. If there are outer portions in the photograph that do not relate to the story being illustrated, they should be eliminated.

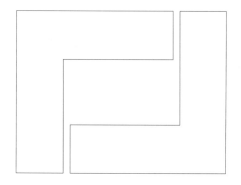

L's, or brackets used for cropping photographs.

The best way to determine how a photograph should be cropped is to make a pair of L's (see illustration on the left) out of mat or illustration board, and use the two pieces to create a frame around the area of the picture that has the greatest amount of appeal. Move the L's around the photograph until you find an interesting area within the frame, and put marks, or masking tape, around the extraneous parts to indicate the desired area to the printer. Eliminate all the unnecessary information that is not vital to the story being told by the photograph.

If you are using a scanner to screen photographs, you will need to use an image-editing program to make adjustments for printing. Scan only the area of the photograph you need. If a photograph has already been scanned, cropping can be done in an image-editing program, or a page layout program.

3. Direction of the action

The action of the photograph should lead the reader into the story, or article, not off the page. You can direct the reader's eye to the information on the page by having the photograph facing in the direction you want the reader's eye to go.

4. Contrast in size

When using several photographs on a page in a newsletter, for example, it is a good idea to stress the differences in the photographs by changing the size and shape of each one, using vertical and horizontal formats.

5. Using boxes to frame the photographs

Some photographs are extremely light on the sides and the edges are not clearly defined. Putting a box around the photograph will frame the photograph and define the edges. The weight of the line of the box should be consistent with the rest of the publication, and should not overwhelm the photograph.

A proportion wheel used for sizing photographs.

6. Sizing the photographs to fit the space

Most photographs do not come in a size that will fit neatly onto the printed page. They must be reduced or enlarged in proportion to fit into the allotted space. Designers use a proportion wheel or scale to determine the percentage of the reduction or enlargement for the printer to make. These wheels are found in art supply stores. Let's say that the original photograph is 8" x 10", and you have allotted a 2" x 3" space for the photograph on the front page of your newsletter. To use the proportion wheel look at the middle wheel, which represents the original size and has the percentage information. Line up the 8" indicator with the 2" indicator and you will discover that the photograph needs to be reduced by 25%. The wheel is simple to use and has directions on the back.

PHOTOGRAPHS AND THE PRINTING PROCESS

Have you ever tried to copy a photograph on a black and white copy machine? Unless the copying machine has the capability of screening the image, you get a black and white image without the grey tones. Photographs are made up of continuous tones of black, white, and the shades of grey in between. When reproducing a photograph for a publication, the image is photographed by a printer with a screen of fine lines laid on top to pick up the continuous tones of grey. This is called a *processed halftone* and it contains all the tones between black and white in a dot pattern.

Desktop or electronic publishing has had a profound impact on the use of the photographic image. Using a scanner, the designer can create halftones, reducing the cost of the printed piece. The task of reducing or enlarging the photograph, another task traditionally performed by the printer, can be done in the scanning program as well, and the photograph can be manipulated in various ways for different effects.

FINDING PHOTOGRAPHS FOR YOUR PUBLICATION

There are several possibilities for obtaining photographs to use in your printed piece. Below are some suggestions.

1. Hire a professional photographer

If your budget permits, hire a professional photographer. Shop around to find one with whom you can work comfortably. Make sure to specify the kinds of photographs you want. Go with the photographer on the shoot to make sure you get the images you have in mind.

2. Buy from stock photo agencies

Stock agencies have files of photographs with a variety of images in different categories: children, people at work, landscapes, etc. These agencies will give you prints of the photographs you select and will charge a fee for one-time use. There are a number of photo stock agencies which now have a good sampling of photographic images on a CD-ROM disk, like clip art. You can purchase the disks to use with your computer.

There are electronic imaging services that can digitize your photographs and put them on a CD-ROM disk.

3. Use clip art books

If you don't need a photograph of a specific person or event, you can purchase clip art books with generic photographs in different categories. These are photographs meant to be used as clip art. They are not under copyright, and they may be used by cutting and pasting them into your publication manually, or by scanning them onto a page of your publication.

Cover and inside spread of brochure for H & E Machinery Inc., a manufacturer of blades for rotating equipment. The strong photographs emphasize the shapes of the blades enhancing the manufacturer's products and the elegant design.
Designer: Phil Wilson.
Photographers: Sheryl D. Sinkow and Tony DeCamillo, 1993.

CHECKLIST FOR USING PHOTOGRAPHS:

☐ The photograph is a strong, sharp, and clear image.

☐ The photograph illustrates the text and tells a story.

☐ It is relevant to the printed piece and to the audience.

☐ The photograph will grab and keep the interest of the audience.

☐ The photograph has been cropped well.

☐ **You have permission to use this photograph.**

Top left: The roles of the child and the mother in this photograph seem to be reversed. The mother is blowing bubbles while the child looks very serious and concerned.
Photographer: Sheryl D. Sinkow, 1990.

Top right: Bored German family waiting for people to buy their used clothing, toys, jewelry, etc. at a flea market in Kaiserslautern, Germany.
Photographer: Marcelle Lapow Toor, 1989.

Bottom right: This photograph uses a touch of humor. This rather unfashionable-looking mannikin made out of stockings was found sitting in a trendy Greenwich Village, New York City boutique.
Photographer: Harry Lapow, 1978.

Top left: Decorative windows on a house in
Amsterdam, Holland.
Photographer: Marcelle Lapow Toor, 1987.

Top right: A view of the New York City skyline with
interesting angles.
Photographer: Harry Lapow, 1960.

Bottom right: Photograph of San Francisco's famous
Golden Gate Bridge from an interesting angle.
Photographer: Sheryl D. Sinkow, 1983.

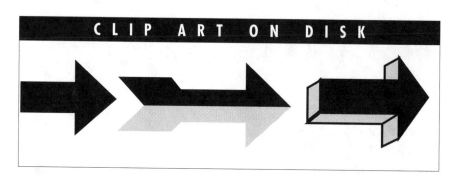

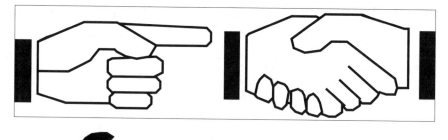

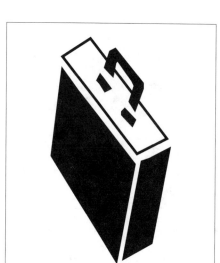

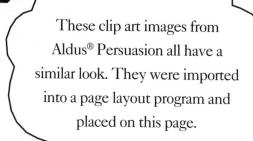

These clip art images from Aldus® Persuasion all have a similar look. They were imported into a page layout program and placed on this page.

USING ILLUSTRATIONS

THE ILLUSTRATION

An illustration can be a drawing, collage, painting, or any non-photographic image created to communicate visually. Many designers do not create their own illustrations; they hire people to do drawings for their printed pieces. An illustration can show details that cannot be shown in a photograph. An illustration can look realistic, but not real like a photograph, or purely fantastical, surreal, or cartoon-like. An illustration looks like it was created by a human hand. This may or may not be the look you want for your printed piece.

Your drawing ability may be limited. If you cannot draw, or cannot draw well and you want to use drawings to illustrate your text, several options are available depending upon your budget.

FINDING ILLUSTRATIONS FOR YOUR PUBLICATION

Where do you find illustrations that are appropriate to your printed piece without depleting your entire publication budget? There are several options.

1. Hire a professional illustrator

Hire a professional illustrator, if you can afford one. Each illustrator has an individual style—and price. You will need to find an illustrator with a style that fits with the piece you are designing, taking into consideration the audience and the message. Someone whose best style is cartooning is not the right person to do drawings for a serious corporate publication. You must let the illustrator know exactly what you want. If there is a certain style you've seen that you like, show it to your illustrator. Work closely with this artist to make sure you get the best results for the piece you are designing.

2. Use clip art books

Although it is always preferable to hire an illustrator to create drawings specific to a publication, budgets don't always allow for such luxury. The solution to using illustrations on a low budget job is clip art, an old method used by graphic designers limited by deadlines. Clip art books are available from a number of different publishers. These books include drawings for every occasion and publication, in all kinds of styles. There are monthly clip art subscription services that have elaborate drawings in a variety of styles, created by illustrators who do drawings specifically for that purpose. You will often see clip art from these publications in advertisements for small businesses in your local newspapers.

3. Use clip art on disks

Clip art is also available on disk from a number of software publishing companies (see Software Bibliography). Before purchasing clip art from these companies, make sure you see what the final printed product will look like. You want drawings that are not bit-mapped and are professional in appearance. The act of purchasing a disk with clip art gives you the right to use the art for your publication needs.

4. Find source Books

The Encyclopedia of Source Illustrations, Volumes One & Two
The title page describes these volumes as "a portable picture library of steel engravings originally reproduced in the *Iconographic Encyclopaedia of 1851.*" The original encyclopedia was created as a treasure trove for designers, and so is this reproduction. The illustrations are beautifully rendered drawings, and they are presented according to subject: mathematics and astronomy, botany, physics and meteorology, art, animals, etc. All of the illustrations are in the public domain, which means they may be used without permission.

There are many other books that contain source illustrations that are copyright-free. Ask the librarian at your local library.

5. Old books and magazines

Libraries, bookstores, and antique shops are good sources for old books that are now out of copyright and in the public domain. Depending on the look you are trying to achieve, old woodcuts can be effective illustrations for certain publications .

Hint: If you see an illustration that you like, contact the publisher or artist to get permission for its use.

Simple, stylized figures like the people and the cars in the publications below, can be done in a drawing program, and repeated to create a pattern.

6. Computer graphics

Simple or very complex drawings can be created on the computer in drawing programs (see software Bibliography). You can import clip art on disk into a drawing program, autotrace it, and alter the line weight, shape, and fills to eliminate the "canned" clip art look, and create a new drawing that will satisfy your needs.

Hint: When using clip art it is important to maintain a unified style. If the images have all been rendered using different techniques, your page layout will look busy, awkward, uninviting, and unprofessional. If you have doubts about the graphic image you have chosen, leave it out!

7. Type

If you cannot find an appropriate graphic image, an enlarged letter, number or word can be used to create visual excitement on your page. Special software programs give you the ability to manipulate type in order to make a graphic statement. You can also manipulate type, single letters, or words in drawing programs and image-editing programs in order to create interesting effects.

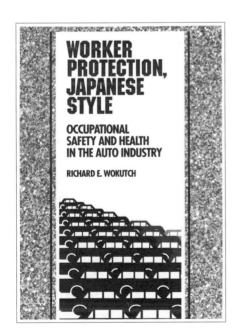

Above: *Worker Protection Japanese Style* is a book about safety in the Japanese auto industry. ILR Press, Cornell University.
Illustrator & designer: Marcelle Lapow Toor. 1992.

DRAWINGS AND THE PRINTING PROCESS

A drawing is referred to as line art, as opposed to a photograph which is a continuous tone. Most drawings, clip art included, that are rendered with pen and ink or pencil use solid tones of black and white, so your printer will not have to make a halftone to reproduce your drawing. Line drawings can be placed directly on the page, by manually cutting and pasting, or scanning them into the computer as line art, not grey scale, or halftone. They can be included in your mechanincal as camera-ready art. An illustration created in a drawing software program can be imported into your page layout program, placed on the page in the intended space, and enlarged or reduced to fit.

A CHECKLIST FOR USING ILLUSTRATIONS

☐ The drawing has the right feel for the printed piece.
☐ The drawing has the right look for the audience.

- ☐ It reproduces well.
- ☐ The style of the clip art is appropriate to the piece.
- ☐ The clip art has a consistent style throughout the piece.
- ☐ The drawing contains all the necessary information.
- ☐ All the illustrations in the publication go well together.

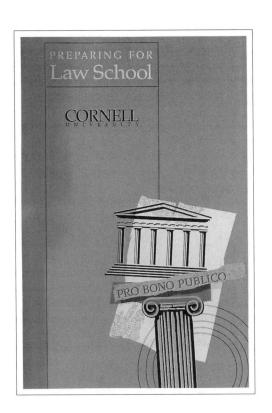

Top and bottom: Cover and inside spread for brochure for Cornell Law School with computer illustrations. Illustrator and designer: Phil Wilson, 1992.

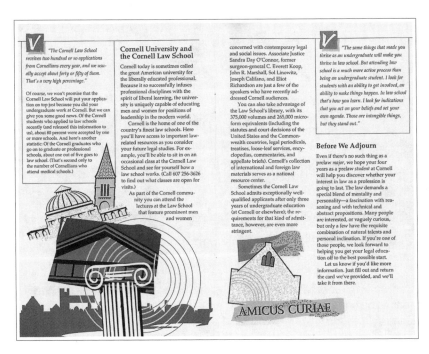

"The Cornell Law School receives two hundred or so applications from Cornellians every year, and we usually accept about forty or fifty of them. That's a very high percentage."

Of course, we won't promise that the Cornell Law School will put your application on top just because you did your undergraduate work at Cornell. But we can give you some good news. Of the Cornell students who applied to law schools recently (and released this information to us), about 80 percent were accepted by one or more schools. And here's another statistic: Of the Cornell graduates who go on to graduate or professional schools, about one out of five goes to law school. (That's second only to the number of Cornellians who attend medical schools.)

Cornell University and the Cornell Law School

Cornell today is sometimes called the great American university for the liberally educated professional. Because it so successfully infuses professional disciplines with the spirit of liberal learning, the university is uniquely capable of educating men and women for positions of leadership in the modern world.

Cornell is the home of one of the country's finest law schools. Here you'll have access to important law-related resources as you consider your future legal studies. For example, you'll be able to sit in on an occasional class at the Cornell Law School and see for yourself how a law school works. (Call 607 256-3626 to find out what classes are open for visits.)

As part of the Cornell community you can attend the lectures at the Law School that feature prominent men and women

concerned with contemporary legal and social issues. Associate Justice Sandra Day O'Connor, former surgeon-general C. Everett Koop, John R. Marshall, Sol Linowitz, Joseph Califano, and Eliot Richardson are just a few of the speakers who have recently addressed Cornell audiences.

You can also take advantage of the Law School's library, with its 375,000 volumes and 265,000 microform equivalents (including the statutes and court decisions of the United States and the Commonwealth countries, legal periodicals, treatises, loose-leaf services, encyclopedias, commentaries, and appellate briefs). Cornell's collection of international and foreign law materials serves as a national resource center.

Sometimes the Cornell Law School admits exceptionally well-qualified applicants after only three years of undergraduate education (at Cornell or elsewhere); the requirements for that kind of admittance, however, are even more stringent.

"The same things that made you thrive as an undergraduate will make you thrive in law school. But attending law school is a much more active process than being an undergraduate student. I look for students with an ability to get involved, an ability to make things happen. In law school that's how you learn. I look for indications that you act on your beliefs and set your own agenda. Those are intangible things, but they stand out."

Before We Adjourn

Even if there's no such thing as a prelaw *major*, we hope your four years as a prelaw *student* at Cornell will help you discover whether your interest in law as a profession is going to last. The law demands a special blend of mentality and personality—a fascination with reasoning and with technical and abstract propositions. Many people are interested, or vaguely curious, but only a few have the requisite combination of natural talents and personal inclination. If you're one of those people, we look forward to helping you get your legal education off to the best possible start.

Let us know if you'd like more information. Just fill out and return the card we've provided, and we'll take it from there.

INFORMATIONAL GRAPHICS

INFORMATIONAL GRAPHICS AS VISUAL INTEREST

Informational graphics—charts, graphs, tables, maps, and diagrams—are another way of adding visual interest to a page while providing statistical data as well. Informational graphics have become a significant art form and a daily presence in our information-ridden society. Charts, graphs, diagrams, and other visual displays of data should be used to present facts that cannot be shown with photographs or other forms of illustrations.

Informational graphics have a long history. They did not begin with *USA Today*. Charts were used in the 11th century as a way to show the orbits of planets, while maps were used early in our history to show location and direction. Informational graphics today have become a way to communicate statistical information, or data, in an interesting visual way.

Edward Tufte, a professor at Yale University and an author of several books on the presentation of statistical information, relates charts to art. In the December 1991 issue of *Yale* magazine, Tufte states, "Graphical excellence is that which gives the viewer the greatest number of ideas in the shortest time with the least ink in the smallest space…. Data graphics should draw the viewer's attention to the sense and substance of the data, not to something else."

September 15, 1982 marks an event that significantly changed both the use of informational graphics, and the newspaper industry. The newspaper, *USA Today,* made its first appearance on newsstands. This newspaper devotes a great deal of space and attention to charts and graphs to provide its readers with a way of grasping information visually. *USA Today* has left its impression and created an impact on the communication of information in publications. We talk about the "*USA Today* look" when we refer to the use of illustrative charts and graphs as a means of presenting information.

The Japanese love statistics, but most people in the United States consider them boring. If a publication needs to show some kind of statistical information, it is the designer's job to present the information in a way that is both aesthetically pleasing and illuminating. Charts and graphs provide visual interest on a page, and they should be used to illustrate data that might otherwise be uninteresting.

Several software programs will convert your statistical information

"On inspecting any one of these charts attentively, a sufficiently distinct impression will be made, to remain unimpaired for a considerable time, and the idea which does remain will be simple and complete."

—William Playfair,
The Commercial and Political Atlas, 1786.
Playfair was a political economist and one of the fathers of informational graphics. This quote refers to a new method of presenting information, the bar chart.

BAR OR COLUMN CHART

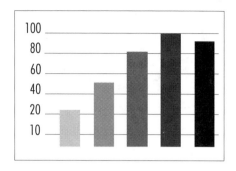

PIE CHART

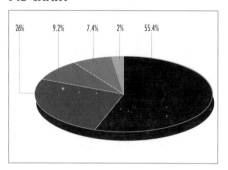

MAPS ON DISK

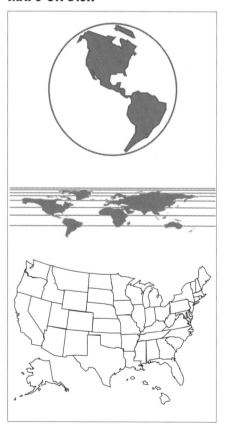

Different styles of map clip art.

into graphs and charts. The numerical information is entered, and the program sorts it out and turns it into a bar chart or other chart or graph of your choice. The graphs and charts produced by these programs have a "canned" look, and should be reworked in a drawing program for a more professional look.

WHICH FORMAT DO YOU WANT TO USE FOR YOUR PUBLICATION?

1. Bar and column charts

This format is a good one to use to show comparisons in a way that is easy to identify. The data is displayed in bar and column charts in a horizontal or vertical format.

2. Pie charts

The pie chart is created in the form of a circle or oval and cut like the wedges of a pie to show the data or information as parts of the whole.

3. Diagrams

The diagram is a method of indicating visually how a system works. The diagram translates complicated events or concepts into a simplified drawing.

4. Illustrative graphs

The illustrative graph shows information by using graphic images or illustrations related to the data rather than to bars or lines. *USA Today* uses illustrative graphs daily to present information and show comparisons to an audience that is visually-oriented.

5. Maps

Maps are one of the oldest means of graphic communication, and they are used as a means of indicating locations. Maps serve to provide information to the reader geographically, topographically, and geologically.

6. Tables

Tables are a way of providing data containing information of importance to the viewer in the form of lists. Tables are easier to design than charts or graphs and should be thought of graphically. Newspapers use tables to display daily items like the weather, the stock market report, baseball and football scores, and other items of interest to their readers. Since the function of a table is to display data, the information should be organized well in clearly-defined columns in a typeface that is readable. The tables should have labels or headlines to identify the information being displayed.

7. Bulleted lists

A bulleted list is used to show related items that do not have a specific order.

8. Numbered lists

Numbered list are used to indicate related items that have a definite order.

TIPS TO REMEMBER WHEN USING INFORMATIONAL GRAPHICS

☐ Check your facts before putting them into a chart or graph.

☐ Make sure you have all the necessary information.

☐ Do not let the graphic display overwhelm the information.

☐ Make sure you have a good grasp of the information so that you can present it in a clear, precise way.

☐ Label all your informational graphics clearly.

☐ Communicate ideas visually with clarity.

A CHECKLIST FOR USING ILLUSTRATIONS AND PHOTOGRAPHS

☐ The illustrations have captions that identify them clearly.

☐ The captions identify the creators of the work.

☐ The illustrations are appropriate to the audience, the message, and the printed piece.

☐ The illustration is an attention getter.

☐ The illustration enhances the page.

☐ Illustrations vary in size, shape, and color.

☐ All the illustrations have the same feel, and they look like they belong together.

☐ The illustrations tell a story.

☐ The art used illustrates the printed piece; it is not merely decoration.

☐ You have permission to use art that is copyrighted.

SUGGESTED EXERCISES

1. Start a file of illustrations from different publications.
2. Find illustrations that you think do not pertain to the story they are illustrating. What is wrong with them?
3. Find informational graphs and charts that at first glance communicate well visually Evaluate their effectiveness.
4. Find some articles that do not have any illustrations. What illustrations would you use to enhance these pages visually?
5. Using your L's, experiment with cropping photographs. See how many ways you can crop them to change the image, its message, and its impact.

COPYRIGHT BASICS

What is a copyright?

The word "copyright" pertains to ownership. An idea itself cannot be copyrighted, but the expression of an idea in a tangible medium of expression is subject to copyright. A copyright is normally held by the creator of the work, and is a form of protection provided by the laws of the United States (Title 17, U.S. Code) to the authors of "original works of authorship" including literary, dramatic, musical, artistic, and certain other intellectual works. This protection is available to both published and unpublished works. Section 106 of the Copyright Act generally gives the owner of copyright the exclusive right to do and to authorize others to do the following:

▶ To reproduce the copyrighted work in copies

▶ To prepare derivative works based upon the copyrighted work

▶ To distribute copies of the copyrighted work to the public by sale or other transfer of ownership, or by rental or lease

▶ To display the copyrighted work publicly, in the case of pictorial, graphic, or sculptural works, including the individual images of a motion picture or other audiovisual work

Who can claim copyright?

Copyright protection exists from the time the work is created in fixed form. It is an incident of the process of authorship. The copyright in the work of an author immediately becomes the property of the author or person who created it. Only the author or those deriving their rights through the author can rightfully claim copyright. Mere ownership of a book, manuscript, painting, or any other copy does not give the possessor the copyright.

What works are protected?

Copyright protects "original works of authorship" that are fixed in a tangible form of expression. The fixation need not be directly perceptible, so long as it may be communicated with the aid of a machine or device.

Copyrightable works include the following categories:

1. Literary works

2. Musical works, including any accompanying words

3. Dramatic works, including any accompanying music

4. Pantomimes and choreographic works

5. Pictorial, graphic, and sculptural works

6. Motion pictures and other audiovisual works

7. Sound recording

8. Architectural works

These categories should be viewed quite broadly. Computer programs and most "compilations" are registrable as "literary works"; maps and architectural plans are registrable as "pictorial, graphic, and sculptural works."

When in doubt about any material you wish to use, check your source, or contact the copyright office (address below).

© Materials in the public domain

Materials in the public domain include photographs and art where the copyright has expired and no longer applies, and works that have never been copyrighted. All materials produced by U. S. Government agencies are also in the public domain. Any materials in the public domain can be used without having to pay a fee or ask permission.

© The fair use clause

There are some copyrighted materials that can be used without gaining permission if they are used for educational, charitable, or religious purposes. This is called "fair use," and the material may be used but the source must be identified.

© Obtaining permission to use copyrighted material

If you want to use work that is under copyright, you must get permission from the person who holds the copyright. You may have to pay a fee for a one-time use. If you are unsure of the status of the work you want to produce, contact the original source.

The above information was excerpted from Copyright Basics produced by the Copyright Office, Library of Congress, Washington, D.C. 20559. Contact the office if you need more information.

11.
WORKING
WITH COLOR

INSIDE THIS CHAPTER

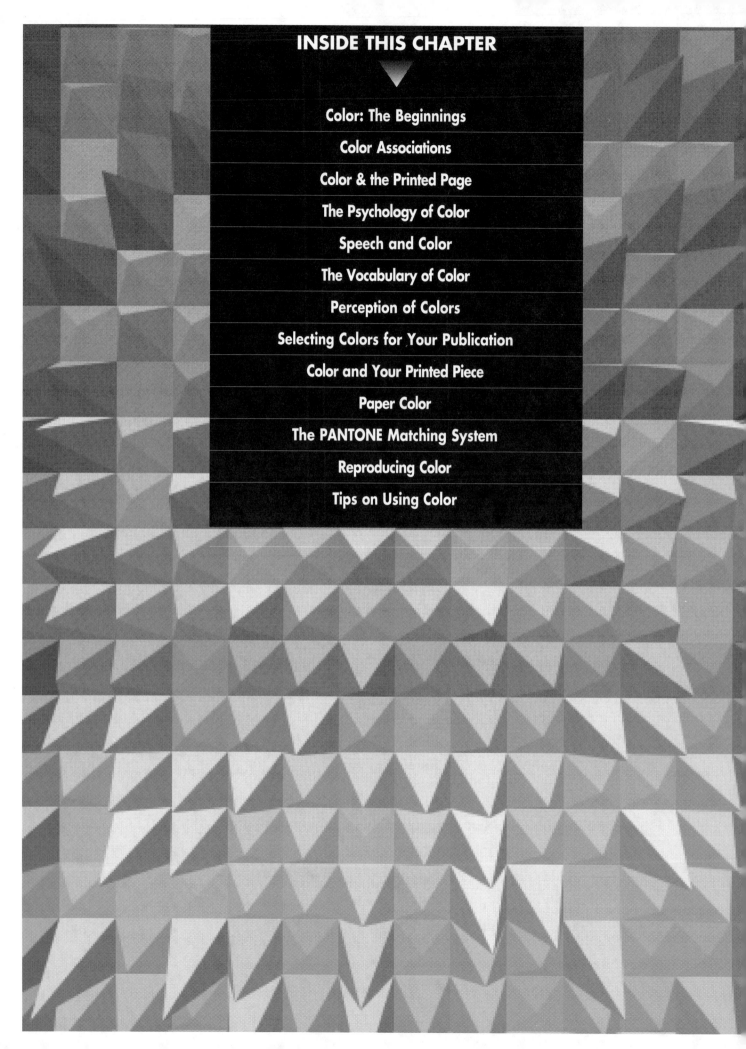

WORKING WITH COLOR

COLOR: THE BEGINNINGS

lthough color has always surrounded us in our natural environment, the ability to reproduce it freely for use in clothing and other decorations did not occur until the nineteenth century. The oldest dyes and paints were created out of organic materials: shells of walnuts, stones like lapis lazuli (blue), and soils for what we refer to as the earth tones (brown, umber, sienna, yellows, and dull reds). White came from chalk, gypsum and lime. The number of colors produced were limited and expensive to produce, and their use was limited to fabrics and other decorative materials that only the very wealthy could afford. Modern chemistry has provided us with ways to produce endless combinations of colors in every hue and intensity. Computer users with color monitors and the right hardware have between 256 and 16 million colors available at their desktops.

With all the color options today, it is necessary to have some understanding of the psychology of color and its value as a marketing tool. Trial and error research has proven that products packaged in certain colors will not sell. If you look at the shelves in a supermarket, you will notice that similar products from different manufacturers use the same colors, or colors that are close. For example, sugar is normally found in a package with the color blue on it. Research has proven that the consumer will not buy sugar that comes in a green package. Like odors, colors evoke emotional responses in us. The color blue makes us think of sweetness, while green gives the feeling of astringency that we associate with mint and the freshness of limes. Marketing research has shown that when certain colors are used in packaging, the product will not sell. For instance, when the color brown is used in cosmetic packaging the product stays on the shelves.

Color specialists are in great demand these days. They range from consultants who "read" your colors to help you choose the colors most flattering for you to wear that work well with your complexion, and your personality, to color experts, often graphic designers, consulted in the selecting of colors for the decor of interiors like doctor's offices, supermarkets, and airline interiors.

For example:

Many people experience varying degrees of panic when flying, and airlines are aware of this fact. This awareness has influenced the selection of colors for the interiors of airplanes, usually soft pastels, to create a sense of well being, to foster a calming effect on the passengers. Imagine how you'd feel if you were in the cabin of an airplane, surrounded by bright red. If you were apprehensive about the flight to begin with, the color red would enhance your fears, not allay them.

Have you ever noticed the colors used in supermarket walls and signs? They are often painted in browns and oranges, earth tones, the colors of domesticity.

The design of the interiors of buildings used to be the domain of the architect. Many architectural firms now hire graphic designers, not only to design the signage for a building, both inside and outside, but also to select colors to create a specific mood for the interior space.

COLOR ASSOCIATIONS

Peoples' color preferences are very subjective. Our surroundings, our experiences, and even our memories influence the associations we have with colors and affect our predispositions and the choices we make.

COLOR AND THE PRINTED PAGE

When competition for products is severe, the designer or visual communicator must take advantage of every possible method to attract the consumer.

A few years ago, a New York City advertising agency was hired to design a new coffee package. They did some marketing research in order to determine the color to use for the package. The same coffee was placed into three different bags, a yellow bag, a green bag, and a red bag. Consumers were asked to do a taste test and give their impressions of each coffee. The coffee that came out of the green bag was said to be acidic and bitter. The coffee packaged in yellow was described as weak and watery. Rich, robust, and flavorful, were the words used to describe the coffee packaged in the red bag, which was exactly the same as the other two.

> **Hint: While color plays a major role in the success of a particular product or printed page, a design with a weak concept that relies heavily on color will not be successful.**

In the previous chapter, we discussed the use of graphic devices and illustrations to make a visual impact. Properly used, color can be a powerful communication device. Steve Hannaford, a computer writer with a specialty in graphic design, talks about the use of color in an article in *ITC Desktop: No. 2.* "Color sets a mood and tone, strengthening the psychological impact. For example, pastel shades soften a message, while vibrant colors can underscore important points. In addition, color brings a sense of style to a piece… And when used properly, color acts as a subtle roadmap that directs the eye through the terrain of text." In the same article, Hannaford talks about the effect of color in ads, how ads with one spot of color are noticed 200% more often than pieces done in only one color, while ads that use full color show a 500% increase in interest.

Our world is not black and white. Color is a significant presence in our daily existence and adds vitality to our lives. We select certain colors to wear according to our moods, other colors to make a specific impression.

In order to get a reaction or response to your printed piece, the colors you select should appeal to the audience you have identified. Color preference is complex because it relates not only to triggered emotional responses, lifestyle, gender, and age, but to style and fashion. Just as color trends in fashions change, so do the colors used in printed materials. Often the two correspond. The fashionable colors for the '90's seem to be the same for clothing as well as printed materials, including magentas, purples, teals, turquoise, bright pinks, and some lighter, pastel versions of these colors.

THE PSYCHOLOGY OF COLOR
Color and emotion

The colors red, yellow and all the blends of these are considered "warm" colors because of our associations with them: fire and sun. Blues and greens are colors generally associated with the natural world: the sky, sea, and the wilderness. They are referred to as "cool" colors.

Colors can have a stimulating, or calming effect on our nervous systems. Below is a list of colors and the emotions associated with them. This information can be used as guide to aid in the selection of colors for a printed piece for a particular audience.

■ **Red**

The color red has a stimulating effect on our nervous system. Red stands for aggression, passion, and conquest. It is the color of success and impulse. Red excites the bull in a bullfight, and has a similar effect on us. A dramatic color, red is a favorite color of sports car owners, the color of power. Perhaps you noticed that all three presidential candidates in the TV debates before the last election were wearing their red "power" ties.

■ **Orange**

The color orange is related to red, a combination of red and yellow. We think of orange as a happy, festive color—bright, but not as dramatic and daring as red.

■ **Blue**

Dark blue, a cool color, has a relaxing and calming effect. It represents tradition. If you are designing a printed piece for an established corporation, like a bank or an investment broker where tradition and stability are to be stressed, dark blue is the color that will represent that feeling. Blue is calm, orderly, free from upsets. It is reminiscent of the constancy of the sky and the sea. The dark blue of night is associated with the end of the day, the winding down of the body for rest and quiet. Light blue, a cool color, evokes a feeling of cleanliness and has a soothing effect.

■ Purple

Purple, the combination of red and blue, is also a color for the daring in spirit, the color of the artist. Purple pigments traditionally were expensive, originally affordable only by the very wealthy. It became a color for royalty, a color we think of as regal.

■ Violet

The color violet is a mixture of red, blue, and white, a unification of dramatic red and calming blue. Violet is a color that can create a sense of intimacy in interior spaces. It is the opposite of bright yellow.

■ Yellow

Bright yellow heralds the beginning of the day, the commencement of activity. Yellow, like red, raises blood pressure. When it is used in combination with black in road signs, it indicates danger. It is a warm color, the color of sunlight, optimism, and health. The emperor in Imperial China was the only person allowed to wear yellow because he was the symbol of enlightenment and supreme wisdom. Yellow is used frequently in food packaging because it conveys a feeling of health and well-being.

■ Green

Green is a color we associate with nature, regeneration, and self-preservation. It is a cool color and reminds us of trees and gives a soothing feeling, an association with cleanliness. The color green is used in soft drinks, products with menthol, cigarettes, cleansers for the home, and products that remind us of the environment.

■ White

Color has a different association for different cultures, and the color white is a good example of this. In the West, white is a symbol for purity, a color worn by brides to suggest innocence. In China white is worn to funerals because it is the color associated with death and mourning.

■ Black

The color black has a number of different associations. In the West it is the color of mourning, also the color of danger. It can have a sinister connotation, or, when used in lingerie, a sexy one. It can signify elegance when worn for a formal evening out, for "a black tie affair."

SPEECH AND COLOR

We refer to color often in our speech as a way of illustrating a point:

- "Painting the town red," is an expression we use when we refer to having a wild night out.
- "Seeing red," is an expression used when referring to anger.
- The expression, "seeing the world through rose-colored glasses," is used when we refer to looking at the world through the eyes of an optimist, in search of a blissful existence.
- The expression "blue blood" is used to describe someone who appears to be aristocratic.
- "A bluestocking" is a person who appears very cultivated and intellectual but snobbish.
- "Greenhorn" is used for a person who is inexperienced.

THE VOCABULARY OF COLOR

Every color has three characteristics or qualities: hue, value, and saturation.

1. Hue

The word hue is used interchangeably with the word color. Hue is either a pure color, red, blue, yellow, or a mixture of colors: teal, violet, brown.

2. Value

Value in color refers to the lightness or darkness of a color, as in the difference between a dark blue or a light blue. The addition of white or black will affect the value of a color.

3. Saturation

Saturation is a term we used to describe the purity or intensity of a color. Full color is considered intense or fully saturated. Adding the opposite of a hue, the complement of a color, or gray, will decrease or lessen the vividness or intensity, and neutralize the color. Colors of low intensity are colors that have been "toned down," and are referred to as "tones."

PERCEPTION OF COLORS

Placing colors on a background of white or black will change the way the color is perceived. Colors on a black background will stand out and look intense, whereas colors placed against a white background may look somewhat washed out.

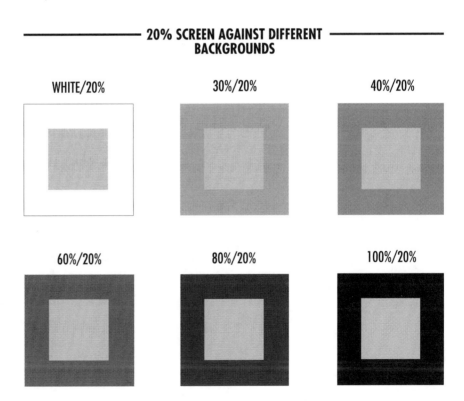

—— 20% SCREEN AGAINST DIFFERENT ——
BACKGROUNDS

WHITE/20%   30%/20%   40%/20%

60%/20%   80%/20%   100%/20%

USING SCREENS

Color changes when placed against different tinted backgrounds. The diagram above shows different percentages of black placed on screened backgrounds. Notice which ones stand out and which ones recede.

SELECTING COLORS FOR YOUR PUBLICATION

The colors selected and preferred by children are not the same color choices adults would make. In general, children prefer bright, loud colors: yellows, reds, and hot pinks, while adults tend more towards the subdued blues and greens.

The psychological responses to color and color preferences, as well as age and gender of the audience, should be taken into consideration before making choices for the printed piece you are designing.

Before selecting colors for your printed piece ask yourself the following questions:

1. Who is your audience?
2. What kinds of colors appeal to this audience? Look at magazines targeted at this audience to help determine the color preferences.
3. Color preference is often determined by culture. Does this audience have cultural differences?
4. Of the colors that appeal to the intended audience, which will best represent your client?

   A store that sells children's toys would be best represented with the bright colors that children like, whereas the colors for a museum or a library should be muted to provide a calming, meditative atmosphere conducive to viewing art or reading books. Financial institutions prefer the more conservative colors of stability, blues and grays.

> *Hint: The eye is attracted to pure colors and to unique hues: red, yellow, blue, white, black, green. Color should have character.*

COLOR AND YOUR PRINTED PIECE

Color is reproduced by the printer on an offset press (see Chapter 12) in two ways, spot color and process color. Each color added to the page increases the cost of the printing job. Using several colors in a printed piece is an expensive proposition because of the labor involved with the addition of each color.

1. One color

If your budget is limited, your design will most likely have one color. When we talk about a printing job being one color, that is exactly what we mean. It means that one color of ink will be used throughout the entire piece to be printed black, red, green, or blue, depending on the color you select. All the photographs, illustrations and text will be printed in that one color.

It is possible to create interesting designs with black as the only color. Using different tints of black will add color to the page and will still be considered a one-color job.

Dressing up the page using one color

▶ **Bleeds**

A bleed occurs when an illustration or inked area runs off the edge of a page. This can be an impressive way of making a piece look more professional while still using only one color. In order to create a bleed, the printer must print on larger paper, and cut the printed piece so that the ink extends to the edge of the page. Since there is more labor involved, and often a larger paper size, the cost of your piece might be increased slightly.

▶ **Reversals or drop outs**

Reversing type, or dropping it out, refers to white type against a black, colored, or screened background. Type used in this way will help create some color and add visual interest to your page. If you create the reversal on the computer, the printing cost will not increase. Bolder type in a reversal is easier to read. The reversed type will be the color of the paper you are using.

> **Hint: Although color, like spice, will beef up a design and get attention, terrific designs can be created with the use of only one color. A strong design will work well whether it uses one color or five.**

2. Spot color

Spot color is the addition of an extra color on the printed page. Using one additional color in strategic places can be very effective in guiding the reader through the printed piece. The color you select can be used separately, or combined with the dominant color to produce a range of colors. If your budget will allow the use of one additional color, select that color carefully, and use it to make an impact. Using black and another color will enable you to use black for your half-tones, for photographs and text which reproduce best in black, while the other color can be used to highlight and decorate selected areas on the page. If you have a design with bold lines, spot color can be used to emphasize the lines. Or, you can use spot color for bullets, or drop caps, that have been used as graphic devices.

3. Multi-colors

If you have an ample budget for your printed piece, you may want to use more than two colors. Sometimes the printing of a three-color job will cost as much as a four-color one. The additional color might give your piece that extra edge. Talk to your printer to get some dollar figures before deciding on the number of colors you will use for a job. A four-color piece using tints can give you a great variety of color combinations. If the printing cost is the same for four-colors as it is for three, you might want to use four colors.

Type and color

Type must be readable! If a light color is selected for the body copy, it will be hard to read. A printed piece that is unreadable will not serve its function. If you do use a color other than black for text, make sure the typeface for the text, and the color selected, are dark enough to be readable.

A headline is meant to stand out. If you use a color for a headline, use one that will emphasize the headline and be bold. Using color in a headline or title can be an effective way to call attention to the words.

Combining colors

Working with color to come up with pleasing, appealing combinations takes practice and a great deal of trial and error. It is possible to make a weak color look interesting by putting it next to a strong color. Colors that are next to each other in the rainbow spectrum are colors that will work well together. Magazines are a good source for ideas in color use. Many magazines use color combinations that are dazzling and exciting.

PAPER COLOR

Paper comes in many hues and the color of the paper can be considered another color, in a one-color job. The choice of paper, including the color and texture, is part of the design decision. The way the ink reacts to paper is another aspect to consider when making a decision about paper. A muted color paper that is uncoated, might provide an interesting backdrop for spot color and produce an intriguing result.

Hint: Selecting an interesting paper color will enhance a one, or two-color piece.

Tint screens

Computer programs enable you to screen colors in order to change the intensity. When using black, for example, you can select an 80% screen that will change the black to a dark gray, as shown in the example below. Screens are also used to change the value of a color.

——— TINTS OF GRAY ———

10%	20%	30%	40%	50%

60%	70%	80%	90%	100%

THE PANTONE® MATCHING SYSTEM

If you have ever selected paint for the interior or exterior of your house, most likely you looked at color charts in the paint store in order to make your selection. "THE PANTONE MATCHING SYSTEM" is an international color language that helps the designer communicate colors for reproduction in the form of publications that are color guides using numbered ink colors. These publications help you communicate color choices to a printer. When you select a PANTONE color, the printer uses these guides that tell which

A PANTONE Publication used as a guide for printers to match colors selected by the designer. PANTONE MATCHING SYSTEM® and PANTONE® are registered trademarks of Pantone, Inc.

combination of inks will create the color specified by the designer. For example, if you specify the color PANTONE 331C, the printer knows to mix 3.1% PANTONE Green with 96.9% PANTONE Transparent White. The C in the number stands for coated stock. The same color on uncoated stock would be PANTONE 331U. There are PANTONE Guides for coated and uncoated stocks, one for metallic color inks, and one for pastel color inks.

PANTONE by Letraset Color Markers

PANTONE by Letraset Color Markers are color-coordinated to the PANTONE Color inks and can be used on your dummy to specify where and how the color will appear on your printed page, a good guide for both you and your client to visualize the final product. PANTONE Publications and markers can be purchased at art supply stores.

Hint: The more sophisticated page layout programs and drawing programs support the PANTONE Colors, but keep in mind that the computer monitor is not always an absolutely reliable source for the exact color match. Use your PANTONE Publications for the exact colors you want.

USING DUOTONES FOR PHOTOGRAPHS

If your budget permits, and you want your photographs to have rich tones with good contrast, you might want to have your printer make a duotone, a halftone in two colors. The addition of a second color in a duotone enhances the richness and density of a black and white photograph. The making of a duotone increases the cost of the printing job, because it involves two plates for each photograph instead of one: one plate to print the black to get contrast and dark tones, and the other plate for the color. The best candidate for a duotone is a photograph with a good range of black and white tones. A duotone can create a dramatic effect. Ask your printer to show you examples of printed duotones before deciding to go that route.

REPRODUCING COLOR
4-Color Process and Color Separations

The term 4-color process, or full-color printing, refers to the mixing of four ink colors basic to the printing process: cyan, magenta, yellow, and black. These colors when combined in varying intensities will reproduce any color found in the rainbow including the gray tones, shades, and shadows for details.

In order for a color photograph to be reproduced for the printed page, it must be scanned or rephotographed with special filters and screens applied, similar to the halftone process used for black and white photographs. The filters separate out the primary colors. Four individual printing plates are made for each ink color and four runs will be made on the printing press. Registration marks are needed for the alignment of each plate to produce a proper register.

Color separation is a critical process. If the plates are not aligned properly the colors will be off creating a disturbing 3-D effect. This effect is clearly visible when newspapers attempt to use color. You can see some colors bleeding into others. The registration marks (see Chapter 12) should be carefully aligned on the mechanical.

Selecting colors for a printed piece can be compared to selecting appropriate typefaces. There are numerous typefaces to choose from, and millions of color possibilities. Color can enhance the printed page or detract from the message.

Hint: Color, like type, must be selected to enhance and reinforce the message of a printed piece. Colors that are soft and muted may be appropriate for an airline interior, but they are not the best choice for advertising a circus or a toy store.

TIPS ON USING COLOR

☐ The intended audience, the format of the printed piece, and the image of the organization or business should all be considered before selecting colors for a piece.

☐ The viewer's perception of color has psychological, cultural, and environmental influences.

☐ Cool colors, like blue, dark green, and violet recede on a page.

☐ Warm colors advance and are prominent on a printed page.

☐ Some colors such as red and yellow will overwhelm if used in excess.

- [ ] The psychology of color associations is important to keep in mind when selecting colors for your printed piece.
- [ ] Colors used in a printed piece should be selected carefully so as not to repel the intended audience.
- [ ] Color printed on a black background will stand out.
- [ ] Color printed against white will appear less dramatic than when printed on black.
- [ ] Spot color can help organize information on a page.
- [ ] Spot color can be used to highlight certain bits of information like a bulleted list, lines or rules, boxes, etc.
- [ ] Spot color is a way to direct the viewer's eye to specific information.
- [ ] All colors on a page should have a unity to bind them together.
- [ ] Color, like type, should be used with purpose, not merely for decoration.

SUGGESTED EXERCISES

1. Look at magazines on a newsstand to find out what colors are used to appeal to the readers of the magazines.
2. Set up a file of interesting color use in magazine and newspaper ads.
3. Look for examples of two-color printing using screens to give the appearance of multiple colors.
4. Experiment with PANTONE markers to see which colors work well together.
5. See if you can find examples of cultural differences in the use of color in publications for people of different nationalities.

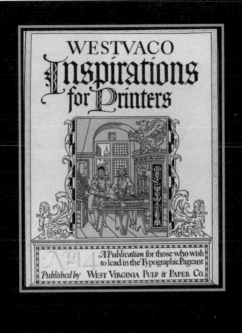

WESTVACO
Inspirations
for Printers

A Publication for those who wish
to lead in the Typographic Pageant
Published by WEST VIRGINIA PULP & PAPER Co.

12.
THE
PRINTING PROCESS

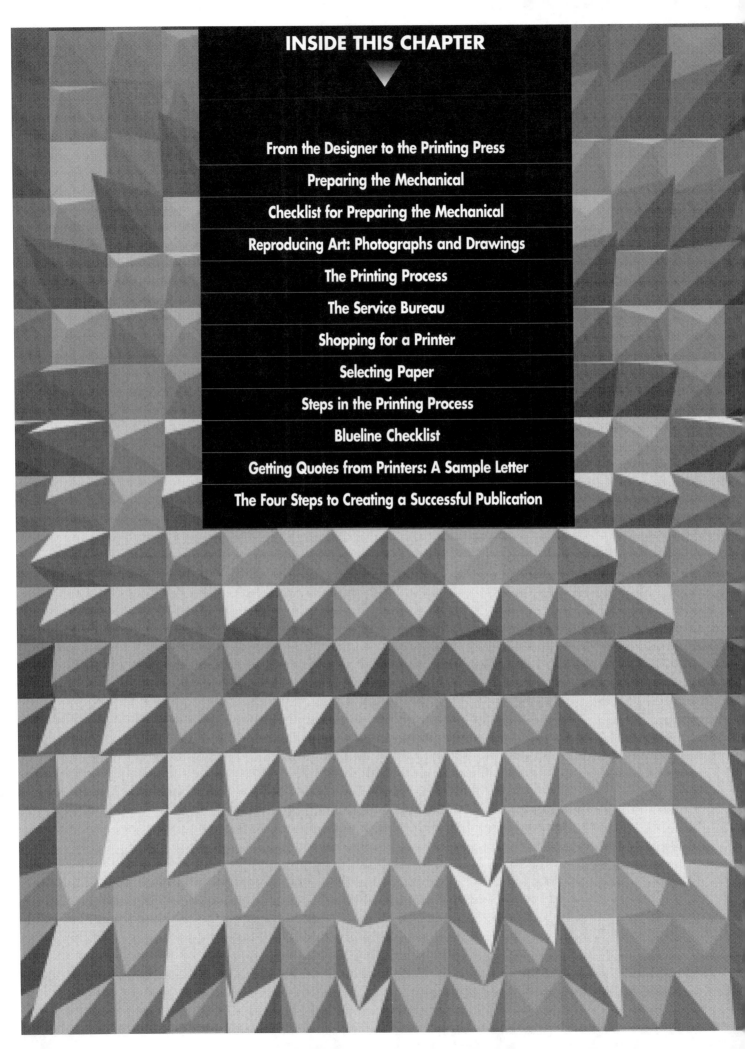

INSIDE THIS CHAPTER

THE PRINTING PROCESS:

FROM THE DESIGNER TO THE PRINTING PRESS

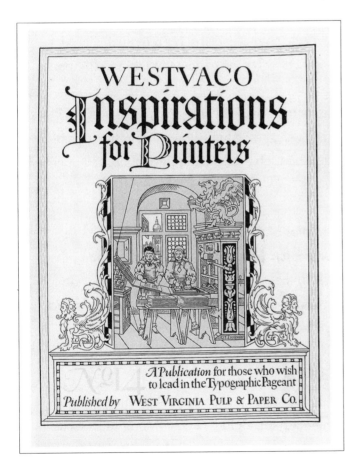

Cover for a book, *Westvaco Inspirations for Printers,* published by Westvaco Corporation, 1926.

fter the design for a printed piece has been completed, and the final layout approved, the document must be prepared for reproduction. Whether the final printing is done on a laser printer, or by a professional print shop, the document to be printed must be put into final shape and made camera-ready. This means all the type—captions, headlines, body copy—must be in place, and all illustrations or photographs must be reduced or enlarged, cropped, and ready to be placed or scanned onto the page in the desired position, with all the elements squared up. Camera-ready refers to everything that is to appear on the final document. When preparing the camera-ready art on the computer, each page in the printed piece must be examined in a magnified view to make sure all the type is lined up using the guide lines in place of T-squares and triangles. The camera-ready piece is called the mechanical. It is the product that goes to the printer.

Establishing a relationship with a printer well in advance of your pre-press tasks will make your job easier, more pleasant, and possibly less expensive. Printers perform a service. The printer will meet with you to discuss your printing needs and expectations. If you feel uneasy and unsure about the printing process and preparing your mechanical, the printer or a salesperson should be able to answer your questions and any concerns about your print job. You should have a dummy of your printed piece with you when you go for the initial meeting. The printer might offer suggestions to help you get the results you desire and should tell you exactly how to prepare the mechanical, what needs to be included, and what tasks the print shop will perform to aid you in the process. Printers, like designers, operate on a tight schedule. Clients want their jobs yesterday, and each job is a custom order that includes ink, paper, and some binding process. Your printed piece is not the only job the print shop is handling. It is one of several that are being printed simultaneously.

If you want your publication to be printed according to the time frame promised by the printer, it is your responsibility as the designer to make sure the job gets to the printer on schedule. Any number of things can go wrong with a print job. The possibilities are endless and might begin with the printing press breaking down. The printing press is a sensitive piece of equipment, and things can go wrong. Humidity slows the drying process of the ink and can delay the completion of a job. Sometimes the paper you selected does not take the ink well, or is too porous and absorbs too much ink. Make sure to give the printer enough time to get your job done properly and to your satisfaction.

The relationship between printer and designer should be thought of as teamwork, a partnership where each person is concerned with doing the best job possible. A printing job well done will enhance a good design.

Hint: Ask to see samples of previously printed pieces before selecting your printer. Some printers are better than others and take pride in their craft, while others do quick and sloppy work. Other designers may be able to provide you with names of printers who do quality work.

PREPARING THE MECHANICAL

The mechanical is the finished layout, the final product that goes to the printer as camera-ready art. Before personal computers were available, designers or layout people prepared mechanicals by hand, at a drawing board, using T-squares, triangles, rubber cement, and wax to line up art and type—a long, tedious, and careful process.

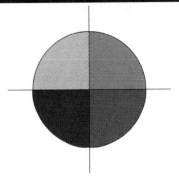

Top left: A registration mark created in a drawing program.

Top right: Preparing the page with registration and crop marks.

Bottom left: The dummy.
The photograph has been scanned for placement only.
The original will be screened by the printer.

Bottom right: The mechanical.
The mechanical prepared for the printer. The globe is from clip art and has been placed directly on the final mechanical since it does not need to be halftoned. Note the box, or window, that has been prepared for the screened photograph the printer will drop in.

CROP MARKS

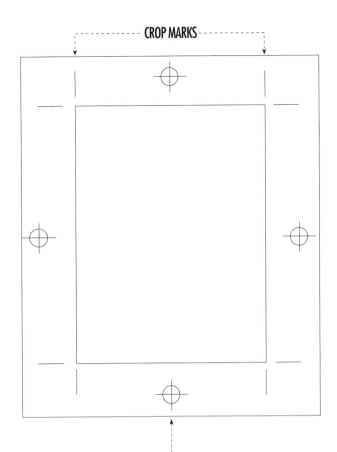

REGISTRATION MARK

THE DUMMY

VOLUME NO. 3

Postscript
THE NEWSLETTER FOR THE DESKTOP PUBLISHER   MAY 1994

DESKTOP PUBLISHING: THE GLOBAL ISSUES

Tlorem ipsum dolors consecter adipcingel, nonummyb heuismod tincidunt ut laoreet dolore magna aliquamer volut patitti. Utwisi enimad minimveniam, quis nost rudexerctatio ullam corperi, suscipit ull tatio ullamcorper suscipit lobortis nislut aliquilexea commodo consequat. Duis aute vel eum iriure dolorin.dolore magna aliquameratvolutpatittihendrein, vulput.

In this Issue

1.
The French Designer
2.
DTP in Asia
3.
The English Designer
4.
Magazine Publishing

THE MECHANICAL

VOLUME NO. 3
Postscript
THE NEWSLETTER FOR THE DESKTOP PUBLISHER   MAY 1994

DESKTOP PUBLISHING: THE GLOBAL ISSUES

Tlorem ipsum dolors consecter adipcingel, nonummyb heuismod tincidunt ut laoreet dolore magna aliquamer volut patitti. Utwisi enimad minimveniam, quis nost rudexerctatio ullam corperi, suscipit ull tatio ullamcorper suscipit lobortis nislut aliquilexea commodo consequat. Duis aute vel eum iriure dolorin.dolore magna aliquameratvolutpatittihendrein, vulput.

In this Issue

1.
The French Designer
2.
DTP in Asia
3.
The English Designer
4.
Magazine Publishing

Many designers still prefer to do mechanicals by hand, but many have switched to creating mechanicals on the computer. Some advertising agencies in large cities have created computer departments for this task.

Preparing the mechanical is the responsibility of the designer, or, in a large design or advertising agency, the pasteup or layout artist. The person preparing the mechanical must be very meticulous, since it must be prepared with great care and precision. Mistakes that are not caught before the piece goes to press will appear on the final printed pages. If you have a print run of 30,000 copies, each copy will exhibit the mistake, and that mistake will most likely be the first thing you will see when you pick the job up from the printer. The printer's responsibility is to take your piece and reproduce it according to your instructions.

Using the tiling function for oversized dummies

If the size of your publication is larger than the standard, 8½" x 11" letter size, and you need to prepare an oversized dummy for the printer, you will need to select the tiling option in the print option box. The tiling function breaks your page into several pieces that, when pieced together, will recreate a full page. It is like putting together a jigsaw puzzle.

If you want to design a large poster on your computer, or large signs for a conference, you can set the custom image size in the page setup and use the tiling option, paste the pages together, and reproduce the page on a large document copy machine.

CHECKLIST FOR PREPARING THE MECHANICAL

Remember, consultation with your printer before preparing the mechanical and well in advance of the printing job can save you a great deal of work, time and money.

☐ All the type is aligned and squared up on the page.
Scroll through the pages of your publication at a magnified view (400%) to make sure that all the type is aligned. Make sure all columns of type and pictorial elements are squared up using the computer's vertical and horizontal guide lines.

☐ All the extraneous elements have been erased from the page.

Scroll your pages at a magnified view (400%), and use the "select all" function to identify items that should not be on the page, as well as ones that had not been erased previously.

☐ The pages have been proofread to check for spelling, typos, and grammatical errors.
Do a spell check to make sure you have not made any obvious spelling errors or typos.

☐ Errors in typography have been checked: smart quotes, widows and orphans, en and em dashes, etc.
(See Chapter 6 Type Terminology and Typesetting Basics.)

☐ An accurate dummy has been prepared for the printer.
The dummy shows your pages the way you want them to look after they are printed. The dummy should have photocopied or scanned illustrations, at accurate sizes, placed exactly where you want them on the pages of your document.

☐ All the line art has been pasted or scanned onto the camera-ready page.
If you have access to a scanner, scan all art onto your page to size it. If you do not have a scanner, use a proportion wheel to determine the percentage of reduction or enlargement needed. Scanned images can be used in your publication if you have a high-end scanner, (i.e. one that will give you high resolution) and know how to manipulate the images in an imaging program for final printing. If your scanner cannot scan at a high resolution, use it only for your dummy to indicate the size and placement of your illustrations on the page.

☐ Windows, (black boxes) have been put on the page for photographs or illustrations to be dropped in after they have been screened.

☐ Clear, precise instructions have been prepared for the printer to follow.

REPRODUCING ART: DRAWINGS OR PHOTOGRAPHS

Illustrations fall into two different categories: line art and continuous-tone art (see Chapter 10, Using Illustrations).

1. Line art

Most drawings, pencil or ink, fall into the category of line art and can be pasted directly onto the mechanical. They are camera-ready. The exceptions to this are drawings that have a variety of grey tones and values and might need to be screened. If you have doubts about your drawings and whether or not they need to be treated as halftones, consult your printer.

2. Continuous tone

Photographs are considered continuous-tone art because, like elaborate drawings, they contain variations of tones and values. In order to reproduce photographs, they must be screened, a task performed either by the printer or your scanner. If the printer will be processing the halftones, you need to calculate the percentage of the reduction or enlargement needed for the photograph to fit the allotted space on the page.

Registration marks

If your design is to be printed in several colors, you will need to add registration marks to your mechanical. The registration marks help the printer match each additional color that is added to the page. If you are using a service bureau ask them to include registration marks on all your pages.

Registration marks can be purchased on tape at your local art supply store or stationery store, or they can be created in a drawing program.

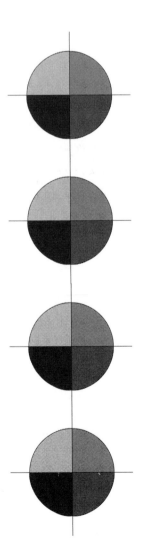

Crop marks

Crop marks are used to indicate the boundaries of your page so that the printer knows where to cut the pages after printing to give you the size piece you specified. If you are using a service bureau it will include crop marks for you.

THE PRINTING PROCESS
The Service Bureau

Before the advent of desktop publishing, the finished design—the mechanical—was taken to a print shop to be printed. The printer had all the necessary equipment to reproduce the printed piece. When personal computers became available to designers, and designers had to assume the task of typesetting, they were unhappy with the quality of type from the laser printer. Output from the laser printer could not be used for the mechanical because it was not of the same standard of printing of professionally-typeset documents. It still isn't, but the decision to use a service bureau depends on your budget, the function of the printed piece and the intended audience, the method of reproduction, and how professional you want your piece to look. If you want the type and illustrations on your printed page to look sharp and crisp, you will want to take your disk to a service bureau.

If you have designed a flyer that will be reproduced on a copy machine and hung on a bulletin board in the library, it would be a waste of money to use a service bureau. However, if you have designed an annual report that must impress a board of directors, using a service bureau is a necessity.

Service bureaus began to spring up in the mid-1980s as cottage industries offering a specialty service for high-end printing, an intermediary service between the designer and the printer. The service bureau takes the file or files from your disk or modem and prints the pages of your document on an imagesetter at a high resolution, between 1200-4000 dots per inch, depending on the equipment. To understand what this means in terms of sharpness of image, consider the dot matrix printers you might be using for proofing. These printers—the ImageWriter and others like it—print out pages at between 72-144 dpi. The type is jagged, not easily read, and you can see the bitmapped effect clearly. Most personal desktop laser printers print out pages at 300-600 dpi, depending on the printer. You can easily see the difference between the dot matrix printer and the laser printer with the naked eye. While a print-out from your laser printer looks considerably better than one produced on a dot matrix printer, if you have sharp eyes, or if you look at your laser proof with a magnifying glass, you will see that the edges of your type and graphics are slightly fuzzy.

RESOLUTION AND DOTS PER INCH
High vs. low resolution
When a page is printed at 1200-4000 dots per inch, all those extra

dots make a huge difference in the final appearance of type and graphics. A light typeface will become lighter and thinner when more dots per inch are added, and a typeface that is very bold will look slightly less bold when printed out to an imagesetter. If you have created a box using a gradual fill, you can see all the dots when you print it out on your laser printer. When the same box is printed on a Linotronic, or other imagesetter, the fill will be gradual, and the dots will fade into each other.

Hint: It is not essential to take your publication to a service bureau. Hard copy from a laser printer may be sufficient for your job. The pages from an imagesetter will give you a higher quality mechanical than one you get from your desktop printer, but it will also add to the cost of your job.

Your service bureau will give you the option of printing out to paper or to film. The choice depends on whether you have scanned photographs, gradual fills, or straight line art. If you have used screened tints or photographs, you might want your output for those pages on film. Consult your printer about the best output (film or paper) for your job. Film is an important factor in the quality control of a job, and your service bureau may not use the highest quality or the right kind for your purposes. Service bureaus charge by the page, and the prices can vary greatly. It is a good idea to do some comparison shopping to get estimates, and to do a quality comparison.

Some print shops have their own imagesetting equipment, and it might be easier, with less wear and tear on you, to have the final printer do the entire job. Get estimates for every aspect of the job before making a decision.

Hint: Careful advanced planning might save you a great deal of money and time. If you don't plan ahead, and end up needing a rush job, the cost of your job will increase substantially.

Questions to ask before selecting a service bureau:

1. What kind of imagesetter will be used?

2. What kind of resolution can you expect?

3. What is the cost of film output? What kind of film is used?

4. What is the cost of paper output? Will you get a discount if the job is a large one?

5. Does the service bureau have the fonts specified, both the screen and printer fonts?

6. Is your technology, hardware, and software compatible with that of the service bureau?

7. If your publication is too large to fit on a high-density disk, how will you get your document to the service bureau? Ask the service bureau for suggestions.

Hint: Ask the service bureau print to out a few test pages so you can see the results. Do some test runs on pages that have complex images to see how they will reproduce. Your service bureau will need a dummy that includes each page of your document to use as a reference and a guide.

Information you will need to give the service bureau:

1. Your name, address, telephone, and/or fax number

2. The name of your publication

3. The titles of documents to be output as they appear on your disk

4. The files for support documents (TIFF, EPS, etc. files) that appear in your publication or postscript files. (If you have created illustrations in a drawing program, or if you have included scanned images and imported them onto your page layout, include these files on your disk.)

5. A list of all the software programs used with their version numbers

6. The page setup of your document

7. The type of output you want: paper, film negative, film positive

8. The output size you are requesting

9. A list of all fonts used in your publication, including fonts used in drawings or logos

10. Special instructions (crop marks, registration marks, percentages of reductions or enlargements)

11. Any additional instructions (If you have used a tint screen or graduated fill, you will need to note the percentages of the fills.)

THE SERVICE BUREAU

INFO FOR THE SERVICE BUREAU

Date: _____

Client:
Name _____
Address _____
_____
Telephone number _____

Contact person:
Name _____
Address _____
_____
Telephone number _____

Name of project: _____

Publication size:
Size (opened) _____   Folded _____

Disk(s) Titles:
# of Disks
1 disk labeled _____
1 disk labeled _____

EPS or TIFF files included:
Drawings and scans
Clip Art
(All these files must be on the disk you prepare for the service bureau.)

Desired output:
☐ Paper

☐ Film

Software programs used (Name & Version #):
1. _____
2. _____

Fonts used, include name of software manufacturer:
1. _____
2. _____

Please phone contact person at (000-0000) if there are any problems.

ADDITIONAL INFORMATION:
Include registration marks, crop marks
Boxes in grey - screen at 40%

SHOPPING FOR A PRINTER

If the printer you selected for your first job was satisfactory, your relationship with that printer may turn out to be a long-lasting one. Or, you may never want to use that print shop again.

How do you find a good printer?

1. Reputation

Good printers, ones who are skilled and take pride in their craft and workmanship, have an established reputation. Ask other designers for recommendations of printers. If you don't know anyone who has used a printer, check the yellow pages and conduct some interviews.

2. Getting quotes

If you have a newsletter, or other publication that you will be producing with regularity, you might want to send out letters to several printers asking for quotes. Compare prices from different printers, and set up some interviews.

3. Interviewing printers

Set up interviews with printers after receiving their quotes. Ask for a tour of the print shop to see the facilities and the equipment they are using. Since the printer/designer relationship is an important one, spending time talking to the printer or salesperson should give you a good feel for the kind of relationship you will be able to establish with this print shop. Request some samples of work and references.

Hint: If you are a novice at desktop publishing and design and this is your first experience with production, you will want to choose a patient printer who will spend time talking with you and answering any questions you might have; a printer who will lead you through the experience as painlessly as possible.

4. Service

Since printing is a service industry, a great deal of value should be

Designed by
Macdonald Gill for the
Westminster Press
London

An English printer's mark for the Westminster Press, London, 1850, designed by Macdonald Gill. From *Westvaco Inspirations for Printers*, Westvaco Corporation, 1926.

placed on the printer who offers you the kind of service that will make your job easier and give your publications a professional appearance.

5. Additional services

Find out what other services your printer offers. Some printers offer a pick-up and overnight delivery service. If you have selected a printer in another town, this kind of service will be invaluable to you. Find out in advance if there are hidden charges for the special services offered.

SELECTING PAPER

Selecting the appropriate paper for your publication, whether it is a brochure, stationery, or a newsletter, is another decision that has to be made as part of the design process. The selection of paper, color, weight, and texture is as important as the type and color choices you made previously. The paper used in a publication plays a significant role in the appearance of the final printed piece. The cost of the paper comprises 30-50% of your invoice and should be selected carefully. Your printer will be able to recommend papers for your job and will show you sample books with different grades, colors, and finishes. You might want to ask the printer for sample books of your own for future reference.

If you intend to reproduce your printed piece on a photocopy machine, or through the services of a quick print copy shop, you might want to order special paper from a paper catalog. If your print run is small, and you intend to use your laser printer as a short-run printing press, you might want to purchase specialty paper to upgrade the appearance of your printed piece so that it looks like it has been professionally produced.

Paper weight

Paper is defined by weight, grade, and finish. All printing paper has a basis weight, a weight based on the weight and grade of 500 sheets (a ream) of paper in its basic size and is referred to in terms of pounds. Very few paper stocks come in the letter size (8½" x 11") that we use in our laser printers. Some papers, offset and coated stock, for example, come in the same basic size, 25" x 38". The paper is cut to size after the job is printed. When communicating paper weight to the printer, the # sign is used: (e.g., 80# coated).

Hint: If the size of your publication can be printed on a standard paper size, you will save money on the paper.

PAPER FINISHES
Uncoated stock

Paper comes in two finishes, uncoated and coated stock. Most of the paper used in laser printers, duplicating machines, copy centers, and most commercial print jobs is uncoated paper. It is a frequently used paper stock that comes in a variety of colors, weights, and differing qualities. It comes in both rough and smooth finishes: the rough are vellum and antique, while the smooth finishes are English and lustre. Uncoated paper is most frequently used for newsletters, brochures, flyers, and announcements.

Coated stock

Paper that is coated is used for high-quality printing and is best when reproducing photographs. It is often used for annual reports and other magazines, catalogs, and slick brochures with lots of photographs. The most commonly coated stock has a glossy finish. If you look at magazines at a newsstand you will notice that most of the slick magazines are printed on glossy coated paper. The glossiness of coated paper is rated from 1-5, with the lower numbers standing for the higher quality, more expensive papers. Coated stock also comes in a matte and dull finish, with a non-glare surface, and mostly in off white colors.

GRADES OF PAPER

Paper comes in different grades with each grade serving a different purpose. Below is a list of printing paper grade classifications with the basic size for each grade.

1. Bond

Bond stock has a surface that will accept ink from pens, the printing press, or the laser printer. Bond is commonly used for letterheads and other business materials. The standard size for bond is 17" x 22".

2. Text

Text stock comes in many colors, textures, and finishes, and is most commonly used for booklets, flyers, brochures, and announcements. It comes in 70, 80, and 100 lb. weights. The standard sheet size is 25" x 38".

3. Cover

Cover stock comes in both uncoated and coated finishes and is used most frequently for covers of catalogs, booklets, reports, menus, and invitations. The colors of cover stock can be matched and coordinated with other stock like bond, so if you are designing a catalog and want to use the same color stock for the cover and inside pages the colors will match. Cover stock comes in 60, 65, and 85 lb. weights. The standard sheet size is 20" x 26".

4. Book

Book stock is the paper used in both trade books and textbooks. It is an inexpensive paper and comes coated or uncoated, in both smooth and antique finishes, in the same size and weights as text paper.

6. Offset

The paper generally used in duplicating machines and laser printers, and offset presses is offset stock. It is the least expensive of all the paper stocks and comes in a variety of colors and finishes in weights of 50, 60, and 70 lb. The standard sheet size is 25" x 38".

7. Newsprint

Newsprint is an inexpensive paper that newspapers are printed on. It does not have a long life and will yellow and crumble in a few years. Its basic weights range from 28-35 lb. The standard sheet size is 24" x 36".

Recycled paper

Since there is a growing concern for our environment, recycled paper is in high demand these days. Paper manufacturers are producing recycled papers in a wide range of choices, colors, textures, and weights in both coated and uncoated stock. Some of these papers are extremely beautiful and elegant in appearance; however, some do not take ink very well. Ask your printer's advice about the best paper for your job before making a selection.

GETTING PAPER SAMPLES AND PURCHASING PAPER

1. Paper catalogs

The use of paper has proliferated since desktop publishing began, and a whole new industry—the paper catalog company—has grown as a result. These companies seem to have sprung up overnight, and offer a variety of paper for printing on the desktop. These catalogs often include sample books that display all their papers and can be purchased for a minimal fee.

2. Collecting swatch books

Printers often have extra swatch sheets or sample books from paper companies that they will give you. Paper companies will often send you samples of their papers if you phone their 800 numbers. Sending you samples is good advertising for them.

3. Purchasing paper from your local copy center

If you are doing a short press run using your laser printer, you might check out the samples of paper at your local copy center. If you do not need an entire ream of paper, your copy center will sell you paper by the individual piece. Copy centers have a surprisingly large selection of paper, including many choices of recycled stock.

THE PRINTING PROCESS

Unless you are using your laser printer as a short-run printing press, or your local copy or duplicating machine, the printing process that will most likely be used to print your camera-ready art (your mechanical) is called offset lithography. The word "lithography" is from the

Greek, lithos (stone), and graphos (writing) and is a form of printing invented by Aloys Senefelder, a printer and playwright, in 1798 over three hundred years after the development of Gutenberg's printing process. Senefelder based his printing process on the principle that oil and water do not mix.

The Six Steps in the Printing Process

1. Making the negative

The printer takes your camera-ready piece, the mechanical, either produced by you on your laser printer or output from your service bureau, photographs it, and gets a negative. If you use a service bureau for imagesetter output, this step can be eliminated if your copy is printed out to film and results in a usable negative.

2. Making the plate

Using a photographic process, the printer exposes the negative to a light sensitive metal plate. The plate is developed and gets a lacquer-like coating. The exposed areas on the plate, the actual image areas, repel water, while the blank or unexposed areas attract water.

3. Wetting the plate

After the plate, which is made of flexible metal, has been exposed, it is wrapped around a rotating cylinder on the printing press, and a wet watery solution from a tray mists a water roller and wets the entire plate. During the actual printing, the water sticks to the unexposed areas, not the lacquered ones.

4. Inking the plate

The oil-based ink, the color you selected for your piece, is rolled onto the plate and adheres only to the exposed areas.

5. The blanket

The image is transferred to another roller and then onto a rubber blanket that presses against, or "kisses," the plate. The image on the blanket is reversed. This is the part of the printing process that makes it offset.

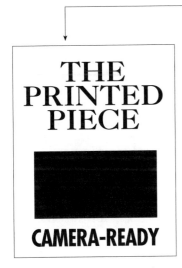

THE PRINTED PIECE

CAMERA-READY

THE DESIGNER

THE DESIGNER AND THE PRINTING PROCESS

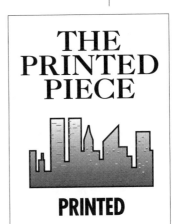

THE PRINTED PIECE

PRINTED

1.

SERVICE BUREAU

Prints high resolution output

2.

THE DESIGNER

Gives printer the mechanical

3.

THE PRINTER

Makes negatives from the mechanical

4.

THE PRINTER

Strips the negatives onto prepared grids

5.

THE PRINTER

Prints out the blueline

10.

THE DESIGNER

Picks up the print job

9.

THE PRINTER

Cuts, folds & binds the printed piece

8.

THE PRINTER

Puts plate on press, adds paper & prints

7.

THE PRINTER

Exposes & develops printing plates

6.

THE DESIGNER

Checks the blueline

6. Printing

The image on the blanket presses against the paper, and a positive image is printed.

Hint: The printer will need a dummy with numbered pages for reference and as a guide.

GETTING A PROOF
The blueline

Once your mechanical goes through all of the above processes, you might want to get a proof sheet, or blueline, before any more copies are run off. This will increase your printing cost slightly, but it will be worthwhile in the long run.

The blueline is an exact reproduction of your printed piece, with all the art, including the halftones made by the printer, printed in blue or sometimes brown. The function of the blueline is to help you catch any errors, either the printer's or yours, and to check the accuracy of the entire publication before the final printing occurs. Making changes at this point can be expensive, if the mistakes are yours, but it is better to catch errors at this stage than after a print run of 30,000 brochures with the name of your organization misspelled, or other errors. After a very careful perusal of the blueline, you will be asked to sign your name to okay the proof. Your signature on the blueline indicates that you have found no errors, either yours or the printer's, and gives the printer the go-ahead to print the job. If the mistakes on the blueline were made by the printer, they will be repaired at the printer's expense. If the mistakes were yours, and changes need to be made, there will be an extra charge—a good reason to check over your mechanical with great care before taking it to the printer.

It is a good idea to ask the printer to notify you when a job is about to go to press so that you can be present when the first pages come off the press, to check for ink coverage, accuracy of color, etc. Your presence and concern will keep the printer on his or her toes. When you pick up the job from the printer, look over a number of the finished printed pieces to check for poor printing, inconsistencies in ink coverage, ink smudges on the pages, or any other errors the printer may have made.

BLUELINE CHECKLIST

When you check the blueline, make sure you have your dummy with you, and do a very thorough check.

Make sure:

- [ ] There are no typos
- [ ] All the pages of the publication are together
- [ ] All the elements on the pages are in the correct places
- [ ] There are no extraneous elements on any of the pages
- [ ] All the type is lined up properly
- [ ] The illustrations and photographs are in the right places and are the right sizes
- [ ] All the screened photographs are sharp and clear
- [ ] Nothing has been left out
- [ ] The printer followed all your instructions

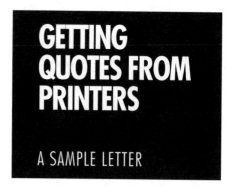

Date

Specialty Printers
Street Number
City, State, Zip

Dear Sir or Madam:

I am designing a 20 page newsletter, *The Communication Express*, for the Business Management Group in (your town). The newsletter is to be published monthly and will be a self-mailer.

I am interested in getting a print bid from your company for this publication based on the spec sheet I have attached. Please send me appropriate paper samples, based on the information in the spec sheet.

Also, please break down the pricing of job by category: negatives, plates, press time, paper, as well as any other relevant pricing information.

If you need more information, you may phone me at (000) 000-0000 or fax at (000) 000-0000.

Thank you.

Sincerely,

(Your name and title)

GETTING QUOTES FROM PRINTERS

A SAMPLE SPEC SHEET

Name of piece to be printed:

Description: (Number of pages)

Frequency of publication: (Weekly, monthly, quarterly)

Size:

Quantity: (Number to be printed)

Mechanical delivery date:

Bleeds: (None)

Color separations: (Supplied for spot color)

Reversals: (Supplied)

Paper: (Would like samples, all one stock, preferably white)

Folds:

Inks: (Three: PANTONE 421, PANTONE 186, and black)

Binding:

Blueline date:

Delivery date:

Contact person:

Your name

Your address

City, state

Telephone number

IN CONCLUSION!

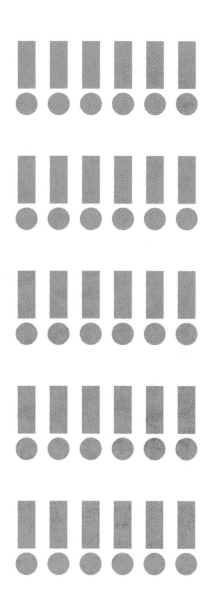

There are many possible solutions for each publication in need of a design. Experimentation and time spent on trial and error will lead to a layout that seems to be just the right one.

Each new piece to be designed can be looked upon as a new and exciting challenge, a different and unique problem to be solved. There is no one right solution. The design that works best for a bank will not be an appropriate one for a children's school. Graphic design has some guidelines, but it does not have hard-and-fast rules.

THE FOUR STEPS TO CREATING A SUCCESSFUL PUBLICATION:

1. Careful planning

Plan your printed piece before you begin to design. Get all the materials to be included, text and illustrations and then start designing.

2. Consistency

Establishing and maintaining a consistency throughout your printed piece is essential to the success of your design.

3. Guiding the reader

A successful design will guide the reader through a page by emphasizing the important elements on the page. This is done by organizing information, both visual and verbal, in a hierarchy.

4. Attention to detail

Before sending a mechanical to the printer, the final piece should be checked, re-checked, and checked again for errors in spelling, inconsistencies and typesetting details.

BIBLIOGRAPHY OF DESKTOP PUBLISHING SOFTWARE

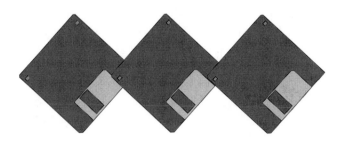

The computer and its software programs are new tools for the designer. At this point there is no one program that enables the designer to accomplish all the necessary tasks for drawing, design, and production.

If we think of software programs as tools, we realize that in learning to use any tools it is important to select the most expedient one for each particular task. This bibliography was compiled to aid you in selecting the appropriate software for the task at hand.

The programs that are listed as PC programs only work with Windows. The version numbers that identify the programs are not listed here, but the information on each refers to the latest version to date.

An effort was made to contact all of the leading publishers of software related to desktop publishing. Some companies have not been included here because they either did not respond to our offer to include them in the book, or they elected not to be included. We will try to include them in the first revision.

Drawing and painting programs should be used to create illustrations, drawings, or paintings, or to trace scanned clip art in order to remove the bitmapped effect and to turn type into graphics for importing into a page layout program.

ADDDEPTH   [MAC]
Ray Dream, Inc.

AddDepth is a Postscript-compatible graphic tool with built-in text and drawing tools that let you add three-dimensional depth and perspective to your type and line art. It imports and exports artwork to Aldus FreeHand, Adobe Illustrator, EPS, and drawing-type PICT formats.

ADOBE DIMENSIONS™   [MAC]
Adobe Systems, Inc.

Adobe Dimensions lets you create, extrude, revolve, bevel, and manipulate simple 3-D objects and effects and integrate them with artwork from popular 2-D graphics programs. You can perform 3-D rendering using Bézier curves and automatically generate shading based on lighting. You can import art from a drawing program and give it 3-D properties, or use it for packaging, logos and other kinds of design projects and presentations, as well as simple animation sequences for digital movies.

ADOBE ILLUSTRATOR   [MAC/PC]
Adobe Systems, Inc.

Adobe Illustrator is a professional drawing program for graphic artists, technical illustrators, and desktop publishers with precise illustration and single-page design capabilities. You can create, manipulate, and refine artwork flexibly and accurately, or draw from scratch and autotrace scanned images. Illustrator's text handling features let you place text along any path, and then edit and transform it easily. Illustrator supports 16-and 24-bit color.

ADOBE STREAMLINE [MAC]
Adobe Systems, Inc.

Adobe Streamline converts bitmapped graphics into scalable Postscript outline graphics. It has the capability of reading TIFF files from a scanner, along with PICT and MacPaint files, and it can convert gray-scale images into posterized line art.

ALDUS® FREEHAND™ [MAC/PC]
Aldus Corporation

Aldus FreeHand is a Postscript language professional drawing and illustration program that combines a wide range of drawing tools, color options, special effects, and advanced text-handling capabilities to produce high-quality graphics. The recent releases for both Windows and Macintosh include support for pressure-sensitive electronic drawing tablets that enable users to create natural-looking lines of variable widths.

ALDUS® GALLERY EFFECTS [MAC/PC]
Aldus Corporation

Aldus Gallery Effects lets you transform color bitmapped and gray-scale images into art that that looks hand-painted. It has sixteen master effects, including, fresco, charcoal, and watercolor.

ALDUS® INTELLIDRAW™ [MAC/PC]
Aldus Corporation

Aldus IntelliDraw is a cross-platform (Macintosh and Windows) sophisticated drawing program that provides users with a way to visually experiment, refine, and show ideas. This is a good program for businesses that need graphics for presentations in a hurry.

ALDUS® SUPERPAINT [MAC]
Aldus Corporation

Aldus SuperPaint is an easy-to-use combination drawing and painting program with plug in features: paint spray, pattern fills, interesting effects, etc. Complex graphics will not import well.

CORELDRAW [PC]
Corel Corporation

CorelDRAW is a drawing program that includes illustration, charting, photo-paint, tracing/OCR, and presentation capabilities. It has word processing features, special effects, hundreds of fonts, thousands of clip art images, and symbols for business applications. CorelDRAW includes CorelMOVE, a new animation module.

FRACTAL DESIGN PAINTER® [MAC]
Fractal Design Corporation

Fractal Design Painter® is a 24-bit color professional painting program with photo design features that include image-retouching, color separations, natural-media tools (like marbling, glass distortion and liquid effects) and straight line tools.

MICROGRAFX DESIGNER [PC]
Micrografx, Inc.

Micrografx Designer is a precision illustration program for Windows. Designer includes Adobe Type Manager, Adobe TypeAlign, and more than 175 Type 1 fonts. It comes with 15 drawing tools.

MICROGRAFX WINDOWS DRAW [PC]
Micrografx, Inc.

Micrografx Windows Draw is a drawing program for Windows, with 9 drawing tools, 2600 clip art images, and special effects like blending, rotating, gradient fills; text along a curve, flip, amd stretch; as well as slant drawing and add patterns.

PIXAR SHOWPLACE [MAC]
Pixar

Showplace lets you create realistic 3-D scenes and pick and place pre-designed objects, cover them with any number of surface appearances, set lights, view the scene from any angle, and create a realistic picture. Showplace plug-ins include: rooms, fractal terrain, and venetian blinds. Postscript fonts can be imported into Showplace.

CLIP ART

Clip art by definition is art in public domain. Most of the numerous clip art software programs have illustrations or photographs based on themes: images of people, places, animals, and art that can be used to enhance publications.

ALDUS® FETCH™ [MAC]
Aldus Corporation

Aldus® Fetch™ is a multi-user, mixed media cataloging, browsing, and retrieval tool designed for the professional production environment. Users can catalog clip art, photo images, presentations, QuickTime movies, and sounds in a common visual database for fast browsing and retrieval.

ART ABOUT BUSINESS [MAC/PC]
Dynamic Graphics, Inc.

This is a collection of images that shows men and women in a variety of business and career activities and pressures. Art styles range from realistic to stylized to cartoon, covering situations that are both serious and lighthearted.

ART ABOUT DINING [MAC/PC]

This is an assortment of images of specific food items or dining scenes including families and couples, chefs and waiters, hot dog stands and fine restaurants, picnics and barbecues, and popular ethnic cuisine.

ART ABOUT EDUCATION [MAC/PC]

This is a collection that includes symbols and scenes from primary school to adult education. It includes images of crayons, computers, pencils, notebooks, as well as several borders for memos.

ART ABOUT FOOD [MAC/PC]

This disk includes images of prepared and natural foods, herbs and spices, meat, poultry, fish, vegetables, fruits, nuts, grains, and seasonal fare.

ART ABOUT HEALTHCARE [MAC/PC]

A collection of health, medical, and fitness images of medical technology, diet, aerobics, and fitness.

ART ABOUT SEASONS [MAC/PC]

This assortment captures the flavor of each time of year. It is good for timely retail promotions and direct mail. The illustrations range from summer picnics and lawn mowing to sled riding.

ART ABOUT SYMBOLS [MAC/PC]

This is a collection of over a hundred images and symbols that range from agriculture and automotive to geography and home maintenance, recreation, travel, and the weather.

ARTS & LETTERS APPRENTICE [PC]
Computer Support Corporation

Arts & Letters Apprentice is a graphics, drawing, and desktop publishing program for small businesses. Apprentice comes with 3,500 art forms and clip art symbols and 35 typefaces, and includes charting, lines, and fill styles and gradient fills, text on a path, as well as other drawing features.

ARTS & LETTERS GRAPHICS COMPOSER [PC]
Computer Support Corporation

This is a graphics and drawing program for non-artists to produce publications. Composer has tools for creating visuals that include 8,000 clip art images, 80 scalable typefaces, and automatic charting to produce pie, bar, area, and line charts. The user can add highlights, blends, shadows, accents, and airbrush effects.

ARTS & LETTERS GRAPHICS EDITOR [PC]
Computer Support Corporation

Graphics Editor contains more than 8,000 clip art images, 90 versatile typefaces, and data-driven charting. The program has advanced features including warp/perspective, hole cutting, shaping and automatic 4-color separation.

ARTS & LETTERS JURASSIC ART [PC]

Computer Support Corporation

Jurassic Art is a complete illustration product, that includes drawing tools, scalable typefaces, special effects, and more than 400 clip-art images—including a collection of dinosaurs, prehistoric plants, scenes, and backgrounds. Included in the package is a 44-page informational booklet with information about dinosaurs.

ARTS & LETTERS SCENERIO [PC]

Computer Support Corporation

The Arts & Letters Scenerio features Instant Art, a composition system of modular art backgrounds with movable props and figures. Scenerio comes with more than 300 Arts & Letters clip-art images, eight outline typefaces, import capabilities, and Bézier curve drawing tools. You can add type, clip art, and drawings to create a finished composition.

ARTS & LETTERS PICTURE WIZARD [PC]

Computer Support Corporation

Picture Wizard is a drawing and graphics program for newcomers to computer graphics. It features concise and easy-to-understand instructions and comes with 1,200 clip art images and 15 scalable typefaces, line and curve drawing tools, and automatic charting.

CLIPPER [MAC/PC]

Dynamic Graphics, Inc.

Clipper is a monthly subscription clip art service with more than 70 output-ready images available either as camera-ready on paper, or on disk in electronic format. The artwork is high-quality and professional in appearance.

BUSINESS AND INDUSTRY (VOL. I) [MAC/PC]

Comstock Desktop Photography

This CD-ROM volume contains 2,940 photographs that focus on the business world. *(Reproduction rights and fees must be negotiated.)*

COMSTOCK ON-LINE ACCESS BBS [MAC]

Comstock Desktop Photography

This is an electronic bulletin board service that makes 10,000 prescanned photographic images available by modem 24 hours a day, 365 days a year. This service is for Macintosh users only. There is a subscription fee, a fee for log-in time, a fee per image, and a charge per minute.

COREL PROFESSIONAL PHOTOS ON CD-ROM [PC]

Corel Corporation

100 royalty-free Kodak CD-format photographs on a variety of themes. You can turn any CD-ROM photo image into a screen saver or wallpaper.

DESIGNER'S CLUB [MAC/PC]

Dynamic Graphics, Inc.

This club is an all-EPS graphics subscription service of contemporary art and design that provides color images, idea-starters, how-to's, and technical support to help the designer create a wide range of projects, including the Designer's Bonus Library that introduces the latest electronic art for more creative options.

DESKTOP PHOTOGRAPHY VOL III [MAC]

Comstock Desktop Photography

This volume of photographs from Comstock Desktop Photography contains 441 color and grayscale images of subjects ranging from families and beauty to sports and nature.

DIGITAL SELECTIONS [MAC/PC]

Comstock Desktop Photography

You can select from Comstock's inventory of 4 million photographs by modem. Fees for images.

DIGIT ART CLIP ART [MAC/PC]

Image Club

BUSINESS CARTOONS

Business cartoons is a clip art package that will help add humor to business documents.

BORDERS & ORNAMENTS SCIENCE & MEDICINE

This collection of clip art has an old world style and contemporary design elements to add a distinctive touch to printed pieces.

FABULOUS FIFTIES

Fabulous Fifties clip art has images from the fifties that will help add a nostalgic look to your printed page. It can be used for brochures, newsletters, and other publications.

WOODCUTS

This collection has 150 hand-rendered images useful to designers. The images have been rendered in a traditional woodcut style, and they are constructed to be customized.

ELECTRONIC PRINT MEDIA SERVICE [MAC/PC]

Dynamic Graphics, Inc.

Electronic Print Media Service is a creative retail advertising, and promotion CD-ROM subscription art service that provides high-quality TIFF and EPS images, with seasonal and topical themes for ad campaigns and sales promotions. It also has suggested layouts for retail use.

ELECTRONIC VOLK [MAC/PC]

Dynamic Graphics, Inc.

This electronic subscription art library service of EPS and TIFF illustrations and designs with themes provides the most useful subjects in a variety of styles.

IMAGES WITH IMPACT [MAC/PC]

3G Graphics

ACCENTS AND BORDERS

This is clip art with decorative elements and representational illustrations inspired by many cultures and artistic styles. It is a resource of images for the desktop publisher that includes frames and borders, tiles and ornaments, symbols, and illustrations for holidays and the four seasons.

PLACES AND FACES [MAC/PC]

Places and Faces is a collection of images suited for projects related to community events, human services, natural environments, recreational activities, and travel.

PIXAR ONE TWENTY EIGHT CD [MAC/PC]

Pixar

One Twenty Eight is Pixar's private collection of high-quality, photographic textures specifically designed for use with paint, photo-retouching, page layout, presentation, video, and multimedia applications. The collection incorporates a patented technology which allows the textures to be tiled seamlessly. As a result, when the textures are tiled to cover a large area, they will appear as a single, smooth image without breaks or lines.

PRINT MEDIA SERVICE [MAC/PC]

Dynamic Graphics, Inc.

A creative retail advertising and promotion art service, Print Media Service provides quality art with seasonal and topical themes for ad campaigns and sales promotions, and it has suggested layouts with fresh solutions for retail use.

QUARK LIBRARIES [PC]

Quark Inc.

Quark Libraries is a collection of Encapsulated Postscript (EPS) clip art on subjects that include: Arts and Entertainment, Business, Calendar, Communications, Health, Holidays and Religion, Leisure, Flags, Maps, and other clip art to visually enhance your publications. The clip art can be used in Quark XPress documents and in documents created in other applications.

VOLK CLIP ART [MAC/PC]

Dynamic Graphics, Inc.

This is a subscription art library service in a compact, self-indexed art file box that provides useful subjects in a variety of styles.

Image-editing software enables the user to touch up and edit photographs in black and white and in color, and to create some interesting special effects: embossing, blurring, posterizing, etc., as well as retouching photographs and graduating tones of color.

ADOBE PHOTOSHOP [MAC/PC]
Adobe Systems, Inc.

Photoshop is a professional photo design and production tool that can be used for creating original artwork, for retouching photographs and other images, and for pre-press professionals producing high-quality color separations and output. You can design artwork with painting and selecting tools, or retouch and correct true color or black-and-white scanned images with image processing tools and filters and special effects like posterizing and embossing. Created images or manipulated photographs can be easily imported into your page layout program. Controls allow for four-color proofing and color separations.

ALDUS®PHOTOSTYLER™ [PC]
Aldus® Corporation

PhotoStyler™ is a professional color image-editing or processing program for the PC. It gives you the ability to acquire images from a wide range of sources and industry-standard file formats, enhance or modify them for use in publications and presentations, and create new images from scratch. This program has the power of a color pre-press system on the desktop. You can work in color, grayscale, or black and white, do retouching and color correction; and produce color separations.

ADOBE™ PREMIERE™ [MAC]
Adobe Systems, Inc.

Adobe Premiere is an image-editing program that lets you combine video, audio, animation, still images, and graphics to create films and videos.

ALDUS® PREPRINT® [MAC]
Aldus Corporation

PrePrint® is a professional color-production tool that generates full-color separations of entire multiple page documents from your desktop, including text, illustration and color photographs.

ALDUS® TRAPWISE™ [PC]
Aldus® Corporation

TrapWise™ is designed for pre-press professionals—pre-press houses, service bureaus, print production departments, and publishing operations. It can trap spot and process colors, vignettes, hairline rules, thin text, and more.

FRACTAL DESIGN SKETCHER™ [MAC]
Fractal Design

Fractal Design Sketcher™ is an image-editing program that duplicates the expressive line of a soft lead pencil or the luminous glow of oil paints. Other features include image retouching, color separations, tear-off tools, tools like marbling, and glass and liquid effects, Type 1 and True Type™ font support, and straight line tools.

PHOTOMAGIC AD COPY [PC]
Micrografx, Inc.

PhotoMagic Ad Copy is an image-editing program that comes with over 250 color clip art images. It has the capability of producing special effects, and it can be used as a companion for word processors, presentation graphics programs, scanners, and paint programs in order to enhance publications and dress up a page layout.

PICTURE PUBLISHER [PC]
Micrografx, Inc.

Picture Publisher is a desktop darkroom—a 24-bit image-editing program with color separation controls. Users can enhance and tint photographic images with masking and retouching tools, and it has over 30 special effects and clip art .

PAGE LAYOUT

Page layout programs are the basis of desktop publishing, giving the designer the ability to lay out and compose an entire publication, page by page. The page layout program acts like an electronic paste-up board. These programs enable you to compose pages and prepare an entire publication for printing, including typesetting and sizing of graphics.

ALDUS® PAGEMAKER™ [MAC/PC]
Aldus Corporation

PageMaker is a desktop publishing program, or an electronic page composition/layout program, that gives you all the tools you need to produce professional-quality publications on the computer. It enables the desktop publisher to integrate text and graphics from many sources into a wide variety of printed documents. Its special features include: built-in color separation, and on-screen control palette; story editor for word processing with spelling checker, and search and replace; extensive typographic precision controls like kerning, letter spacing, condensing/expanding, rotation of text and graphics, text wrap, and multiple open publications. The Macintosh and Windows versions of PageMaker have file compatibility.

CLARIS WORKS [MAC/PC]
Claris Corporation

Claris Works is a drawing program, a spread sheet, and desktop publishing program that you can use to produce professional-quality reports, presentations, plus budgets, charts, labels, and newsletters.

COREL VENTURA [PC]
Corel Corporation

Corel Ventura is an page layout program for Windows with font loading and support for Adobe Acrobat. It comes with Ventura DataBase Publisher for publishing documents from database information.

MICROSOFT PUBLISHER [PC]
Microsoft Corporation

A page layout program for the Microsoft Windows™ operating system for desktop publishers with little or no experience in graphic design. Publisher helps the novice designer create professional-quality publications in a few easy steps. Features include an on-line design advisor, 35 templates, an on-screen demonstration of a variety of desktop publishing tasks, and a layout and print troubleshooter.

QUARK XPRESS® [MAC/PC]
Quark®, Inc.

Quark XPress is a professional electronic publishing system that provides the precision and power needed to create and produce a broad range of publications. It offers a full range of word processing, typographic, and page layout features to enable users to create high-quality publications. Its special features include: built-in color separation, on-screen control palette; story editor for word processing with spelling checker, search and replace; extensive typographic precision controls like kerning, letter spacing, condensing/expanding, rotation of text and graphics, text wrap, and multiple open publications. It is possible to exchange files between the Macintosh and the PC.

TYPE AND TYPE MANIPULATION

Additional fonts and specialty fonts can be purchased from a number of sources. Type manipulation programs enable the user to design new typefaces and alter existing faces for use as illustration and graphics.

ADOBE FONT FOLIO™ [MAC/PC]
Adobe systems, Inc.

Font Folio™ comes on a CD-ROM disc and gives you access to more than 1,700 Type 1 typefaces, including Adobe Originals™ fonts.

ADOBE SUPER ATM™ [MAC]

Adobe Systems, Inc.

Super ATM software solves the problem of on-screen, jagged, bitmapped typefaces. ATM™ creates "substitute fonts" for viewing, editing, and printing files.

ADOBE TYPE ALIGN [MAC/PC]

Adobe Systems, Inc.

With TypeAlign you can create novel type effects: draw a line, arc or freehand curve, type text along it, and shape it any way you want.

ADOBE TYPE LIBRARY [MAC/PC]

Adobe Systems, Inc.

A large selection 1,700 fonts in the Type 1 digital format. Includes the collections of internationally-renowned foundries and special characters.

ADOBE TYPE ON CALL [MAC/PC]

Adobe Systems, Inc.

You buy type as you need it with a phone call.

ADOBE TYPE REUNION [MAC]

Adobe Systems, Inc.

Reunion sorts fonts and displays Type 1 typefaces alphabetically by family names with a submenu that shows styles and weights.

BITSTREAM® TYPEFACE LIBRARY [MAC/PC]

Bitstream Inc.

One of the largest sources of high-quality type for computer-driven printers and typesetters. Includes over 1,000 typefaces, available in the various formats required by Mac and PC users.

EASTERN EUROPEAN LIBRARY™ [MAC/PC]

Casady & Greene

The Eastern European Library has 26 Postscript and True Type fonts that support Albanian, Croatian, Czech, German, Hungarian, Polish, Roumanian, Slovak, Slovenian, and English.

FLUENT LASER FONTS LIBRARY™ 2 [MAC/PC]

Casady & Greene

120 fonts for crisp output.

FONTOGRAPHER [MAC/PC]

Altys® Corporation

This program enables you to create your own fonts or personalize existing ones with control over every aspect of typography. Any graphic or image can become a font and can be used for signatures, company logos, or special symbols.

FONT STUDIO® [MAC]

Letraset® USA

This font creation and modification tool gives you total control over the printer font character outlines and on-screen bitmaps. You can control the shape of the letter, serifs, character width, kerning, stem weights, diagonal strokes—every aspect of the typographic design—to design and customize your own logos, characters, line art, symbols, and typefaces. A good program to use to communicate or illustrate ideas with type.

GLASNOST CYRILLIC LIBRARY ™ 2 [MAC/PC]

Casady & Greene

17 fonts for business documents, desktop publishing, and personal correspondence that support Russian, Byelorussian, Serbian, Ukrainian, Bulgarian, Macedonian, and English.

LETRA STUDIO® [MAC]

Letraset® USA

An easy-to-use type design tool for logotypes, headlines and video titling. You can bring a wide range of fonts onto your screen, turn them into customized display type designs, and then import them into your favorite page layout or graphic program. You can adjust tiny details with precise control. You can condense, stretch, slant, scale, skew, rotate, flip, and reshape your type and create type that conforms to a shape.

METAMORPHOSIS PROFESSIONAL   [MAC/PC]

Altys® Corporation

A font conversion utility that converts type into PICT outlines for editing and reshaping characters and creating fills in numerous drawing programs. Metamorphosis generates outlines that are identical to the original font.

PIXAR TYPESTRY   [MAC/PC]

Pixar

Typestry turns Type 1 and TrueType fonts into three-dimensional images. Once converted, you can rotate, move, and scale any word or individual letter. Letters can be decorated with a number of effects: motion blur, patterns, shadows, etc.

TRUETYPE™ STARTER SET™   [MAC/PC]

Casady & Greene

This Starter Set includes 22 high-quality True Type fonts in a variety of styles for professional-looking printouts on a NON-Postscript printer.

TYPEFACE LIBRARY   [MAC/PC]

Image Club

Image Club's Typeface Library has a large selection of current fonts in Adobe Type One format for high resolution output. They have FontPaks for every need, from starter packages to specialized designer collections.

Word processing software is used both to write and to edit manuscripts and letters. Text can be formatted into headlines, subheads, body copy, and spelling, and grammar checked before it is imported into a page layout program to be fine tuned and used in a design.

DE SCRIBE® WORD PROCESSOR   [PC]

DeScribe, Inc.

DeScribe® Word Processor combines advanced word-processing functions with powerful desktop publishing features, intuitive menus, and extensive drawing capabilities. It has easy-to-use tables, with sort, mail merge, indexing, and full network capability. Text and graphics can be integrated in minutes.

MAC WRITE PRO   [MAC/PC]

Claris® Corporation

MacWrite Pro is a word processing program that offers sophisticated productivity tools. Features like style sheets, one-step table creation, and floating tool palettes help save time. Text can be wrapped around graphics, and you can incorporate non-textual elements and set up variable columns to create a variety of documents. The technology gives you access to more than 20 different file formats on DOS, Macintosh, Windows, and other platforms. You have access to the most current information published by your colleagues; a change in their file is automatically reflected in your document.

MICROSOFT WORD   [MAC/PC]

Microsoft Corporation

Microsoft Word is a sophisticated word processing program that is also used for desktop publishing. Some of its features include the ability to create graphics, style sheets, spell and grammar check, automatic footnotes, page layout, outlining, the ability to generate a table of contents, and more.

SOFTWARE PUBLISHERS LISTED IN THIS BIBLIOGRAPHY

Adobe Systems, Inc.
Box 7900
Mountain View, CA 94039-7900
(800) 833-6687
Fax: (415) 961-3769

Aldus Corporation
411 First Avenue South
Seattle, WA 98104-2871
(206) 628-2320

Altys Corporation
269 W. Renner Road
Richardson, TX 75080
(214) 680-2060
Fax: (214) 680-0537

Bitstream Inc.
Athenaeum House
215 First Street
Cambridge, MA 02142
(617) 497-6222
Fax: (617) 868-4732

Casady & Greene
22734 Portola Drive
Salinas, CA 93908-1119
(800) 359-4920

Claris Corporation
5201 Patrick Henry Drive
Box 58168
Santa Clara, CA 95052-8168
(408) 987-7305
Fax: (408) 987-7440

Comstock Desktop Photography
The Comstock Building
30 Irving Place
New York, NY 10003
(800) 225-2727
Fax: (212) 353-3383

Computer Support Corporation
15926 Midway Road
Dallas, TX 75244
(214) 661-8960

Corel Corporation
The Corel Building
1600 Carling Avenue
Ottawa, Ontario
Canada K1Z BR7
(613) 728-8200
Fax: (613) 728-9790

DeScribe, Inc.
4047 N. Freeway Blvd.
Sacramento, CA 95834
(916) 646-1111

Dynamic Graphics, Inc.
6000 North Forest Drive
Peoria, Il 61614-3592
(800) 255-8800
Fax: (309) 688-5873

Fractal Design Corporation
335 Spreckels Drive
Aptos, CA 95001
(408) 688-8800
Fax: (408) 688-8836

Image Club Graphics, Inc.
Suite 5 1902 11th Street SE
Calgary, Alberta
Canada T 2G 3G2
(800) 661-9410
Fax: (403) 261-7013

Letraset USA
40 Eisenhower Drive
Paramus, NJ 07653
(800) 343-TYPE
Telex: 134430

Micrografx, Inc.
1303 Arapaho Road
Richardson, TX 75081
(800) 733-3729

Microsoft Corporation
One Microsoft Way
Redmond, WA 98052-6399
(206) 882-8080
Fax: (206) 9336-7329

Pixar
1001 West Cutting Boulevard
Richmond, CA 94804
(800) 888-9856
Fax: (510) 236-0388

Quark Inc.
1800 Grant Street
Denver, CO 80203
(303) 894-8888
Fax: (303) 894-3399

Ray Dream, Inc.
P.O. Box 7446
Fremont, CA 94537-7446
(800) 846-0111
Fax: (800) 477-0012

3G Graphics, Inc.
114 Second Avenue South
Suite 104
Edmonds, WA 98020
(800) 456-0234

BIBLIO-GRAPHY

BOOKS AND PERIODICALS

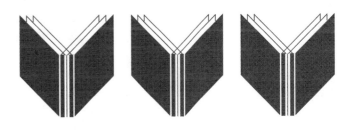

BOOKS

Arnston, Amy E. *Graphic Design Basics*, 2nd Ed. Fort Worth, TX: Harcourt Brace Jovanovitz, 1993.
A basic book for the graphic design student dealing with graphic design concepts, the use of typography, design of logos, ads, using photographs, and preparing camera-ready art for the printer.

Beach, Mark, and Russon, Ken. *Papers for Printing: How to Choose the Right Paper at the Right Price for Any Printing Job.* Portland, OR: Coast to Coast Books, 1989.
A guide to aid in the selection of paper for a publication which demonstrates how paper choice affects the appearance of words and graphics on a page.

Beale, Stephen, and Cavuoto, James. *The Scanner Book: A Complete Guide to the Use and Applications of Desktop Scanners.* Torrance, CA: Micro Publishing Press, 1989.
This book helps guide the reader in choosing a scanner. Demonstrates how to scan and manipulate scanned images.

Blatner, David. *Desktop Publisher's Survival Kit.* Berkeley, CA: Peachpit Press, 1991.
Reveals the secrets of desktop publishing on the Macintosh. Includes tricks and tips about scanning, sorting fonts, and production.

Blatner, David, and Stimely, Keith. *The Quark XPress Book.* Berkeley, CA: Peachpit Press, 1991.
A guide and manual to help the desktop publisher using Quark XPress get the most out of the program, from setting up the page to the final camera-ready output.

Bohle, Robert. *Publication Design for Editors.* Englewood Cliffs, NJ: Prentice Hall, 1990.

Textbook for editors on designing for the printed page. Covers design, typography, and layout using photographs and illustrations, and it includes information on pasteup and production.

Brown, Alex. *In Print: Text and Type in the Age of Desktop Publishing.* New York: Watson-Guptill, 1989.

A look at different typefaces and techniques to make effective use of any typeface.

Burke, Clifford. *Type from the Desktop: Designing with Type and Your Computer.* Chapel Hill, NC.: Ventana Press, 1990.

A basic book on using and understanding type, including helpful tips, aimed at desktop publishers.

Conover, Theodore E. *Graphic Communications Today.* St. Paul, MN: West Publishing Co., 1990.

A basic graphic design book that deals with history of design, use of typography, art and illustrations, and the use of color, paper, and ink.

Craig, James, Barton, Bruce. *Thirty Centuries of Graphic Design.* New York: Watson Guptill, 1987.

An illustrated survey that shows the evolution of graphic design from prehistoric times to the present and puts it in the context of other historical events.

Denton, Craig. *Graphics for Visual Communication.* Dubuque, IO: Wm. C. Brown, Publishers, 1992.

A textbook for students of graphic design that covers basic graphic design issues.

Gosney, Michael, Odam, John, Schmal, Jim. *The Gray Book.* Chapel Hill, NC: Ventana Press, 1990.

How to create effective designs in black and white and all the shades in between.

Holmes, Nigel. *Designer's Guide to Creating Charts and Diagrams.* New York: Watson-Guptill, 1984.

Nigel Holmes is an innovator in the field of processing visual information. This well-illustrated book demonstrates how to convert numerical data into eye-catching graphics.

Hurlburt, Allen. *Layout: the design of the printed page.* New York: Watson-Guptill Publications, 1977.

The keys to the design of the printed page beginning with the source of modern design.

Jewler, A. Jerome. *Creative Strategy in Advertising.* 4th ed. Belmont, CA:
Wadsworth Publishing Company, 1992.
This textbook examines what goes into a successful advertising
campaign. Shows case studies of two nationally known campaigns.

Kuwayama, Yasaburo. *Trademarks & Symbols, Vol. 1 & 2.* New York:
Van Nostrand Reinhold, 1973.
Volume 1 shows trademarks and symbols based on the alphabet.
Volume 2 shows trademarks and symbols using symbols.

Meggs, Philip B. *A History of Graphic Design* 2nd ed. New York:
Van Nostrand Reinhold, 1993.
A comprehensive history of graphic design from its earliest roots to the
present with illustrations that show changes in design styles and trends
through the ages.

Naiman, Arthur, ed. *The Macintosh Bible,* 2nd ed. Berkeley, CA:
Goldstein & Blair, 1989.
Contains practical tips on understanding the concepts behind the
computer as well as tips on the most popular programs.

Nelson, Roy Paul. *The Design of Advertising,* 6th ed. Dubuque, IA:
William C. Brown, 1989.
This book focuses on effective use of typography, space, and color in
the design of magazine and newspaper ads.

Olav, Martin Kvern. *Real World FreeHand 3.* Berkeley, CA:
Peachpit Press, 1991.
Good manual for the drawing program, FreeHand. Gives information
in a straightforward, easy-to-understand manner.

Owen, William. *Modern Magazine Design.* Dubuque, IA:
Wm. C. Brown Publishers, 1992.
A history of the magazine and an analysis of contemporary magazine
design with illustrations of beautifully-designed magazines.

Parker, Roger C. *Looking Good in Print,* 3rd ed. Chapel Hill, NC:
Ventana Press, 1990.
A guide to basic graphic design for desktop publishers with hints and
tips for creating professional-quality publications.

———. *The Make-over Book: 101 Design Solutions for Desktop Publishing.*
Chapel Hill, NC: Ventana Press, 1989.
Before and after examples of design solutions for newsletters, ads,
brochures, flyers, and other printed materials.

Quark, Inc. *Quark XPress Tips*. Denver, CO: Quark, Inc., 1989.
    Tips on Quark XPress, a page layout program.

Shushan, Ronnie & Wright, Don. *Desktop Publishing by Design*. Redmond,
    WA: Microsoft Press, 1991.
    Design and typesetting hints for page layouts using PageMaker.

Thompson, Philip & Davenport, Peter. *The Dictionary of Graphic Images*.
    New York: St. Martin's Press, Inc, 1980.
    A dictionary with 1200 entries of visual images or clichés. A good
    source for understanding visual communication.

Tufte, Edward R. *The Visual Display of Quantitative Information*. Cheshire,
    CT: Graphics Press, 1983.
    Describes different ways to create charts and graphs and guides you in
    making a choice for the right one for your task.

Walker Art Center. *Graphic Design in America: A Visual Language History*.
    New York: Harry Abrams, Inc., 1989.
    Catalog of an exhibition at the Walker Art Center that puts graphic
    design in an historical context from 1829-1989.

White, Alex. *How to Spec Type*. New York: Watson-Guptill, 1987.
    A basic book on using type with techniques to enrich the printed page.

White, Jan. Graphic *Design for the Electronic Age: The Manual for Traditional
    and Desktop Publishing*. New York: Watson-Guptill, 1988.
    A handy reference book for the beginning designer on the principles
    of basic design.

——. *Using Charts and Graphs: 1000 Ideas for Getting Attention*. New York: R.
    R. Bowker, 1984.
    Discussion on the different types of charts and graphs and which kind
    to use to get a specific message across.

Will-Harris, Daniel. *Typestyle*. Berkeley, CA: Peachpit Press, 1990.
    How to choose & use type on a personal computer.

Williams, Robin. *PageMaker 4: An Easy Desk Reference*. Berkeley, CA:
    Peachpit Press, 1991.
    An easy-to-read manual with everything you need to know about
    using PageMaker.

—— . *The Mac is not a Typewriter*. Berkeley, CA: Peachpit Press, 1990.
    The PC is not a Typewriter. Berkeley, CA: Peachpit Press, 1990.
    These are two style manuals to aid the desktop publisher in
    creating professional-looking type on a Macintosh or PC.

Aldus Magazine. Aldus Corporation, 411 First Avenue, South, Seattle, WA 98104-2871. (206) 628-2321.
 Subscription or free to owners of Aldus products. Information on using Aldus products: PageMaker, Persuasion, FreeHand, etc. Each issue includes some articles with tips on design.

Communication Arts Magazine. Communication Arts, Palo Alto, CA.
 Shows examples of new and well-designed work being done by graphic designers. Published 8 times a year.

Desktop Communications. 48 East 43th Street, NY, NY, 10017.
 Magazine for the desktop publishing professional with articles on new technologies but with an emphasis on design. Bimonthly.

National Association of Desktop Publishers Journal. Desktop Publishing Institute, 1260 Boylston Street, Boston, MA 02215.
 Magazine for desktop publishing professionals dealing with current issues relating to the use of computers for design. Monthly.

Emigre. Emigre Graphics, 48 Shattuck Square #175, Berkeley, CA 94704.
 A large format avant garde arts magazine that addresses graphic design issues in words and pictures. It is produced on the Macintosh and is a showcase for unusual electronic graphic design techniques. Published 4 times a year.

Font & Function. Adobe Systems, P.O. Box 7900, Mountain View, CA 94039-7900.
 This publication, a type catalog from Adobe, is sent to registered users of Adobe software and includes articles on typeface designs. Published three times a year.

How. F & W Publications, Inc., PO Box 12575, Cincinnati, OH 45207.
 A magazine that presents ideas and techniques in graphic design in a step-by-step, how-to format.

In-House Graphics. United Communications, 4500 Montgomery Ave. Ste. 700N, Bethesda, MD 20814.
 A magazine with practical advice and hints on graphic design. Monthly.

Newsletter Design. Newsletter Clearinghouse, 44 West Market St., P.O. Box 311, Rhinebeck, NY 12572.
 Each issue shows illustrations from over 20 newsletters, with critiques of the strengths and weaknesses. Good for ideas for newsletters. Monthly.

Newsletter on Newsletters. Newsletter Clearinghouse, 44 West Market St., P.O. Box 311, Rhinebeck, NY 12572.
Deals with issues of concern to creators of newsletters: marketing, graphics, type, and post office regulations. Biweekly.

The Page. P.O. Box 14493, Chicago, IL 60614.
A publication geared towards desktop publishers who use the Macintosh computer. This attractive monthly publication gives a good hands-on view of design. Monthly.

PC Computing. Ziff-Davis, 4 Cambridge Center, 9th floor, Cambridge, MA 02142.
Articles of interest to PC users and others about the state of the present hardware and software.

Print Magazine. Print, 3200 Tower Oaks Blvd., Rockville, MD 20852..
Has examples of some of the best contemporary graphic designs.

Publish Magazine. PCW Communications, San Francisco, CA.
Articles of interest to the desktop publisher including reviews of new software and hardware, as well as articles on design. Published monthly.

Step by Step Graphics. Step by Step Publishing, a Division of Dynamic Graphics, Inc. 6000 North Forest Park Drive., Peoria, IL.
A how-to magazine showing techniques of different designers/illustrators. Ideas for using different techniques for special effects, with some hints on the business side of graphic design.

Upper & Lower case. U&LC Subscription Dept. ITC, 2 Hammarskjold Plaza, NY, NY 10017.
Large format magazine on newsprint that is a showcase for creative and fascinating illustrations and imaginative use of typography. Quarterly.

GLOSSARY

Alignment

The placement of text in relation to the margins: flush left, flush right, justified, force justified.

Ampersand

The symbol for the word "and" (&). Each font has an ampersand unique to that typeface.

Ascender

The part of the letter that rises above the x-height.

Asymmetry

A design based on informal balance, the opposite of symmetry, which refers to formal balance.

Auto leading

The amount of spacing between lines of text in proportion to the type size.

Baseline

The imaginary line on which a measure of text sits.

Basic weight

The weight of a ream of paper at a standard size (cover stock: 20" x 26", book: 25" x 38")

Bit-mapped image

Type or graphics from paint programs formed by a series of dots and jagged in appearance.

Blackletter

A typestyle, sometimes referred to as Old English, that has the appearance of type originally used by monks or scribes.

Bleed

An illustration or inked area that runs off the edge of a page.

Blueline or brownline

A proof in blue or brown prepared by the printer as a final check for the designer to catch mistakes before a job goes to press.

Body text

The main text, or copy, of a document that is usually set in 10-12 point type.

Boldface

A darker and heavier typeface. Each entry in this glossary is boldface (Futura Bold).

Bowl or counter

The circular part or space of a letter (b, e, p).

Bullet

A typographic element for listing items in a publication. The bullet provides graphic interest on a page and helps the reader through the information.

Byline

The name of the author under an article.

Camera-ready art

The completed design including all art, photographs, and text ready for reproduction by a printer.

Caps and small caps

CAPITAL LETTERS, or uppercase letters, come in both small and large capitals. SMALL CAPITAL LETTERS are the same size as the x-height of lowercase letters but are uppercase.

CD-ROM

A system of storing large amounts of information an on a compact disk for retrieval on the computer: clip art, photographs, and fonts.

Centered type

Type aligned in the center of a page.

Character

An individual letter or symbol.

Clip art

Uncopyrighted line art or photographs found in books or on disk, to be used in a layout.

Clipboard

The place where the computer stores a recently-cut element, type, or a graphic from a document to be pasted into another place. Shutting down the computer erases the clipboard.

Closure

The ability of the brain to close off or complete incomplete shapes.

Coated stock

Paper that is coated with an enamel-like, glossy substance. This stock is used for reproducing photographs and other illustrations.

Cold type

Type reproduced through a photographic or process other than hot or foundry type.

Collage

A composite of different materials combined to form one picture.

Colophon

Factual information related to the production of a book that may include typefaces, hardware and software used, and printer's name.

Color separations

Negatives for printing the four primary subtractive colors—cyan, magenta, yellow, and black.

Column guides

Vertical rules on a page layout program for setting up columns for text. The guides can be moved to change the width of the columns.

Comprehensive (comp)

An approximation of the final layout and design of a printed piece.

Computer graphics

Electronically-created graphics or designs.

Condensed type

Type that has been made narrower than normal and allows for the possibility of more type on a page, more characters per line.

Continued line or jumpline

A line of text at the bottom of an article to indicate the page where the article is continued.

Continuous tone art

Photographs or detailed line art with a wide range of tones from black to white.

Contrast

A tonal range from black to white or dark colors to lighter ones in photographs, illustrations, and type.

Cool colors

The colors associated with the natural world: blues and greens.

Copyfitting

Fitting copy (text) into a desired space.

Crop marks

Lines on the camera-ready art that indicate where the page is to be trimmed.

Cropping

The process of eliminating extraneous elements in a photograph to make the image more powerful. It is also a way to change the proportions of a picture to fit within a given space.

Cropping "L's"

Two right angles to help determine where a photograph should be cropped.

Cropping tool

Tool in a page layout program for trimming or cropping graphics.

Cyan

One of the four colors in full-color printing (vivid blue).

Deck, subtitle, or tagline

A line of text beneath a headline that provides more information about a story in a newsletter or magazine.

Default

A preset option on the computer that can be changed and customized to your specifications.

Descender

The part of the letter that descends below the baseline (g, y, j, p).

Desktop publishing

The ability to prepare publishable pages on a computer for reproduction. Desktop publishing began in 1985. The term was coined by Paul Brainerd, President of Aldus Corporation.

Dialog box

A box that appears on the computer screen to help you set up options in a publication.

Digital halftone

A photograph or continuous-line art that has been scanned and turned in into a series of dots (gray scale) and ready for printing.

Dingbat

A decorative element or graphic device for listing items or for decoration on a page.

Display type

Large type, often bold, that is used in headlines to grab attention.

Dot matrix printer

A printer that uses a carbon ribbon and prints out images that are bit-mapped (jagged).

Dots per inch (dpi)

The measurement that refers to resolution, sharpness, or clarity of a printer, a computer monitor, or an output.

Download

To transfer information form one computer or other electronic device (modem or fax) to another.

Downloadable fonts

Fonts that you install in your printer.

Drop cap

A large initial capital letter dropped into the beginning of a paragraph to add visual interest on a page.

Dummy

A sketch of an idea for a page layout used as an aid in working out the full page design. Also the piece given to a printer as a guide to show how the final publication should appear.

Duotone

A process of printing a halftone negative using one color on top of a tinted screen in another color . Produces a rich one-color photograph.

Ellipsis

Three dots (…) used to indicate that something has been omitted.

Em dash

A dash that is the width of the letter m.

Em space

A spacing unit for type the width of a capital M.

Encapsulated PostScript (eps)

A format used in graphics programs to smooth out graphics so there are no jagged edges. The files can be resized in a page layout program.

En dash

A dash that is the width of the letter n.

En space

A spacing unit for type that is the width of the letter n.

Extended type

Type with characters wider than normal.

Face

The name of a particular type design (Caslon, Times, Helvetica). Originally it referred to the raised printing surface of type.

Facing pages

The pages that face each other when a publication is opened (e.g., two-page magazine spread).

Fibonacci Series

A series of numbers based on the golden mean, a proportion found in nature in dimensions of the chamber of a snail shell and an egg. 2:3:5:8:13:….

Figure

A shape (positive space) that stands out from the background.

Flush left

Text is evenly aligned at the left margin and the right margin is ragged or uneven.

Flush right

Text is aligned on the right side leaving the left side ragged.

Folio

The page number.

Font

All the letters, numbers, and punctuation points in one size in a type style.

Footer or running foot

A line of type that appears at the bottom of every page in a publication with the name of the publication, chapter title, and page number.

Force justify

A option in alignment that adds space between letters forcing a line of text to conform to a space.

Formal balance

A format of balance where all elements are symmetrical on the page.

Format

The typographic setup of a publication that includes type specifications, size, and style of a publication.

Formatting

Specifying text for body copy, headlines, and subheads to create a style sheet in a page layout or word processing program.

For position only (fpo)

A photocopied or scanned photograph or other art placed on a page to indicate where the actual art should be placed after it has been screened.

Foundry type

Type that is hand-set.

Four-color process printing

The process of printing color that combines cyan, magenta, yellow and black to reproduce all the colors of the spectrum.

Front-end

The technology (hardware and software) used at the beginning of the production process.

Gestalt psychology

A study of the way the brain perceives and organizes visual information.

Gothic style type

Type with even strokes and no serifs

Graduated fill

A screened fill for an object with tones from light to dark, or from dark to light.

Greeking

Simulating text in bars or lines, or Latin text used to show typeface and style in a rough design.

Grid

An invisible series of lines, rectangles, or squares used by designers to organize elements on a page.

Ground

The background (negative space) that surrounds a figure.

Guides

The electronic rules on a computer that help align text and graphics.

Gutter or alley

The space or margin between two facing pages.

Hairline rule

A very thin line or rule.

Halftone

A screened photograph ready for reproduction.

Hanging indent

The first line in a paragraph that goes out to the left margin. Following lines are indented.

Header or running head

Text at the top of each page of a publication with information on chapter heading, and page number.

High-end technology

Electronic technology that is sophisticated and precise (e.g., Linotronic).

Hot type

Type using raised letters made out of molten metal used in letterpress printing.

Hue

The name of a color.

Icon

A small graphic or symbol used for identification.

Imagesetter

Typesetting machine found in service bureaus and used for high-resolution output.

Informal balance

Design balance that uses asymmetry as opposed to symmetry.

Initial caps

Large letters used as decorative devices at the beginning of a paragraph.

Inline graphic

A graphic inserted into a line of text that becomes part of the text.

Italic type

Type that slants to the right. Used for emphasis.

Justified type

An arrangement of type in a paragraph where each side is aligned on both left and right.

Kerning

Removing or adding space between letters.

Laser printer

An output device that uses laser technology to print pages from the computer.

Layout

The arrangement of elements, type, and graphics, on a page.

Leading

The space between two lines of text measured from baseline to baseline.

Letterpress

A method of printing that uses raised letters.

Letterspacing

The variable spacing between individual letters.

Ligature

Two characters or more that are joined together to form a single unit (Æ).

Lightface

Letters with thin strokes, thinner than normal.

Line art

A drawing composed of lines.

Linotronic

A high-resolution imagesetter or PostScript printer. Resolution runs from 1200 dots per inch to over 3000.

Linotype
The first typesetting letterpress machine that used cast lines of hot type for printing.

Logotype
A logo for an organization using all type.

Lowercase
The small letters of the alphabet.

Magenta
One of the four colors used in full-color printing (purple-red).

Master page
The page that contains information that appears on every page in a publication (rules, page numbers).

Masthead
The copy on a magazine, newspaper, or newsletter that lists editorial information: name of organization, date, volume number.

Measure
A line or column width measured in picas.

Mechanical
The camera-ready art with all the type and graphics in place ready for reproduction.

Megabyte (MB)
One million bytes of information.

Minus leading
Eliminating the space between two lines to make type denser. Used in headlines for impact.

Modem
An add-on device that enables a computer to communicate with other computers through telephone lines.

Moiré pattern
An effect caused by rescreening a halftone.

Nameplate
The name of a publication as a logotype. Also called a flag.

Negative space
The white space or ground. Opposite of figure

Novelty, specialty, or decorative type
Type that is ornamental. It is used in small amounts because it draws attention to itself. Used for headlines or drop caps.

Object-oriented graphic
A graphic created with defined mathematical curves and lines that can be resized in proportion. The opposite of a paint graphic.

Oblique type
A roman typeface that is slanted but the letters keep their original shape as opposed to italics where letters assume a slightly different shape.

Orphan
A single word or part of a line of text at the top of a column.

Output
The paper or film printout, the product of a desktop printer or imagesetter.

Overlay
A sheet of acetate or paper laid over a mechanical with instructions for the printer pertaining to color, bleeds, and other pertinent information for printing.

Page layout programs
Software programs for desktop publishing that enable the designer to import text and graphics in order to create a publication on the computer.

PANTONE® Matching System
Color publication guides to help the designer communicate colors for reproduction.

Pasteboard
The area outside the page in a page layout program that acts as a drawing board for type or graphics that need to be moved to another page.

Photomontage
A collage or composite of different photographs.

Pica
A standard unit of line measurement (12 points or approximately $1/6$ of an inch).

Pict format
A format used to save object-oriented graphics.

Pictograph
A pictorial representation of an object as a symbol

Pie chart
A chart with data in the shape of a pie.

Pixel
Smallest measurement on the computer that determines the clarity or resolution of an image.

PMT (Photo Mechanical Transfer)
A positive screened print made from a piece of art ready for placement on a mechanical.

Point
A traditional unit of type measurement in this country, and most countries. A point represents $1/72$ of an inch.

PostScript

A page description language that allows the computer to communicate with a printer.

Printer font

The font stored in the system of the computer that enables the laser or other printer to recognize the typeface when printing. If the font is not in the system, the printer will select another font.

Pull quotes or breakouts

A quotation or sentence extracted from a paragraph and used as a visual device on a page.

RAM

The random access memory inside the computer where data is stored.

Rebus

The use of pictures to represent words.

Registration marks

The marks used on all pages of a document with color that enables the printer to register the color.

Reversals or drop outs

White type on a black or screened background.

Resolution

The crispness or clarity of an image or type either on a monitor or an output device.

Saturation

The purity or intensity of a color.

Script

A slanted typeface design based on the handwriting of scribes.

Serifs

Type with horizontal strokes on the top and bottom of each letter.

Sidebar

A short article related to a larger article that appears alongside the main one. Sometimes the text in the sidebar is in a screened box.

Silhouette

A technique where the background of an image is eliminated to make an image stand out.

Sizing

Reducing or enlarging an illustration or photograph to fit within a space on the page.

Solid leading

Type where the point size and leading is the same (42/42). Used in headlines to close up spacing between the lines.

Spot color

The addition of an extra color in a design.

Spread

The facing pages (2) in a publication.

Stem

The vertical stroke in a letter.

Stock agency

A business with a collection of photographs in different categories that can be rented for use by designers for specific publications.

Stripping

The method used by a printer to place screened photographs into a film to create a plate for printing.

Style sheets

Setting up typographic commands for a publication in order to maintain consistency in body type and headlines throughout a publication.

Swash

A decorative stroke on a letter.

Template

A design style used as a prototype for a publication that is produced on a regular basis (newsletter, magazine) with all the information for that publication: text styles, grids, and column widths.

Text wrap

A line of text that is wrapped around a graphic.

Thumbnails

A preliminary sketch for the design of a page that shows placement of text and graphics.

TIFF (Tag Image File Format)

A format for storing and importing images into a page layout program.

Tint

A screen that changes the percentage of a color (80% black, 20% red).

Tracking

The control over the spacing between letters within a line of text.

Type family

A typeface of the same design but with varying weights, widths, and styles (bold, oblique).

Typography

The art and design of type.

U & lc

Upper and lowercase letters.

Uppercase

Capital letters.

Value

The lightness, brightness, or darkness of a color.

Velox

A halftone photograph in black and white.

Verso

The left-hand page in a publication.

Warm colors

Reds, yellows, and all the blends of these colors.

Weight

The thickness of a letter (light, medium, bold, extra bold, ultra bold)

Widow

A single word or short line at the end of a column that is less than ⅓ of the column width.

Width

The horizontal measurement of a letter: condensed, normal, or expanded.

Window

A black or red box on a mechanical where a screened photograph is dropped in.

WYSIWYG

What you see is what you get (on the computer monitor or in the printout).

x-height

The height of a lowercase x in a typeface.

APPENDIX

COMMON MISTAKES AND HOW TO AVOID THEM

The following errors will affect the readability and the design of your publications:

☐ Too many lines/rules on a page.

With each line or rule you want to add, ask yourself if you really need this line. Is it absolutely necessary? Does it enhance the design of the page? Does it interfere with readability?

☐ Too many boxes and boxes of different shapes.

Maintain consistency in the boxes on a page. If you are using a box with rounded edges, stick to that shape throughout a publication. Limit the number of boxes.

☐ Text in a box without white space around it.

Leave some breathing room all around text that is boxed.

☐ Two spaces after a period.

Use only one space after a period. If a manuscript has been formatted with two spaces, you can make a global change in your word processing or page layout program that will eliminate one space.

☐ Use of the <u>underline</u> function for emphasis in text.

Use italics or bold face type for emphasis instead.

☐ Too many typefaces on a page—the "ransom-note effect."

Use one typeface, or, use one serif and one sans serif face that are dissimilar to create contrast.

☐ Widows and orphans create an awkward, unbalanced look.